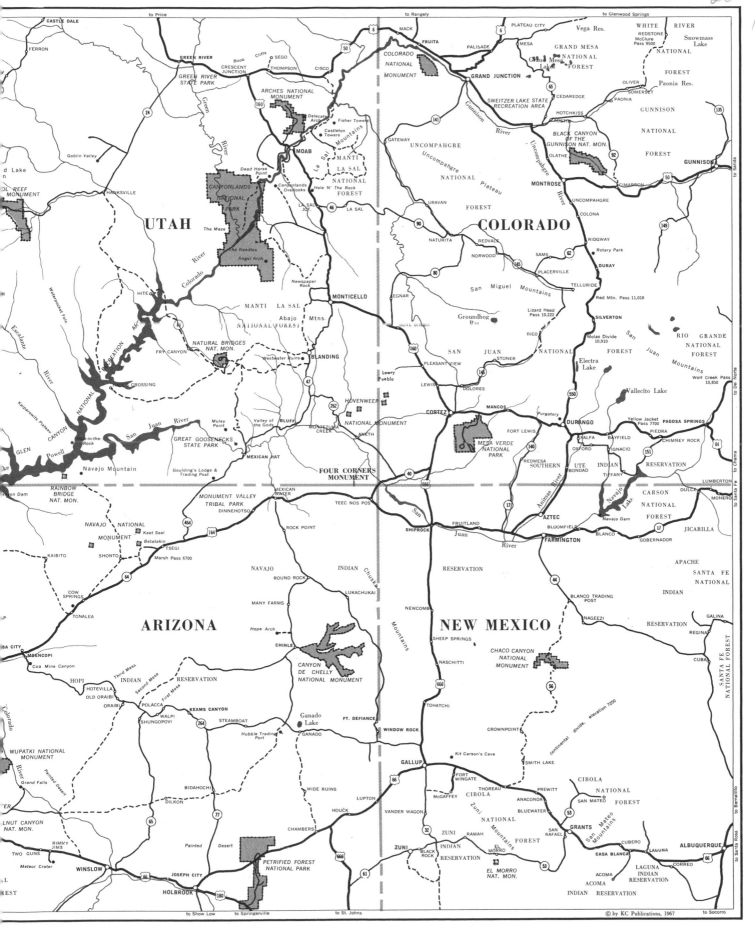

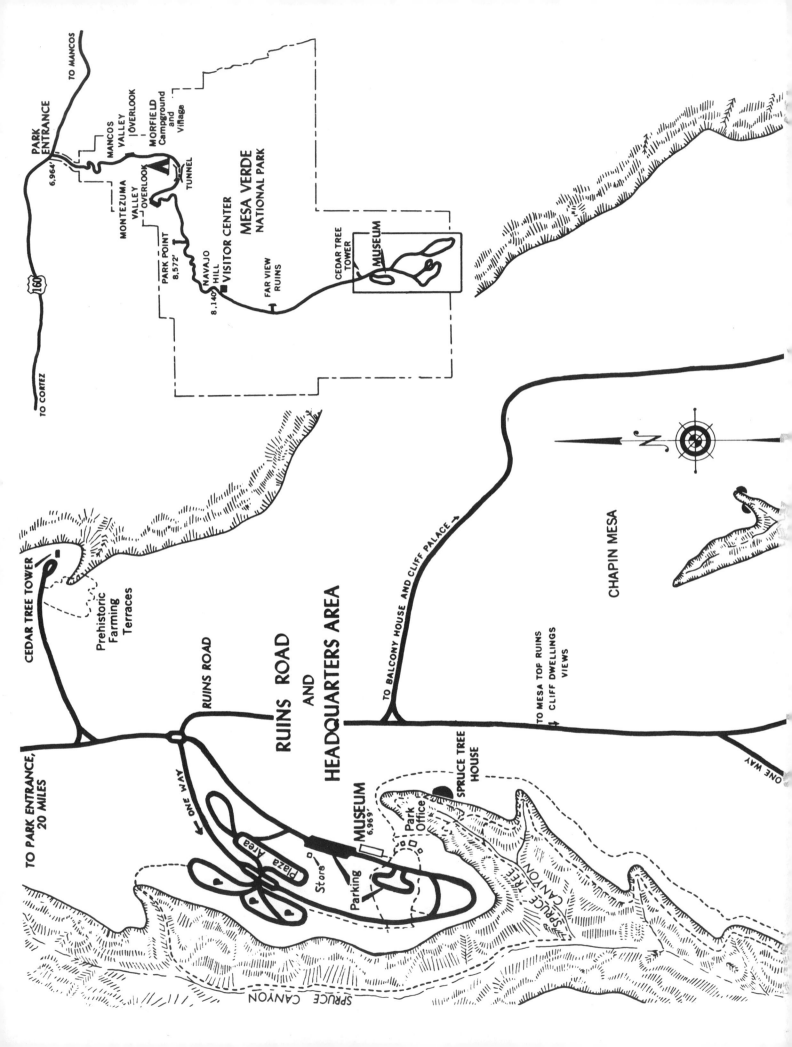

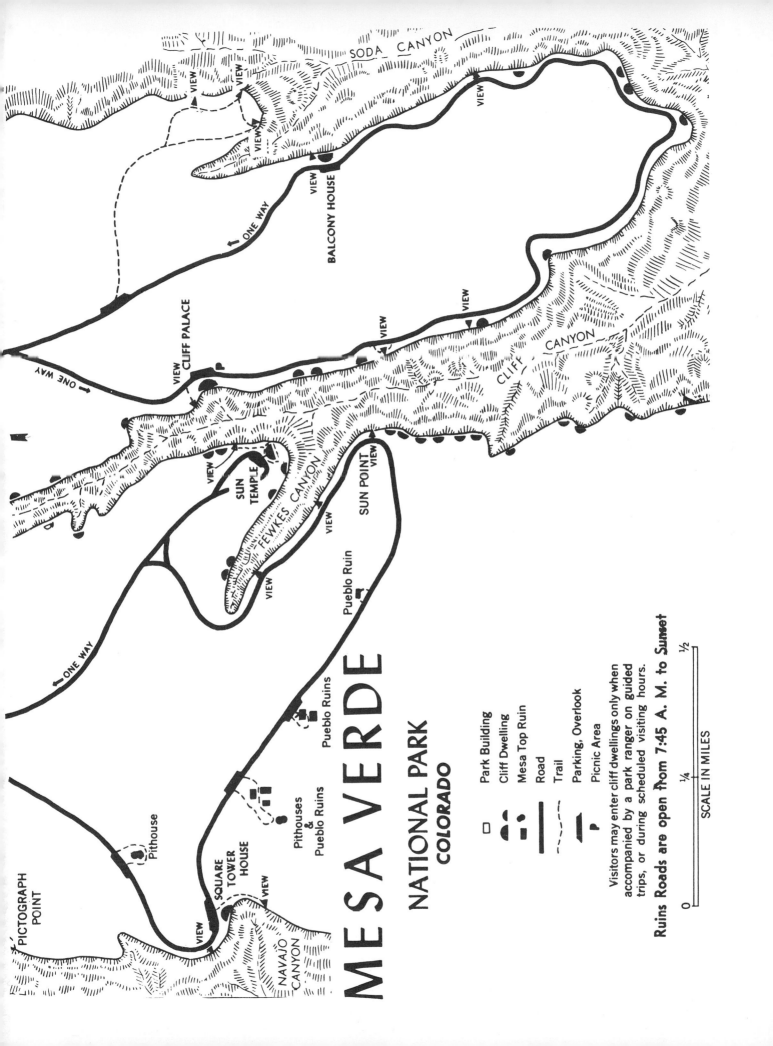

MESA VERDE
NATIONAL PARK
COLORADO

SODA CANYON

VIEW

ONE WAY

VIEW

BALCONY HOUSE

VIEW

CLIFF PALACE

VIEW

VIEW

ONE WAY

CLIFF CANYON

VIEW

SUN TEMPLE

FEWKES CANYON

VIEW

SUN POINT

VIEW

VIEW

Pueblo Ruin

ONE WAY

Pueblo Ruins

Pithouses & Pueblo Ruins

Pithouse

SQUARE TOWER HOUSE

VIEW

VIEW

PICTOGRAPH POINT

NAVAJO CANYON

□ Park Building
⁝ Cliff Dwelling
⁝ Mesa Top Ruin
— Road
- - - Trail
▐ Parking, Overlook
⊿ Picnic Area

Visitors may enter cliff dwellings only when accompanied by a park ranger on guided trips, or during scheduled visiting hours.

Ruins Roads are open from 7:45 A. M. to Sunset

0   ¼   ½

SCALE IN MILES

Litho by INTER-COLLEGIATE PRESS SHAWNEE MISSION, KANSAS

THE CLIFF DWELLERS

OF

THE MESA VERDE

SOUTHWESTERN COLORADO

THEIR POTTERY AND IMPLEMENTS

BY

G. NORDENSKIÖLD

TRANSLATED

BY

D. LLOYD MORGAN

The Rio Grande Press, Inc.

GLORIETA, NEW MEXICO · 87535

First edition from which this edition was reproduced
was loaned to us for this purpose by
MESA VERDE NATIONAL PARK
Ron Switzer, Superintendent

NEW MATERIAL IN THIS EDITION

1. Publisher's Preface.
2. Foreword by Ron Switzer, Superintendent, Mesa Verde National Park.
3. Nordenskiold biographical Introduction by Charlie Steen, former Regional Archaeologist, Southwestern Region, National Park Service.
4. Interpretative Foreword by Robert Lister, Ph. D., former Chairman of Dept. of Anthropology, Univ. of Colo., Boulder. Present Director, Chaco Research Center, a Joint project of the National Park Service and the University of New Mexico.
5. Map of Four Corners country, courtesy K. C. den Dooven, K. C. Publications, Las Vegas, Nev. on endpapers.
6. Endpaper photo of entrance to Park, by Robert B. McCoy.
7. Frontispiece sketch by the late Don Mills.
8. 64 color photographs on 32 color plates, courtesy Mesa Verde National Park collection, Ron Switzer, Superintendent.
9. Map of Mesa Verde National Park, drives and facilities.

Library of Congress Cataloging in Publication Data

Nordenskiöld, Gustaf Erik Adolf, 1868-1895.
    The cliff dwellers of the Mesa Verde, southwestern Colorado.

    (Beautiful Rio Grande classic series)
    Reprint of the 1893 ed. which was published by
P. A. Norstedt & Söner, Stockholm.
    Translation of Ruiner af klippboningar i Mesa Verde's cañons.
    Includes bibliographical references and index.
    1. Cliff-dwellings--Colorado--Mesa Verde. 2. Mesa Verde. 3. Indians of North America--Colorado--Antiquities. 4. Colorado--Antiquities. I. Title.
E78.C6N6713 1979   978.8'27'00497   78-32107

Library of Congress Cataloging in Publication Data
ISBN 0-87380-127-X

A RIO GRANDE CLASSIC
First Published in 1893

Second Printing 1980

GLORIETA, NEW MEXICO · 87535

The moving finger writes,
and having writ

Moves on; nor all your
piety nor wit

Shall lure it back to cancel
half a line

Nor all your tears wash
out a word of it.

Stanza 71
The Rubaiyat of
Omar Khayyam

DONALD MILLS

Publisher's Preface

We are pleased when we can publish another Beautiful Rio Grand Classic (this is the 118th), and we are especially pleased to publish this title. In every sense of the word, *Cliff Dwellers of the Mesa Verde* is a rare book; it is especially difficult to come by on the rare and out-of-print book market. Our good friend and book expert Dick Mohr, of International Bookfinders (P.O. Box 1, Pacific Palisades, Calif. 90272) says he hasn't had or seen a copy offered or sold in twenty years. He suggested he might price a good copy for $1,000 or so, with an immediate lineup of interested buyers. From the strictly materialistic viewpoint, this is indeed a rare book.

But it isn't only money, or even scarcity, that always makes a book "rare"; libraries these days are full of books that will be out of print and forgotten (and rightly so) five years hence (some even sooner). Gustaf Nordenskiöld's work, first published in 1893, is not only a scholarly classic but still a bibliographic masterpiece after 86 years. The Swedish explorer and author wrote with clarity and meticulous detail, so that his work makes good reading today even for the non-scholarly reader. For the hundreds of thousands of visitors who come each year to what is now Mesa Verde National Park, this book should be a real treat. It is big, beautiful, and expensive, but if the visitor enjoys what the Park has to offer, then the visitor will also enjoy what this book has to offer.

We are indebted first to our great and good friend Fred Rosenstock, a former nationally-known rare book dealer (now dealing in Western art) of Denver, who urged us several years ago to reprint this book. Where to find a rare first edition? Even Fred Rosenstock didn't know.

When we approached the superintendent of Mesa Verde National Park, Mr. Ron Switzer, we received eager and willing cooperation. Yes, in their archives was a first edition, and yes, we could borrow it. We invite the reader's attention to Superintendent Switzer's excellent Foreword in the pages immediately following ours. Here the superintendent gives a brief biography of the park, as a park.

From Mr. Switzer, we went to our fellow Westerner friend and colleague Charlie Steen, who lives in Santa Fe and is a former Regional Archaeologist for the Southwest Region of the National Park Service. Mr. Steen was good enough to write some words of his own — a fine recounting of the first discovery and exploration of the ruins at the Mesa Verde. Much of Mr. Steen's Introduction consists of quotations from private correspondence never before published; letters written by Gustaf Nordenskiöld to members of his family, and to some of his friends. These intimate glimpses of the man himself reveal the human side of the scientist. One reads these notes, and has the feeling that author Nordenskiöld might have been a delightful person to know.

In our talks with these men, the name Robert Lister came up repeatedly. A few questions, and we learned that Dr. Lister lived in Corralles, a suburb of Albuquerque, and that he was one of the foremost scholarly authorities on Mesa Verde and its history. One of the abiding pleasures of this business of ours is meeting men like Dr. Bob Lister. He was quite busy in the 1978 pre-Christmas rush, but still he took time to offer a scholar's appraisal of Nordenskiöld's work (as well as the Wetherill brothers') as exemplified in this volume. We are very grateful for his cooperation, and we invite the reader to his words following those of Charlie Steen.

The 64 color photographs, two on each color plate, are from the Park's splendid collection of slide transparencies. We had access to the collection by courtesy of Superintendent Switzer. It was difficult to cull just 64 out of 500 or so; we were limited by the economics of book publishing; color printing doesn't come cheap these days. Even so, we feel we have made an interesting selection which adds beauty as well as interest to this edition. The original slides were duplicated in Chicago by Mr. Jim Berg, owner of Reliable Photocopy Studios. The color separations used for our color plates were made from the duplicate slides.

We would be remiss, we think, if we did not mention our great and good friend Ed Robison of Albuquerque, by profession an Optometrist (and a very good one), and by avocation a self-educated archaeologist, ethnologist, and anthropologist. His office is a veritable museum of beautiful and rare artifacts of the Southwest cultures, and the genial doctor emits a light not even the biggest bushel would cover. A gregarious, outgoing extravert, Dr. Robison confounds people without a sense of humor and delights those who have one. His personal interest in this project went a long way to helping bring our edition into publication, and for his interest, our warm thanks.

There may be some who feel that a reprint of even a rare book is overpriced at the price we are charging for our edition. We have no reluctance to report that a certain publisher in the east reprinted this title in 1973 (it is no longer listed "in print"), adding only a new two-page Introduction and a two-page list of "Selected Reading" titles. The first edition is an oversize book 11 inches by 14½ inches; the 1973 eastern reprint was *reduced* to a small 7 inches by 10 inches. The price of *that* reprint was $84.50. Repeat: $84.50.

Well, that's competition. Or is it?

Mesa Verde National Park is one of the wonders of America. It is set in the midst of even

8

more wonders — the so-called Four Corners country, which is, roughly, adjacent to the Park. Here is a land of wild and primitive beauty, of vivid color contrasts, of breathtaking immensity. Here nature has lavished stupendous and marvelous landscapes; here lies the evidence of rolling seas and vast forests and early man. One should not visit either the Park or the Four Corners country without seeing the other. One wonders, in this gargantuan theater of Time, how the cliff dwellers of Mesa Verde, centuries ago, regarded the natural splendor of their environment. Life was no doubt not very easy or simple in those distant years, but it must have been great to be alive in such a wondrous setting. Maybe we were born too late, and in the wrong place.

Robert B. McCoy

La Casa Escuela
Glovieta, N.M.
March 1979

Foreword

Beginning in March, 1975, the National Park Service initiated a large program to commemorate the historic events and influences that led to the independence and growth of the United States. Among the significant events which have led to the growth of the country was the founding of our National Park System. Inasmuch as our knowledge of the history of many of our National Parks is largely dependent upon books and other written materials it seems timely and appropriate that the Rio Grande Press has chosen to reprint a most remarkable book, *The Cliff Dwellers of the Mesa Verde.* First published in 1893, the volume in a sense commemorates not only the beginning of the science of southwestern archeology, but also the birth of concern for the inestimable worth of the archeological resources that lie within the boundaries of what is now Mesa Verde National Park. The following is a capsule history of the park during the past two centuries which hopefully imparts something of the sense of intimacy with the site that the young Swedish scientist Nordenskiöld experienced eighty-four years ago.

The vast uplifted tableland comprising the Mesa Verde was first seen by Europeans from the base of its northern escarpment by members of one of the most remarkable North American adventures of the nineteenth century. This expedition, led by Fray Silvestre Velez de Escalante from New Mexico into the Great Basain in 1776, skirted the Mesa Verde and even camped at its base on Mud Creek, near the present Mancos, Colorado.

So it was the Mesa Verde became known to the western world. However, the mesa apparently was not visited by Anglo-Americans until about eighty years later when a geologist with the Captain J. N. Macomb Expedition, Professor J. S. Newberry, climbed the north escarpment near Park Point to view the vast green mesa stretching southward below. Newberry, it seems, was the first to use the term "Mesa Verde" (Spanish for green tableland) in print in his 1859 report.

It is generally accepted that a twenty-nine year old photographer named William H. Jackson was the first to explore Mesa Verde cliff dwellings and publish a description of them. In 1874 Jackson was the leader of the Photographic Division of the U. S. Geological and Geographic Survey of the Territories directed by F. V. Hayden, whose purpose it was to investigate and photograph areas of southwestern Colorado. Among the best known cliff dwellings visited by Jackson in September 1874 was Two Story Cliff House in Mancos Canyon. The next year brought W. H. Holmes, later chief of the Bureau of American Ethnology, to the region. The Holmes Expedition described some of the ruins and stone towers and performed the first known excavation in a Mesa Verde cliff dwelling at Sixteen Window House in Mancos Canyon.

It was truly an accident of history that none of the early exploration parties followed up the side canyons of the Mancos River far enough to discover the largest cliff dwellings of the Mesa Verde. Such discoveries were not made until eleven or twelve years later when various members of a local ranching family, the Wetherills of Mancos, made several remarkable finds.

While exploring on foot for ruins during the winter of 1887, Al Wetherill may have been the first to discover Cliff Palace, the largest cliff dwelling. Lacking the time to explore the site, he abandoned the effort, but his discovery was reconfirmed the following winter on December 18, 1888, by his brother Richard and their cousin Charlie Mason. During the ensuing 24 hours after they first saw Cliff Palace, the cowboys also came upon the ruins of Spruce Tree House and Square Tower House. For several years thereafter the five Wetherill brothers and their friends and relatives systematically explored the remaining canyons of the Mesa Verde, naming and excavating ruins and selling large collections of artifacts for profit.

The first woman to visit a Mesa Verde cliff dwelling may have been Mrs. Virginia McClurg, who appears to have visited Balcony House in Soda Canyon as early as 1886, and who later actively led the drive to preserve the magnificent ruins in a national park.

Even though the general looting of archeological sites in the Southwest had begun somewhat earlier in the century, wholesale pot hunting of the Mesa Verde did not occur until after 1888. Such activity caused prodigious damage to the architecture and cultural remains that were everywhere in abundance. However, it is perhaps unfortunate that the Wetherill brothers are so often censured and maligned for digging in the mesa's cliff dwellings; ruthless vandals they were not. While the Wetherills did not employ the techniques and standards of modern archeology, prior to 1900 they made the first extensive efforts to explore and map the Mesa Verde and record the locations of the major ruins. Untutored in science, the collections they excavated with long-handled shovels and documented with painstaking care were at first objects of curiosity. Quickly, however, and quite by historical accident the artifacts became salable antiquities; only later did they become specimens of scientific study. Although many of the Wetherill's collections rest in private hands today, they testify to the care with which their field work was done.

Significant in the history of the park was the archeological work performed during the summer of 1891 by a young Swedish scientist, Gustaf Nordenskiöld. Digging with the Wetherill family, his scientific training overcame his youthful lack of experience in archeology as he carefully measured, photographed and diagrammed the ruins and described the artifacts he found. During his brief stay on the Mesa Nordenskiöld explored and mapped a large number of ruins, including Long House, Mug House, Step House and Kodak House on Wetherill Mesa and several ruins on Chapin Mesa, including the not so well known Painted Kiva House. Perhaps Nordenskiöld's greatest contribution to science lay not in the artifacts he collected, but in his 1893 report *The Cliff Dwellers of the Mesa Verde,* the first major record of archeological work in the United States. Gustaf Nordenskiöld in one summer made the recovery and study of Pueblo artifacts a scientific discipline and set the basic structure of archeological investigations in the Mesa Verde culture area for all scientists who have worked here during the last eight decades.

The hardship and toil of these early explorers was in part rewarded by the protection and preservation afforded Mesa Verde ruins by the act of Congress which created Mesa Verde National Park, June 29, 1906. While there clearly had been some interest in protecting the ruins as early as 1891, it was not until 1900 that the dedicated and untiring efforts of the Colorado Cliff Dwellings Association, lead by Mrs. Virginia McClurg and Mrs. Lucy Peabody, put the legal machinery in motion to obtain national park status for the area.

Within two years after the establishment of Mesa Verde National Park, a permanent superintendent had been appointed by the Secretary, and necessary repairs to the major cliff dwellings had been identified. In 1907 the sum of $2,000 was set aside from the park appropriation to begin a program of excavation and preservation and repair of the cliff dwellings and other ruins. This work was to be done under the immediate direction of Dr. Jesse Walter Fewkes of the Bureau of American Ethnology, commencing in the spring of 1908. Among the more spectacular sites investigated by Fewkes between 1908 and 1922 were Cliff Palace, Spruce Tree House, Sun Temple, the Far View House/Pipe Shrine House complex, Balcony House, New Fire House, Oak Tree House, and Cedar Tree Tower.

By 1916, the year in which the National Park Service was formed, Mesa Verde's annual visitation exceeded the 1,000 mark for the first time and in 1926 had multiplied by ten times that figure. After 1922 archeological work slackened, but Superintendent Jesse L. Nusbaum excavated several pit houses between 1926 and 1929, representing the early periods of occupation on the mesa. Tree ring dating as a means of accurately fixing the time of construction and/or alteration of the well preserved sites was developed by Dr. A. E. Douglas, an astronomer from the University of Arizona between 1923 and 1935. Also during those years a road was brought into the Mesa Verde, providing good access for the ever growing numbers of visitors.

By 1928 the full extent of visitor damage to the ruins had been assessed, and it became painfully apparent that something had to be done. However, even with further appropriations to repair the damage, part of Cliff Palace had to be closed to the public five years later. Fortunately, in 1932 Mesa Verde was the recipient of a public works allotment of $16,500 to carry on a program of ruin stabilization which began in the fall of 1933 under the supervision of Earl Morris, field archeologist of the Carnegie Institution of Washington. In 1934 Morris appointed Al Lancaster and Raymond Dobbins as the nucleus of the permanent stabilization team that was incorporated into park operations. The team still functions at Mesa Verde today under the capable direction of Al Decker, who understudied Mr. Lancaster for a number of years in the art of stabilization.

Lancaster was also an archeologist, and during the course of his 30 years of service at Mesa Verde he worked closely with other archeologists and scientists to fill the many gaps of knowledge about the ruins and their ancient inhabitants.

During the middle 1930's emphasis in research was focussed away from the large multi-stored cliff dwellings to surveying the park for archeological resources and excavating early prehistoric sites as an aid to interpretation. The surveys and excavations were interrupted briefly by World War II, but during the 1950's both programs were reinstated and expanded under the guiding and watchful eyes of Al Lancaster and Chief Park Archeologist Don Watson.

The 1950's saw visitation at Mesa Verde exceed 200,000 persons a year and the necessity to contract with outside institutions for archeological research to relieve the workloads of park staff. Beginning in 1953 the University of Colorado Department of Anthropology, directed by Dr. Robert H. Lister, began an intensive four year program of excavation to add further to the inventory of scientific knowledge. With preservation and research as the hallmarks of National Park Service policy at Mesa Verde, the most important archeological program in its history was initiated in 1958. Named the *Wetherill Mesa Archeological Project*, the interdisciplinary program was sponsored by the National Park Service and the National Geographic Society of Washington, D. C. The disciplines explored during the project included geology, paleobotany, environmental studies and many others that contributed to the total knowledge of the park's prehistoric inhabitants.

With increased visitation during the 1960's it became imperative that a plan be developed to disperse visitors over a wider area of the park. Wetherill Mesa, and the magnificent excavated ruins located there, was chosen for development. A paved access road was constructed to the mesa in 1969, and Long House ruin was opened to the public in the summer of 1973. Further development will take place over the next few years to make additional sites available to park visitors. Visitation at Mesa Verde reached an all time high in 1978 with 650,334 persons making the twenty-one mile drive from the park entrance to view the spectacular ruins.

Current ongoing research at Mesa Verde National Park includes a long term program of intensive site survey under the direction of Dr. David A. Breternitz of the University of

Colorado, as well as studies by other institutions in astroarcheology, seismology, botany, and the application of remote sensing techniques to resources management.

As we study the history of Mesa Verde, our reflections on the past illustrate a measure of concern for archeology that has seldom been so strongly expressed. Today, owing in part to the foresight and perseverance of men such as Gustaf Nordens kiöld and other concerned scientists and citizens, Mesa Verde National Park is the greatest archeological preserve in the United States. Visited by more than one half million people each year, the spectacular ruins and artifacts of a long vanished civilization are protected and preserved as a part of the American heritage and for all people to observe, study and appreciate. The reprinting of Nordenskiold's remarkable book *The Cliff Dwellers of the Mesa Verde* truly commemorates the beginning of the science of southwestern archeology and the sustained effort to preserve park values for future generations.

Ron Switzer
Superintendent

Mesa Verde National Park
Colorado, December 1978

Introduction

During the late summer months of 1891 a young Swede, four cowboys and two laborers were hard at work excavating portions of several cliff dwellings on the Mesa Verde. The Swede was Gustaf Nordenskiöld; the cowboys were brothers — John, Clayton, Richard and Alfred Wetherill of the Alamo Ranch at Mancos. One of the laborers is known only as Earl, because of a couple of references in Nordenskiöld's daily record. We know that the other was named Bill because "he is a rogue" and ate some precious canned fruit which had been intended for Nordenskiöld's table.

The circumstances which led Nordenskiöld to be on the Mesa Verde make a fascinating story.

NORDENSKIÖLD'S EARLY LIFE

Gustaf Nordenskiöld was a scion of a prominent family of Swedish Finns. A Seventeenth Century forebear, Johan Erik, was steward to a Count Wrede and in that position went to Finland to take care of his employer's estates. He established an estate there and acquired three farms near the present city of Turku; the farms remained in the possession of the family until the end of the Nineteenth Century. The family was prominent in scientific and political activities in both Finland and Sweden.

Nils Adolf Erik Nordenskiöld, Gustaf's father, graduated with honors from the University of Helsinki in 1853 and was considered to be a coming scholar. The Russians, however, thought him too radical and in 1855, after an address at the University, he was advised to leave the country which he did, between sundown and sunup. His family followed later. Nils Nordenskiöld then established himself in Stockholm and became prominent in the academic and scientific life of Sweden. He made a number of mineralogical studies in the Arctic, particularly in Spitzbergen but his great accomplishment came in 1878-79 when he led the Vega expedition in the only circumnavigation of Eurasia.

Nil's wife, nee Anna Maria Mannerheim, was the aunt of the future Marshal and President of Finland, Carl Mannerheim. Gustaf Nils Adolf Nordenskiöld was born to this couple on June 29, 1869. He was the second child between two girls, Maria (1864) and Anna (1871). His brother Erland, born in 1877, became professor of Ethnography at the University of Göteborg and an authority on the Indians of South America. Gustaf early was attracted to studies in Natural History and had a particular interest in Lepidoptera. During his secondary school years he made long trips of several weeks at a time, on foot, to collect plants and butterflies as well as mineralogical specimens for his father.

In 1887 Gustaf matriculated at the University of Uppsala. There he applied himself and received his bachelor of arts degree, with high honors, in three years. Among his close friends at the University were Axel Klinckowstrom (who would be with him on the expedition to Spitzbergen in 1890) who became an important student of the arctic and Sven Hedin who was to become a world famous explorer of central Asia.

From this brief description of Nordenskiöld's early life one might picture him as being overly studious. This was not the case. There are many family letters and personal recollections which show that the Nordenskiöld's family life was a lively and happy one — full of visits to and from relatives and friends and with at least its full share of parties, picnics and balls. Gustaf's son-in-law, Olof Arrhenius, has written of his university life, "He seems to have worked very hard, and had little time for the social life of the University. Only occasionally did he take part in student fun. He was more frequently seen at balls in Stockholm where he was a popular partner in great demand."

During the spring of 1890 an expedition was outfitted at Tromso, Norway, for Spitzbergen. The purpose of the voyage was to study fossiliferous strata, collect fossils, map the recession of the Spitzbergen glaciers and make studies of the flora and fauna of the islands and of the animal life of the surrounding waters. The expedition apparently was intended to pay for itself, for among the personnel of the ship were three quarrymen, and a quantity of explosives for mining the rock phosphate deposits of Spitzbergen was carried along. The scientific investigations were to be made by Gustaf and two of his classmates from Uppsala.

The three young men joined their ship, the sailing vessel Lofoten, at Tromso and they sailed for Spitzbergen on May 27. For two months on the island the three scientists and the crew of the Lofoten led extremely rigorous lives. A rich collection of fossils was made, measurements and photographs were made to record the reduction of the glaciers since measurements had been taken 50 years earlier. Nordenskiöld was the photographer for the expedition and his photographs were so captioned and located that subsequent investigators could photograph from the same spots he did in order to record further movements of the ice sheets. In addition more than a ton of phosphate was loaded onto the Lofoten and a large amount stockpiled to be picked up at a later time.

The hard work in the extreme Spitzbergen climate proved to be too much for Gustaf's body. In late summer he returned home ill and developed tuberculosis. His father took him to a sanatorium in Berlin where he stayed from December 1890 to February 1891. He was not bedridden for while in Berlin he wrote an account of his Spitzbergen investigations and his letters home described a rather active social life. While in Berlin he resolved to seek a cure in warmer climates and decided on a trip around the world. He particularly wished to visit Egypt and India.

He left Berlin at the end of February and traveled in a leisurely manner to the south. He stopped in Munich, Rome and Naples, visiting so many museums that "I felt dizzy." After visits to Pompeii and Herculaneum he spent the month of April on Capri.

WESTWARD TRAVELS

Then came a change of plans. Nordenskiöld decided to travel westward rather than to the east. He must have given some reason for this about-face, but present day members of the family do not know why. At any rate, he set sail from Naples on May 1; his steamer , the Algeria, dropped her propeller near Civita Vecchia and he had to take another ship into Marseilles. He continued overland to Paris where he spent a week with Dr. Herman Fritjof Antell. Dr. Antell was another Swedish Finn and a family friend; he will appear again near the end of this narrative of Nordenskiöld's life and career.

On May 27 Nordenskiöld arrived in New York. His description of the city sounds, in part, rather familiar. "New York is an extremely noisy and dirty town, rather better some distance from the center. Thanks to the elevated railroad it does not take long to get between two points in the widespread town. Communications are better than at any place I have visited. I went to New Haven yesterday, and to the Peabody Museum there. There I met Dana, Brush, Marsh, Penfield, who send regards to father. Marsh himself showed me his famous collection of fossil bones, the most extraordinary and interesting things. From New Haven at night straight to Niagara, where I have walked around today. Mother knows how beautiful and magnificent it is, so I won't have to describe it. I shall not go to Boston and Philadelphia."[1]

[1]

From a letter to his family translated, without date, by O. Arrhenius.
The gentlemen at the Peabody Museum at Yale were:
  Dana, James Dwight, 1813-1895, geologist and mineralogist,
  Brush, George Jarvis, 1831- date of death not available, mineralogist,
  Marsh, Othniel Charles, 1831-1899, palaentologist,
  Penfield, Samuel Lewis, 1856-1906, mineralogist.

From Niagara he went to Washington where he spent several days and described it as one of the most beautifully planned cities in the world, thence to Charleston, South Carolina to spend a few more days not only to enjoy the town but also to inquire into phosphate rock production in that region.

He struck inland from Charleston. One of his stops was at Mammoth Cave, Kentucky, where he took the regular guided tour through the caverns. This so fascinated him that he stayed another two days and employed two of the cave guides to take him on some special explorations through the caves. From Kentucky he went to Chicago and from that city to Denver.

An item in his notebook from the days in Denver reads "Cliff dwellers. Pueblo Alto near Chaco Canyon. Met Miss Alice Eastwood in the library at Denver. She gave me letters to Durango and Mancos."[2]

"Denver, Co., June 27, 1891. Just a few lines to tell you I have arrived here safely. As I wrote in my last letter, I have a free ticket from Chicago. I have now also a free pass down to Durango in South Colorado and back here again. I am going there to look at the cliff dwellers (sic); on my way back I shall visit Pikes Peak and many other places. I have no money to buy minerals or, at least very little. ———The cliff dwellers I mentioned are about 45 miles from the railway station at Durango, a stretch that must be covered on horseback."

ON THE MESA VERDE

"Mancos, Montezuma Co., Colorado, July 11, 1891. I mentioned in my last letter that I was going to S. W. Colorado to see the so-called cliff dwellings in Mancos Canyon. I went by train to Durango and from there by coach to Mancos. There I stayed with a farmer Wetherill, who drives his cattle in the tract where the cliff dwellings are, and thus knows them well. He himself, is old, and stays at home while the boys drive the cattle down into the valley. I decided to go with them to a place where they camp, and then go with one of them to visit the ruins. My intention was to stay about a week at Mancos Canyon. Now the week has gone, and I have made up my mind to stay for one or two months.

2
    This, and the following items from his notebook as well as the quotations from letters were translated by O. Arrhenius. Miss Eastwood, well known western botanist, was at that time teaching in Denver and later went to the University of California. She was a friend of the Wetherill family of Mancos, Colorado, had recently visited the Wetherills and was familiar with the recently discovered cliff dwellings of the Mesa Verde.

"First I will tell you about my first trip down to the ruins. The first day we rode twenty-four miles along the Mancos Valley down to Blowout. The following day we rode up on the mesa, one of the plateaux of the canyon, and from there about ten miles to Cliff Canyon, on to Navajo Canyon, where there is a small spring of good water; otherwise water is scarce in these regions. In the last-named canyon we visited a small cliff dwelling. It could be reached from the top of the canyon wall; the descent was made easy by steps cut once upon a time by the inhabitants of the house. The dwelling was in the wall, and the overhanging cliffs above formed a roof. The rooms were small, the walls well preserved. From this cliff dwelling we rode back to a branch of Cliff Canyon, which we crossed on foot, leaving our horses on smoother ground; on the other side there was a large number of cliff dwellings on a high shelf of rock. The place is called 'Cliff Palace.'

"If I can I will send you a view of it in the letter. It will be sent as printed matter, with a photograph of Wetherill's collection. From there we returned to the camp, where we arrived in the evening. The following day we rode down Mancos Canyon to look at some figures cut in the rock, some of which I drew. The next day I took two men with me and rode along the bottom of Cliff Canyon to a small cliff dwelling, which I decided to excavate. We camped the first night at the bottom of the canyon. The first afternoon, a whole day and the following morning we spent digging. The dwelling contained eleven rooms, two round, the rest square, all formed according to the cliffs. The ceilings of the two round rooms had caved in, and the walls were partly ruined; in the first of these I found most of the things mentioned in the list below. After digging was finished I returned to Mancos, after exactly a week in camp in the open air.

"I mentioned in my first letter that the only scientific expedition that has studied the dwellings was that of Holmes and Jackson in 1874.[3] They determined the situation of several ruins, that was practically all. A stone axe, a few earthernware pots, grains of maize were all they found. They noted specially the absence of human beings and animals (see my list, numbers 69; 115; and 118.) One reason why they did not dig more thoroughly was probably that the Indians were then hostile, now they are quite harmless. A few years ago Wetherill's

3
Jackson, William H.
  1876 - Ancient Ruins in Southwestern Colorado
        8th Annual Report U.S. Geological and Geographical Survey of the Territories for 1874. Washington
Holmes, W. H.
  1878 - Report on the Ancient Ruins of Southwestern Colorado 10th Annual Report
        U.S. Geological and Geographical Survey of the Territories for 1876. Washington

sons (cowboys, but with a surprising degree of education) started digging in the ruins. On the first visit a considerable collection of practically all kinds of household implements, several skulls, a couple of mummies, i.e., dried human bodies, etc., was found, almost exclusively in 'Cliff Palace'. The collection was sold to a museum in Denver for $3,000.00".

Now he went to work. The Wetherills had a base camp in Mancos Canyon from which they managed their range herd. This camp was also used as the headquarters for the diggers. We do not know the exact arrangement between Nordenskiöld and the Wetherills but John Wetherill was employed as foreman at $3.00 per day. The other brothers worked on the mesa whenever they could be spared from regular ranch chores and two day laborers were employed. There is no record of the pay rate for any of the men except John.

Apparently the routine of work consisted of John and the labor force of the day digging in a cliff dwelling of John Wetherill's selection. Whenever the number of artifacts found diminished, the crew would move to another, more lucrative appearing ruin. Nordenskiöld frequently left the dig and went exploring with one of the younger Wetherill brothers; he investigated ruins in Mancos and Johnson Canyons, south of the Mesa Verde, as well as in most of the canyons on the mesa.

A soon as he had decided to spend two months on the mesa he sent home for his camera; this was a view camera which exposed glass plates. In addition to the plates there are about 50 cellulose negatives, 7.5 x 10 cm. of the ruins and of the trip to the Grand Canyon which was to follow the digging. One suspects that he had bought or borrowed a roll film camera to use until his large camera arrived.

Life on the Mesa Verde during the Nordenskiöld/Wetherill excavations can best be described in Nordenskiöld's words:

"Navajo Canyon July 31, 1891

"Just now our camp is at Navajo Canyon, about forty-five miles from Mancos, the outpost of civilization. Imagine a wood of low pines and a kind of tall juniper called cedars, but by no means of the same type as the so-called cedars of Lebanon. Our cedars are not much taller than a twenty or thirty year old spruce or pine at home in Sweden. The soil is sandy and half bare. A large piece of sail-cloth stretched between two trees is our bedroom, i.e., mine and my foreman's. Ten paces from there is a dirtier piece of sailcloth; two Mexicans[4] sleep under that.

4

Twice Nordenskiöld refers to the laborers as Mexican. With one named Bill and the other Earl this does not seem likely. It is known that there were Utes at the Alamo Ranch and it is probable that these men were Indians.

One of them speaks a little English. He is a rogue; I once sent him to Mancos to buy provisions and fetch some preserves to vary our monotonous diet of cereals. On his return he told a story of how one of the horses had bolted and lost part of its pack (five or six of the most delicious tins of fruit were missing.) But I understood what had happened; he and his friend had eaten at least four large tins of preserved fruit that I had bought for my own private consumption. When I rode over the same trail a little later, I saw with sorrow a whole lot of opened tins with the most tempting labels lying by the roadside. Bill — that is the rogue's name — had also got a dollar in advance on his wages, had spent it in whiskey and come home drunk. I am glad he did not leave the country with all my three horses.

"But that is enough about Bill; let us return to the camp. If you go under my roof you will find an excellent bed, i.e. a frame of split juniper trunks. This is for protection from a very unpleasant species of animal, which I will return to later. Beside the bedstead is a large heap of saddles, saddlecloths, spurs, bridles, etc. Two paces outside my room is a table, a real table, somewhat a la Robinson Crusoe, but nevertheless a table. A cloth — a piece of sailcloth, dirty and blotched — is spread over it. Under the table is a raised compartment for some of the provisions, to protect them from the above implied enemies. A little way from the table is the kitchen, still more unpretentious than the dining room. It consists most often of half-burned bits of wood, when it is not cooking time, for then there is a cheerfully blazing fire.

"Below the kitchen, about twenty or thirty paces away, is our spring, which explains why we camped there, a mile and a half from the place where we are working. Springs are rare in these tracts. Ours has the advantage over some others in that it does not contain a kind of bitter water which, when consumed in tea, coffee, porridge and so on, has an effect far greater than that of castor oil.[5] The spring also provides water for our horses, now grazing near the camp with their forelegs tied together. My experience as a horse owner, like that of many other people in the same category, is not the most pleasant. The same day it was found that one of my horses had gone astray, another was lame and the drunken Mexican managed to get the third saddle-galled. The stray returned, but the lame one remained lame, and 'Old Rigg' still had a bad back.

"Our day begins at six o'clock in the morning. I have the privilege of lying a little longer while Bill fetches the horses, and John Wetherill, the foreman, (who has three dollars a day, almost as much as a professor in the Old World) makes breakfast. This usually consists of bread, baked at the camp in the frying pan, fried bacon, porridge, coffee, tomatoes, sometimes rice and boiled apples. We cannot have fresh meat, for it keeps only two or three days in the

5
Many of the springs in the Four Corners area have a high gypsum contest.

23

heat. At the signal, 'Breakfast ready!' we gather round the dirty table, which is cleared of everything eatable in an incredibly short time.

"Then we wash up, whereupon we saddle our horses, the water bottles are filled, and we set off along the narrow path to a place on the mesa above the ruin where we are working. We unsaddle our horses and tie their forelegs together. Then we climb a long, roundabout way down to the ruin. There we dig, sketch, photograph, label finds and so on till the sun is high in the sky. Then we have dinner, a tin of corned beef and a loaf of bread is all we get, for we cannot have much with us; then we resume work again until the sun begins to sink in the west and the shadows on the side of the canyon grow long. Then up in the saddle again and back to camp. Soon the campfire blazes up, the tea can is put on the flame, and supper, with about the same menu as breakfast, is eaten rather faster if possible. Sometimes we try, always in vain, to trap the unpleasant animals hinted at above. Then to bed, I in my sleeping bag (I have introduced this incomparable article to these regions).

"Just as I am about to fall asleep I hear a suspicious rustling sound close to me. I look to the left and see a large bushy tail. An inexperienced person would take his revolver, shout, or in some other violent way try to get rid of the uninvited guest. But woe to him if he does that! The long tail belongs to a skunk, a small beast of prey which, at the first hint of danger, 'makes a big stink', that is, it spreads an odor that is unbearable. People known for their love of veracity maintain that a skunk can be smelled at a range of six miles, which there is perhaps reason to doubt, however. One thing is certain — if we make them let off their 'stink' we could not stay here by our spring any longer, but would have to move another site. That is why I hurriedly lay aside my revolver and with a slow movement gently urge the beast to go away. But this is not the only one; round our camp flock of about a dozen of the horrid creatures. They are attracted by our bacon, and disturb us the whole night; I am afraid we must surrender the bacon to get rid of them. Despite all the skunks we soon fall asleep and wake up the following morning to begin a new day, very similar to all the others, but which always brings new events and enriches the memory with new experiences."

On September 5 the men completed their work on the Mesa Verde and returned to Mancos. Nordenskiöld intended to dig for an additional month on the Ute Mountain Indian Reservation, and applied for and received permission to do that. Before starting out on this new endeavor he packed the Mesa Verde artifacts in nine crates and took them to Durango to ship to the Swedish Consul in New York.

The Durango and Denver newspapers then began a campaign in which it was claimed that this foreigner had illegally excavated artifacts and was now trying to sneak them out of the country. On September 16 Nordenskiöld was arrested by the U.S. Marshall, at the request of Agent Bartholomew of the Ute Reservation; he was granted bail on surety of $1000. After a month of charges in the press the court decided that no law had been violated and ordered the impounded artifacts to be released.[6]

TO THE GRAND CANYON

The delay, and the costs of the court action, made Nordenskiöld change his plans and he confined his activities on the Ute Reservation to a quick survey of a part of Mancos Canyon and Johnson Canyon. Then, on November 4, Gustaf Nordenskiöld, Al Wetherill and a third man we know only as Rob left Mancos on a horseback trip to the Grand Canyon. They rode through Cortez and thence to Noland's, a trading post on the San Juan River. One difficulty with overland travel in those days was bad stock and Al's horse was a wild one; it sometimes took until noon to get the horses packed and on the trail. This was the case on the first day and again on the day they left Noland's.

At Noland's they hired a Navajo guide to lead them across the reservation to the Hopi villages. They rode well to the north and west of Shiprock then around the northern spur of the Chuckaluck (Chuska) Mountains, then up the Chinle Valley and over Black Mesa. On November 15 they arrived at a village at the foot of Hopi First Mesa.

". . . . . We stayed with Tom, an English and Spanish speaking Moki who has a rather large house at the foot of the mesa. Tom himself is a friendly man and can express himself tolerably well in English. He has a large fat wife. A younger woman, not at all bad looking, is presumably his daughter . . . . . ."[7]

On the sixteenth the men visited the villages on First Mesa and learned that there would be a dance at Walpi on the following day so they stayed on to watch it. Gustaf's brief description of the dance is reproduced here in its entirety.

"Nov. 17. Dance. Bought several things. Half naked men and youth with yellow, blue, white lines under their eyes, jumped in time, two (flashes of lightning) ran in the final act, in which all took part in front of the row past each other. The first dance, each estufa alone. Final act all together. White doctor in the village. The girls were difficult to photograph; boys a nickle a time."

6

    The first of the U.S. laws to deal with antiquities was the "Act for the Preservation of American Antiquities" approved June 8, 1906. (34 Stat L. 225) Neither this nor any subsequent law prohibits artifacts being taken from the country; the only restrictions are that artifacts recovered from public domain be deposited in a public institution and that a report of the results of the excavations be made to the government.

7

    Tom was probably Tom Polacca, for whom this village is now named. Polacca established a home at the foot of the mesa in 1890 and several other Hopi soon built houses nearby.

There is not much meat for ethnologists there. One wonders about the "white doctor in the village". Alexander Stephen[8] was at Walpi that day and described this dance on page 959 et seq. of the *Journal*. Stephen wrote that "T.V.K. drove me over to Walpi. I took up quarters in Wik-ya'-tiwa's house to watch Naash'naiya." the ceremony began on the tenth of the month and what Nordenskiöld saw were the last public dances, almost the last acts of the ceremony. Presumably Tom Kean, The T.V.K. of Stephen's *Journal*, did not stay at Walpi and Stephen and the Nordenskiöld party were probably the only Europeans present.

The *Journal* is concerned only with the ceremony, but if the men met, it seems strange that Nordenskiöld failed to mention Stephen. Did the men look at each other in the small crowd of spectators and not speak? Does "doctor in the village" refer to Stephen? ¿Quien sabe?

On the eighteenth they rode to Oraibi where they stayed until the twenty-first. From Nordenskiöld's description of the country it seems that on the next day they rode northwest around the head of Coalmine Canyon then dropped into Moenkopi Wash to the Mormon settlement at Tubu (Tuba City). One of the Mormons agreed to guide them to Grand Canyon; he had a mining claim in the inner gorge. So off they went on the twenty-fifth down the Moenkopi to the Little Colorado which they followed for a short distance then cut across to Lee's Tank which they reached on the thirtieth. The tank was dry and the nearest water was in the Colorado River. The route they followed into the Canyon is uncertain but they reached the river after dark that night.

They stayed in the Canyon three days and visited the Mormon's claim which lay on the right bank of the river; they crossed the stream on a driftwood log raft the Mormon made. In the notebook for the three days there is no word of the canyon as a spectacle. They were near the upper end of the Inner Gorge and from their camp would not have seen the great colorful vistas which we see from the rims of the canyon; steep granite walls, a thousand feet high, would have hemmed them in. About all we are told of the canyon bottom is that it was summerlike down there.

Perhaps by this time they were too much engrossed in personal problems to be entranced by scenery. Their clothes were worn out, their shoes were falling apart and had to be mended with such tools and materials as they had, and, very important indeed, they were about out of food and had virtually no money. When they reached the plateau again they had passed from the warm days in the canyon to bitter cold with strong winds and snow. They rested for a couple of days at Tubu , exchanged one of their pack horses for food, then started on toward

8
Stephen, Alexander M.
1936 - Hopi Journal. Edited by Elsie Clews Parsons. 2 volumes, Columbia University Press, New York.

Mancos. The return route led past Red Lake (Tomalea) and probably Marsh Pass to the San Juan River. The weather was bad with cold and snow and, on one day, fog. Several times they took a wrong trail and had to backtrack and their provisions were quite low. On the morning of December eighteenth breakfast consisted of bread made with baking powder, but that afternoon they reached Bluff, Utah, bought some food and on the evening of the twenty-first were back at the Alamo Ranch.

BACK TO SWEDEN

The trip to the Grand Canyon ended Gustaf's American adventures. He returned to Sweden and began work on a report of his excavations on the Mesa Verde. He published a small book in Swedish (the translated title is "From the Far West") which was compiled from his travel notes and letters home. At this time he also translated several of Jules Verne's stories into Swedish, and in 1892 he took about fifty of the Mesa Verde artifacts to Madrid where he exhibited them at the Columbus Jubilee.

In 1893 he published the archaeological report *Cliff Dwellers of the Mesa Verde.* The work was printed in both Swedish and English and the volume for which this introduction is written is a copy of the English version.

1893 was one of the most important years of Nordenskiöld's life. In addition to seeing his book published he became engaged to Anna Rudolfina Smitt. Banns for the marriage were published on December 17 that year, but we have no record of the exact date of the wedding. A daughter, Anna Eva Amalia, was born in 1894.

Nordenskiöld's health deteriorated. There is an undated letter from him (probably late spring of 1894) to Richard Wetherill in which he stated that his health had not been good for the preceding month and he had not been out of bed since May 5. During the following winter he grew worse and, in the spring, asked to be taken to the mountains of Jamtland. He died there June 5, 1895 at Morsil Station and then was buried at Västerljung with other members of his family.

AN EVALUATION OF NORDENSKIÖLD'S WORK AND COLLECTION.

When the *Cliff Dwellers of the Mesa Verde* was published, the collection of artifacts was acquired by Dr. Antell with whom Gustaf spent a week in Paris in 1891. There is no record of a purchase but Antell probably bought the collection. In a letter home, on July 11, 1891, Nordenskiöld discussed sale of the artifacts to pay for the expedition. Dr. Antell had extensive collections and willed them to the people of Finland. On his death in 1897, the Mesa Verde artifacts were first lodged in the old State Museum of History and Ethnography. When the present Kansallismuseo (the National Museum of Finland) was established in 1909 the collection was transferred there. It is still housed in the Kansallismuseo, not on display but well stored on the upper floor with other foreign collections. Museum staff members plan for the day when an addition to the museum building will permit display of their important foreign collections but that day has not yet come.

Gustaf Nordenskiöld was an extraordinary young man. Here was a fellow who had no training in archeology (not unusual for there was practically no training in the subject in the Nineteenth Century) who supervised a remarkably efficient excavation. Some of the direction of the job must be credited to the Wetherills who had already dug one large collection from the Mesa Verde cliff dwellings but by far the most credit must go to the Swede.

His studies in mineralogy must have included work in geology and, by 1890, stratigraphical studies were well established techniques in geology. In *Cliff Dwellers of the Mesa Verde* there are several references to comparative age as shown by stratigraphy. Also, his studies would have stressed the importance of keeping a record of the work and he transferred the system of recording mineralogical work to archaeological.

The various ruins he visitedwere carefully marked with a prefix N, for his name and then numbered in sequence as he recorded them. At each ruin this number is neatly engraved in the sandstone cliff. There can be no confusion as to the location of the ruins Nordenskiöld described.

A ground plan was prepared for each ruin and the rooms were numbered. The excavation notes and the catalogue of each artifact found give the name of the ruin (if it had one) and the numbers in Nordenskiöld's survey system as well as the room number. Artifacts were catalogued as to where they were found and their association with other artifacts. In order to appreciate Nordenskiöld's careful recordation of his work one must go to the poorly prepared and scant notebooks of some of his comtemporaries.

In addition to these practices Nordenskiöld apparently felt that there must be more to archaeology than simply removing artifacts from the ground. The collection has a number of items that probably no other excavator of 1891 would have kept yet a digger of the present day would carefully save for future study. For instance:

Specimen # 210, from Long House, is dessicated human excrement.
An excavator today would have that analyzed to determine just what that human had been eating and would also have the specimen checked for remains of intestinal parasites.
Specimen # 711, from Ruin 9. This is a small quantity of wood ash from a firepit.
Specimen, uncatalogued, from Cliff Palace. A small quantity of dust and small trash from a room floor.

These are only a few samples; there are numerous specimens of unworked twigs, bark, etc., in the collection. One has the impression that Nordenskiöld sensed that information could be gleaned from such material but the technology and interest of the day was not ready for this type of investigation.

All in all, Gustaf Nordenskiöld was a much more careful and observant an excavator than were most of his contemporaries. What is particularly important is that he quickly got his notes in order and produced a good solid report of the excavations in so short a time.

Charlie Steen

Santa Fe, N.M.
December 1978

Interpretative Foreword

"Nordenskiöld's monumental work on Mesa Verde appeared in 1893, describing field work during the summer of 1891. The report is magnificently illustrated and describes sites, associated artifacts, kiva paintings, and reservoirs of the Mesa Verde proper. It includes a description of the largest ruin on the Mesa, Cliff Palace, which had not been found by Jackson and Holmes. With true nobility Nordenskiold gives full credit to his nonacademic associates. 'The honor of discovery of these remarkable ruins belongs to Richard and Alfred Wetherill of Mancos.'

"At the outset Nordenskiöld exhibited technical caution which is or should be, common practice today. Before attacking the more complicated large ruins, he conducted a 'trial excavation' in a small ruin in Cliff Canyon, clearing 2 kivas and a few rooms. After this the main excavations were begun on Wetherill Mesa. One month was spent at Long House with a crew consisting of John Wetherill and 2 Mexicans. Another laborer was added for 2 weeks' work at Kodak House, so called because a camera was kept hidden in one of the rooms. And one more digger was added for 2 weeks' more excavation at Mug House and Step House. Projected excavations at Spruce Tree House were abandoned, because of difficulty with the authorities over shipment of specimens to Sweden. During the delay thus occasioned, 2 weeks were spent in exploration, in the mapping of ruins, and in taking of 150 photographs.

"It is impossible to discover from the report, and this is a fault when judged by modern standards, how many rooms were actually cleared. Judging by the descriptions, by the size of the crew, and by the time spent, the total could not have been very great. The main value of this work lies in the excellence of presentation, the reasonably clear descriptions of the artifacts, the photographs and plans, and the general observations on physiography and ecology, important aspects of archaelogical research generally ignored during the 1890's."

The above, written by John Otis Brew of Harvard's Peabody Museum in 1946, is contained in a discussion of the history and extent of Mesa Verde archeology, a part of his comprehensive report upon the *Archaeology of Alkali Ridge, Southeastern Utah.* It is a brief discription and an evaluation of Nordenskiöld's investigations and the report he wrote following his field work by a noted present-day archeologist who, long after the young Swede's time, also delved into the prehistory of Mesa Verde. Brew's comments reflect the opinion generally held by archeologists, particularly those who have worked in Mesa Verde or are familiar with its ancient cultural remains, regarding the scientific merit of Nordenskiöld's work. Prior references to *The Cliff Dwellers of the Mesa Verde* appeared in earlier archeological literature upon the Southwest, but they do not contain opinions about the quality of the report. However, the fact that leading Southwestern archeologists frequently referred to Nordenskiöld's work, especially the illustrations and descriptions of artifacts, indicate the respect afforded him by later professionals.

Alfred V. Kidder in his 1924 volume, *An Introduction to the Study of Southwestern Archaeology,* the first full review of the subject wrote,

> "The minor arts of the Mesa Verde culture have been well described by
> Nordenskiöld, Fewkes, and Morris."

He went on to note that good illustrations of Mesa Verde type pottery are to be found in several reports, including that of Nordenskiöld. Earl Morris in his voluminous monograph, *Archaeological Studies in the La Plata District,* published in 1939, indirectly judged the caliber of Nordenskiöld's study when in discussing the perishable remains from the cliff houses, he stated

> "Considerable quantities are present from the Mesa Verde in the various widely
> scattered collections from that district, but few of these have been even presented
> as illustrations except those figured by Nordenskiöld."

Morris' report makes 15 additional references to Nordenskiöld's illustrations and quotes his descriptions of artifacts in two instances, attesting both to the quality of the figures and the accuracy of the descriptive accounts.

Ironically, recognition of Nordenskiöld's contributions and ways of doing archeology came late. American archeologists, and there were but few around in the 1890's, were not ready to properly evaluate his findings and accept his methods. He simply was ahead of the times. And, the public looked upon Nordenskiöld's book as another travel account of the unexplored West. It was a custom then for scions of wealthy European families to travel through many of the lesser known territories of the United States, to write books about their experiences, and to display their collections of ethnographic and archeological specimens, paintings, and photographs of the American Indians and their ancestors at fairs and in private showings.

Many of Nordenskiölds's deductions about the Indians and culture of Mesa Verde, and the techniques he used in arriving at those conclusions, would later be accepted as correct interpretations and standard practices. For example, he recognized the circular rooms in the cliff dwellings as being earlier counterparts of the modern Pueblo kiva, and correctly identified certain features on the mesas as reservoirs. While digging in Step House, he astutely considered a crudely made pottery vessel found in a trash deposit in the cave to be unlike the fine pottery of the Cliff Dwellers, and surmised that it might have belonged to an older people who had inhabited the cave before the erection of the cliff village. Thirty years later his supposition would be proved correct when excavators found a number of Basket Maker pithouses in that portion of the cave where Gustaf had dug up his unusual piece of pottery.

He was not content to simply describe the form and decoration of the pottery vessels he collected, but identified methods of manufacture and even a distinction between the materials used in cooking jars and decorated pots. The age of Spruce Tree House was judged to be at least 200 years, after he had cut down a spruce tree growing through a masonry wall and counted its annual growth rings — a forerunner of the tree-ring method of dating Southwestern ruins. And, he even taught Richard Wetherill to dig with a trowel rather than a shovel.

One of Nordenskiöld's contributions to Southwestern archeology appears to me to have been overlooked. It is true that *The Cliff Dwellers of the Mesa Verde* has been called "the first major record of archeological work in the United States," but his bringing of scientific methodology to archeological investigations went well beyond his personal experiences at Mesa Verde. Kidder stated in his pioneering treatise on Southwestern archeology,

> "Apparently the first application of the principle of stratigraphy to Southwestern problems was made by Richard Wetherill, when in the nineties he defined the Basket-Maker culture, and then determined, by discovering its remains below those of cliff-houses, that it represented an earlier chronological period rather than a mere local development."

I wonder if Gustaf Nordenskiöld should not be given some credit for this? Let's review the circumstances in reverse order.

In 1893, Richard Wetherill led an expedition to the Grand Gulch country of southeastern Utah to obtain a collection of archeological specimens for the wealthy Hyde brothers of New York. The brothers, Talbot and Fred, had become deeply interested in securing "relics" from the Southwestern ruins and Richard and his brothers were experts at the business; so, a partnership was formed. Frank McNitt in his excellent book, *Richard Wetherill: Anasazi*, has described the following events.

Before leaving for Grand Gulch, Richard wrote Talbot Hyde, proposing the methods of work which he would use:

> " 'I arrived here night before last and will commence on Monday to outfit with such articles as cannot be procured at Durango. I send a form of work (a record sheet twelve by thirteen inches and ruled off in squares) that will meet all requirements unless something else occurs to you that would be of special interest. I find there are none printed but I can do as heretofore, secure blanks and mark them myself in this manner — viz:

1 number of house or ruin	2 number of article	3 name of article	4 number of room
5 number of section	6 depth	7 number of floors if any	8 remarks

'Every article to be numbered with India ink and fine pen or with tube paints white, red, or black. Plan of all houses & sections to be made on paper with numbers and name. Photograph each house before touched, then each room or section and every important article as found.

'I think you will find this will meet all the requirements of the most scientific but if you have any suggestions whatever I will act upon them. This whole subject . . . is in its infancy and the work we do must stand the most rigid inspection, and we do not want to do it in such a manner that anyone in the future can pick flaws in it.'

"Richard knew that whatever he brought out of Grand Gulch would be given by the Hyde brothers to the American Museum of Natural History. The value of the collection would depend entirely upon his ability to document every phase of his work . . . Richard was a groping, untutored but ardent pioneer. He had nothing but his own past experience and his ingenuity to guide him. He knew his limitations, his lack of scientific training or education, but he hoped that his work would stand 'the most rigid inspection' of the scientific men who had not yet ventured out into his country."

The Grand Gulch party was in the field for four months. Besides Richard Wetherill it included his brothers John and Al, a photographer, and four others. They amassed a collection weighing over a ton and numbering 1,216 specimens. McNitt continues his narrative,

"Richard's party had proceeded no farther than the ruins of Cottonwood Wash when he began to find proof of a people which had used the caves before the arrival of the Cliff Dwellers. Far below the floor level of the cliff dwellings he uncovered burial remains which in most respects were foreign to anything he had ever seen before. These remains he found in burial pits, round or oval cysts which in some cases had been used previously for storing food.

After additional digging Wetherill was able to list some sharp contrasts in cultural practices and supposed physical attributes between the two groups of people.

"There was no doubt in Richard's mind that he had made a significant discovery, when he wrote from his camp on Cottonwood Wash to Talbot Hyde one evening in December, 1893:

'Our success has surpassed all expectations . . . In the cave we are now working we have taken 28 skeletons and two more in sight and curious to tell, and a thing that will surprise the archaelogists of the country is the fact of our finding them at a depth of five and six feet in a cave in which there are cliff dwellings and we find the bodies under the ruins, three feet below any cliff dweller sign. They are a different race from anything I have ever seen. They had feather cloth and baskets, no pottery — six of the bodies had stone spear heads in them   '

"Talbot Hyde asked Richard for specific information. In reply, Richard for the first time referred to 'the Basket People' to distinguish the older people from the Cliff Dwellers. He said he could 'now easily separate the two classes of people and their belongings,' and added: 'I named the cliff dwellers, and you should have the honor at least of naming these, since it is your expedition.' "

"Talbot Hyde followed Richard's suggestion that he name Richard's 'Basket People,' replying he thought they might be called Basket Makers."

Thus, as Kidder had stated, Richard Wetherill, using stratigraphic evidence, had defined and named, with Talbot Hyde's help, the Basket Makers. Furthermore, in conducting his excavations he had employed a standardized system of recording, cataloguing, sketching, and photographing his finds. Were these archeological techniques, which were quite advanced for the time, the result of "his own past experience and ingenuity?" A past experience may well account for them.

Two years prior, in 1891, Gustaf Nordenskiöld had spent the summer digging in the Mesa Verde cliff dwellings. He stayed with the Wetherill family and they assisted him in his investigations. Although John Wetherill served as Gustaf's guide and foreman most of the time, Richard accompanied them in the field whenever his ranch duties would allow. Richard carefully observed Nordenskiöld's progress and methods and sometimes joined in the digging. Although lacking training in archeology, Nordenskiöld successfully applied his background in natural history and his field experiences in observing and collecting scientific data and specimens to his archeological endeavors. He understood the principle of stratigraphy from his work in geology, was a keen observer of details, kept detailed written and photographic records, made plans and maps, and carefully catalogued all articles recovered. Richard Wetherill's background was quite different, but he had become thoroughly engrossed in archeological exploration and was an eager learner. Undoubtedly he absorbed a great deal by observing Nordenskiöld's techniques and listening to the remarks, suppositions, and queries put forth by the young foreigner in an English that was amusing and sometimes hard to understand. It is only logical to believe that when Richard Wetherill planned and conducted his Grand Gulch explorations he applied many of the techniques Nordenskiöld had used at Mesa Verde. In addition, Richard soon would embark upon a long-term excavation program in Chaco Canyon, backed again by the Hyde brothers, where he also employed some of the technical skills he presumably had learned from Nordenskiöld. Richard had learned well, and that certainly is to his credit, but Nordenskiöld's likely influence upon him has gone unrecognized.

Robert H. Lister
Professor of Anthropology
University of New Mexico

Albuquerque, N.M.
December 1978

List of References

Brew, John Otis
    1946. Archaeology of Alkali Ridge, Southeastern Utah. Papers of the Peabody Museum of American Archaeology and Ethnology, Harvard University, vol. 21. Cambridge.

Kidder, Alfred Vincent
    1924. An Introduction to the Study of Southwestern Archaeology with a Preliminary Account of the Excavations at Pecos. Papers of the Phillips Academy Southwestern Expedition, no. 1. New Haven.

Morris, Earl H.
    1939. Archaeological Studies in the La Plata District, Southwestern Colorado and Northwestern New Mexico. Carnegie Institution of Washington, publication 519. Washington.

McNitt, Frank
    1957. Richard Wetherill: Anasazi. University of New Mexico Press. Albuquerque.

G. Nordenskiöld

* 29/6 1868 † 6/6 1895

G. NORDENSKIÖLD

THE CLIFF DWELLERS

OF

THE MESA VERDE

THE CLIFF DWELLERS

OF

THE MESA VERDE

SOUTHWESTERN COLORADO

THEIR POTTERY AND IMPLEMENTS

BY

G. NORDENSKIÖLD

TRANSLATED

BY

D. LLOYD MORGAN

P. A. NORSTEDT & SÖNER

STOCKHOLM
RIDDARHOLMEN

CHICAGO, ILL.
WASHINGTON STR. 163, 165, ROOMS 14, 16.

STOCKHOLM 1893

ROYAL PRINTING OFFICE

CONTENTS.

Errata.

Plate XXX   (the text) under the number of the plate, *for* Scale $^1/_3$ *read* Scale $^2/_5$
„   XLII: 2—8   „   *for* Rooms 13 and 14 *read* Rooms 39 and 40.
„   XLV: 4   „   „ cotton twine   „ yucca twine.

———◆•◆———

PREFACE.

The summer and autumn of 1891 I passed in Colorado, engaged upon investigations of the remarkable cliff-dwellings scattered in the cañons of an extensive plateau, the Mesa Verde, in the south-west of the State. The present work is the result of those researches. It contains a description of the ruins, an account of the excavations carried out there and of the objects discovered. In order to trace as far as possible the development of the cliff-dweller culture, I append a survey of the ruins in the South-western States akin to the cliff-dwellings of the Mesa Verde, a description of the Moki Indians, the descendants of the ancient Pueblo tribes, and an account, based on the relations of the first Spanish explorers, of the manners and customs of the agricultural town-building Indians in the middle of the sixteenth century. A special part of the work is devoted to a description by Prof. G. Retzius of the crania found during the excavations.

In order to give my descriptions of the ruins and of the objects found in them as great objectivity as possible, I have almost exclusively employed in the illustrations direct methods of reproduction. The ruins have been reproduced from my photographs, partly in autotype by Messrs. Angerer & Göschl of Vienna, partly in photogravure at the Librairies-Imprimeries Réunies in Paris. The pottery, implements, etc. are heliotyped from photographs of the originals by Mr. Chr. Westphal of Stockholm.

Stockholm, 14 August, 1893.

G. Nordenskiöld.

CHAPTER I.

The Mesa Verde.

Before describing my first excursions to the cliff-dwellings of the Mesa Verde and the investigations carried out there, I shall give a short account of the chief geographical features of these regions.

South-western Colorado was some decades since a mere wilderness, where roving bands of Ute Indians rendered travelling dangerous for the few parties of explorers who ventured on horseback so far beyond the outposts of civilisation. But further and further west poured the crowds of settlers. It was found that the mountains of these regions contained rich stores of gold and silver, and step by step the Indians were forced to relinquish the land that had belonged to their forefathers. All that is now left to them is the narrow strip of country forming the Ute Indian Reservation. With this exception South-western Colorado now possesses a fairly dense population, and is easily reached by the railway running from Denver to Durango, a little mining town of about 3,000 inhabitants. Durango is situated just north of the Ute Indian Reservation, in a beautiful valley surrounded by lofty mountains, and watered by a rushing stream, which bears the pretty name of the Rio de las Animas.

At the time of my arrival, there was no railway to the west from Durango, though one was in course of construction. I made the journey from Durango to Mancos, a distance of 45 kilom.,[1] with a buggy and pair.

After crossing the Rio de las Animas the way led through a narrow glen, Wildcat Cañon, over a plateau thickly overgrown with tall pines, past several settlements surrounded by patches of cultivated ground, through narrow dales and over extensive plains. At last we ascended a long steep hill, from the summit of which a free and magnificent view opened towards the west. Below us lay Mancos Valley with its settlements. Far in the distance towered the volcanic cone of Ute Peak. By a long slope we descended into the valley, and drove on to the village of

---

[1] In this work the Metrical System is employed throughout.

G. Nordenskiöld, Cliff Dwellers.

Mancos. I continued my journey to WETHERILL's Ranch, situated about 3 kilom. south-west of the village. B. K. WETHERILL was one of the first settlers in Mancos Valley. His sons are better acquainted than any others with the ruins of the Mesa Verde, and have done considerable service by their exploration of them. I had a letter of introduction to Mr. WETHERILL, who gave me a most friendly reception. His ranch was from this time my home, when I was not engaged in wanderings among the ruins.

FIG. I. MAP OF THE MESA VERDE.

Colorado consists almost entirely of an alpine landscape not unlike the fells of Northern Scandinavia. In the southwest of the state, however, the landscape is of a different stamp. There we are met by the tableland, with its level plateaux (mesas) rising like terraces above each other, bounded by steep cliffs of sandstone, and intersected by deep cañons.

View of Cliff Palace essentially as it is in 1979. Much restoration and stabilization work has been done on most of the ruins described by Nordenskiöld. Photo courtesy MVNP.

A better view of three kivas in Cliff Palace. Date of photo not given, but scene is essentially same as it is in 1979. Photo courtesy MVNP.

Another view of Cliff Palace, emphasizing the round tower and kiva structure. Photo not dated, but scene is essentially the same as it is in 1979. Photo courtesy MVNP.

A detailed view of two of the kivas at Cliff Palace. Photo is not dated, but scene is essentially the same as it is in 1979. Photo courtesy MVNP.

Mancos is the name of a little village and a number of settlements round it, in a broad valley of the same name. Cortez is another village about 25 kilom. further west, in Montezuma Valley. In the neighbourhood of Cortez there are numerous farms, and also along McElmo Cañon, which begins 7 kilom. west of Cortez and extends in a south-westerly direction for a distance of 50 kilom. down to the banks of the Rio San Juan, a tributary of the Colorado. McElmo Cañon crosses the boundary between Colorado and Utah, and about 40—50 kilom. west of its mouth lies the Mormon village of Bluff City. In these districts, on the boundary between Colorado and Utah, the Mormons form a considerable percentage of the population. Bluff City is the last inhabited spot to the west on this side of the Colorado. An old Mormon road connects Bluff City by way of Colorado with Salt Lake City in Utah. It was from Salt Lake City that the first settlers immigrated to these regions.

The plain, surrounded by mountains and high plateaux, that bears the name of Mancos Valley, is traversed from north to south by a little stream, the Rio Mancos. To the north-east the mountains of La Plata tower to a height of 4,000 metres with their snow-capped peaks. To the east and south we are confronted by an unbroken range of plateaux. To the south-west, 8 kilom. from the spot where the road from Durango to Cortez crosses the Rio Mancos, rises a perfectly level tableland, which is abruptly cut short to the north and continued by a low ridge, the line of watershed between the valleys of Mancos and Montezuma. This tableland bears the Spanish name of the Mesa Verde. A steep slope of 300—500 metres ascends from the valley to the plateau.

A waggon road follows the Rio Mancos downward. The plateaux on both sides of the stream gradually approach each other, and about 12 kilom. below the spot where the village of Mancos is situated, the valley has passed into a cañon, whose steeply sloping cliffs rise immediately on both sides of the river-bed. Here lies the last settlement, and here the waggon road ends and is replaced by a narrow trail. Two kilometres below this point the Mancos receives a tributary from the east through Webber Cañon, which is separated from Mancos Valley by a high mesa. This is the only running water that joins the Rio Mancos between Mancos Village and the Rio San Juan, into which the Rio Mancos flows. Somewhere near the mouth of Webber Cañon runs the northern boundary of the Ute Indian Reservation, though the spot is not fixed by any boundary mark. The Indian Reservation consists of a rectangular strip of land 180 kilom. from east to west, 20 kilom. from north to south. The hilly and stony path winding along the cañon slope is an Indian trail. Still, it is rather seldom that you meet an Indian here in the upper part of Mancos Cañon. Further down towards the San Juan, where the cañon again widens, you sometimes come across a solitary Ute family. Like most of the North American tribes the Ute Indians are rapidly dying out, and form but the last remnant of a once great and powerful nation.

A proposal has already been mooted to remove the surviving Ute Indians to another territory in some part of Utah where the hunting is said to be more productive, and the pasturage better, and where, above all, no white neighbours as yet dispute the possession of the soil. The present reservation should in that case be thrown open to settlers. Considerable parts of the latter might then, it is said, be improved by means of irrigation into excellent arable land. But in Mancos Cañon there does not seem to be much land suitable for cultivation. On both sides of the narrow bed that the stream has scooped out in the layers of gravel and clay, rise steep barren talus slopes, strewn with dislodged boulders, and sometimes overgrown with thin brushwood consisting of piñon and cedar.[1] About 100—150 metres above the

FIG. 2. WETHERILL'S RANCH; THE MESA VERDE IN THE BACKGROUND.
(From a photograph by the author.)

bottom of the valley, at the top of this talus slope, rises a perpendicular wall, 50—100 metres in height, of yellow sandstone. Along this wall at different heights run long ledges of rock, on which a scanty vegetation of bushes and small trees has found a foothold. Cactuses of several species, with leaves of singular form and sharp prickles, are extremely common everywhere along the slopes and in the crevices of the rock. To climb from one of these ledges to another is often difficult and dangerous; but when once a ledge is reached, it is often possible to follow it for a long distance, until it grows too narrow, or entirely disappears.

---

[1] Piñon (*Pinus cembroides*) and cedar or juniper (*Juniperus occidentalis*), are the commonest coniferous trees of these regions.

THE KODAK HOUSE

To this point the cañon has been narrow and winding; it soon widens somewhat. The narrow level on each side of the stream is densely overgrown with low, gray sedgebrush.[1] Here and there along the bed of the stream thick copses of cottonwood with their leafy tops and fresh greenery form a sharp contrast to the vegetation that grows, parched by the blazing sun, on the rocky slopes. It was in one of these copses, where the Indians had formerly camped, that we used to pass the night on our expeditions from Mancos to the still more distant ruins where we carried out our excavations. This place lies about a day's journey from the village and about 25 kilom. beyond the last settlement. Here the cañon is already rather broad, and still further down it almost deserves the name of a valley (fig. 3). The sides grow more and more sloping, and there are no perpendicular cliffs at the top. Finally the cañon opens into the plain or, more correctly perhaps, into a lower plateau, and the stream soon afterwards joins the Rio San Juan.

Besides cottonwood several other species of trees grow at the bottom of Mancos Cañon where the stream gives moisture to the soil. A rich growth of bushes also flourishes there, and forms impassable thickets on both sides of the stream. The trunks of the trees often bear traces of the beaver's teeth, and this animal seems still to be quite common along the whole course of the Rio Mancos.

On both sides of Mancos Cañon there extends a complicated system of lateral cañons, which in their turn send out numerous branches, the whole system thus forming a perfect labyrinth. The beds of the streams at the bottom of these lateral cañons are dry without exception, save after the melting of the snow, or after the violent showers of the rainy season. To the north Mancos Cañon receives four main side cañons, namely Moccasin, Cliff, Navajo, and Ute Cañons, as well as some smaller ones.

The accompanying map[2] (fig. 1) may give some idea of the different main cañons and their ramifications. In appearance these lateral cañons resemble Mancos Cañon, but they give a still stronger impression of desolation. The bottom is dry; no green willows or tall cottonwoods break the gray monotony of the sedgebrush. The slopes are quite as steep, and at the top the perpendicular cliffs of yellow sandstone rise like an insurmountable wall. The height of the mesa above the bottom of the valley is between 200 and 250 metres. In the smaller ramifications the depth of the cañon decreases, as the bottom slowly rises. These smaller cañons, the outermost and finest branches of the system, generally end in a semicircular cliff, in which there have formed, in consequence of the more friable character of some of the strata, deep, horizontal hollows or caves, sometimes only one in number, sometimes several, one above another (see Plate I). These caves sometimes attain

---

[1] *Artemisia.*
[2] The map has kindly been placed at my disposal by Mr. WETHERILL. A number of the details are erroneous, and several of the smaller cañons are omitted; but, to the best of my knowledge, this is the only existing map in which the district appears in detail, and it at least gives a good idea of the principal topographical features.

a depth of 40 metres and a length of more than 100 metres. With their massive, vaulted roof of sandstone, the immense weight of which is not borne up by any support, they present an aspect at once singular and imposing. It is these sheltered spots that the former inhabitants of the tract have chosen for the erection of their fortress-like dwellings, the appearance and construction of which I am presently about to describe.

In these smaller cañons, in the shade of the towering cliffs, there often flourishes a more luxuriant vegetation than on the sunny slopes. Here and there a spruce[1] rears its huge trunk like a giant above the dwarf piñon and cedar. Dense thickets of stunted scrub-oak often render the passage difficult or impossible. At

FIG. 3. MANCOS CAÑON.
(From a photograph by the author.)

many places the flora seems to be extremely rich in species. The verdure is especially luxuriant where some spring trickles from the sandstone and supplies moisture to the soil.

Let us from the Rio Mancos follow one of the larger lateral cañons, that of Navajo for example. The cañon winds on mile after mile in innumerable curves; but the landscape still retains the same gloomy, half-desert character. Here and there, high up in the sandstone cliffs, the erosion of running water or sandstorms has hollowed out a vaulted gallery, where we may descry the ruins of human dwellings, perched like an eagle's eyrie half-way up the most inaccessible precipices. [2]

---

[1] *Picea Engelmanni.*
[2] One of these cliff-dwellings may be seen, though only indistinctly, in fig. 4 to the extreme right, in a hollow high up the cliff.

Gradually the depth of the cañon diminishes as it nears the mesa or tableland. At a distance of 25 kilom. from the entrance the depth of the cañon is hardly more than 30 metres, and the sides ascend more slowly without any perpendicular wall of sandstone. Here the cañon is cut short by a broad valley running N.E. and S.W., the valley of Montezuma, which lies spread out like a map at our feet, 2,000 feet below us. Undulating cornfields and darker patches of uncultivated ground alternate like the squares on a chessboard. Here and there lie farmhouses small as toys, and in the middle we see a larger group of buildings — the village of Cortez. Beyond the valley grow dark woods of piñon, and far away in the blue distance rise some snowy mountain-peaks.

FIG. 4. NAVAJO CAÑON.
(From a photograph by the author.)

Most of the large forks of Moccasin, Cliff, Navajo, and Ute Cañons, extend, like the cañon just described, from north to south until they reach Montezuma Valley and are terminated by its steep slope. Here their depth is reduced, and measures only between 30 and 40 m.; while they lie so close to each other that they are divided only by narrow ridges. The map will give a better idea of the landscape described above. A ride on the plateau along Montezuma Valley is attended with very great difficulties on account of all the cañons that must be crossed. The way lies uphill and downhill without a pause. During a ride from the north-east corner of the mesa, Point Lookout, to a branch of Navajo Cañon, a distance of perhaps 9 kilom., I counted more than 20 cañons in the line of route. It was only seldom, however, that I was compelled to ride this way.

It is difficult to explain the source of all the water that has once hollowed out these cañons. Possibly the formation of Montezuma Valley dates from a period subsequent to the completion of the Mancos system of cañons. Or perhaps we must have recourse to the Glacial Period in order to explain erosive action so great within limits so narrow.

The Mesa Verde, the plateau through which all these cañons have ploughed their deep furrows, is a perfectly level plain, overgrown with woods of piñon and cedar, so dense that it is usually no easy task to force one's way through them on horseback. It is these woods that have given the mesa its name of *Verde* (green), as opposed to the more barren regions further south. That portion of the Mesa Verde that lies north of the Rio Mancos, the field of my researches, forms an independent plateau entirely surrounded by valleys. To the east it is bounded by Mancos Valley, to the north and west by Montezuma Valley, to the south by Mancos Cañon and the plain north of the Rio San Juan. This plateau slopes at an angle of about 1° towards the south, or in the same direction as that in which most of the cañons run. Its highest point (the Summit, 2,600 m.) is situated between two branches of Cliff Cañon, quite close to the steep slope that descends into Montezuma Valley. From this point we may enjoy the most magnificent view over the whole plateau with its intricate labyrinth of cañons. Far in the south we see the peaks of the Chuckluck Mountains, in the territory of the Navajo Indians, on the other side of the Rio San Juan, and east of them Shiprock, a high, isolated cone of volcanic origin. Fashioned by one of nature's strange caprices, this mountain resembles a gigantic castle with battlements and towers, set on the crest of a precipice.

The portion of the Mesa Verde that lies south-east of the Rio Mancos slopes slowly to the west, and the general direction of its cañons is from east to west. Only on one occasion have I followed one of these cañons to head. Beyond this point there seemed to lie an extensive sandy plain without any cañons, bounded to the east by a broad valley with steep walls.

The strata of which the Mesa Verde is composed, and through which the cañons have cut their deep channels, consist of thick beds of light yellow sandstone with extremely indistinct, if any, stratification, and here and there interleaved with shale. The American geologists refer these strata to the Cretaceous Period. Coal is sometimes found in fairly thick seams, and unrecognisable impressions of plants occur in the shale near the coal. In the neighbourhood of Grass Cañon, south-east of the Rio Mancos, are burning coal-beds, which make their presence known by gaseous exhalations through holes in the ground.

The coal-beds and shale are often aquiferous; but the water that percolates through them is always more or less salt, generally with sulphate of magnesia. On the sandstone itself we find numerous snow-white efflorescences of the same substance. A characteristic quality of the sandstone is its tendency to vertical cleavage; hence the origin of the steep sandstone walls. The caves or vaults in these sandstone cliffs have been formed by the erosion of running water or sandstorms, though neither of these forces seems now to exert any appreciable influence. Dikes of basalt appear here and there, running straight up through the horizontal layers of sandstone. They are generally of no great thickness; but now and then they expand into masses of considerable size.

I mentioned above that the erosion of wind and water has now ceased to operate in any considerable degree upon the Mesa Verde. The sandstorms of Arizona scarcely reach so far, and the sand on the mesa is bound by the vegetation. As regards the erosion of water, the rainfall in these regions is so slight that the river-beds, with the exception of that of the Rio Mancos, which rises in the La Plata Mountains, are dry almost all the year round. Only during the melting of the snow or the week of rainy weather that comes at the end of July or the beginning of August, do we find running water in these channels. During the short rainy season the downpour is often incessant and extremely heavy for several days. The rain falls in streams, and the water rushes in torrents down the cliffs. But after a few days' sunshine the ground is again dry, and the watercourses are empty.

CHAPTER II.

The Ruins of the Mesa Verde.

In New Mexico and Arizona, in South-western Colorado and Southern Utah, along the banks of the Rio Grande and the Rio Colorado with its tributaries the Colorado Chiquito and the San Juan, in several tracts which are now in part almost destitute of inhabitants, we find numerous ruins, which in certain respects remind us of the buildings constructed at the present day by the agricultural Indian tribes of Arizona and New Mexico. These ruins may be divided into two distinct groups:

I. *Ruins in the valleys, on the plains, or on the plateaux.*

II. *Ruins in caves in the walls of the cañons.*

In a subsequent chapter I shall give a short account of the most important ruins that have been examined within the above limits, both of those situated in the valleys and the true cliff-houses, as they have been described by American explorers. — In Colorado ruins similar to those that have been found in Arizona and New Mexico, and belonging to both of the above distinct groups, have been discovered at several places, but only in the south or south-west of the state, which in the character of the landscape resembles the two states just mentioned. Further north, in the alpine region proper, such ruins do not seem to occur.

On the Mesa Verde, the principal geographical features of which have been described in the preceding chapter, we meet at every step with ancient remains showing that these regions, now almost deserted, were once inhabited by a large population. Ruins the size of which shows that they must be the remains of no insignificant buildings, may be found at several spots in the cañons of Mancos, Navajo, etc., though the walls are entirely destroyed by weathering. Nor are heaps of ruins uncommon on the mesa. In many cases their extent is such that they must be assumed to represent whole villages or small towns. In others they may be quite insignificant, the ruins of a single room.

Burial places too occur both on the mesa and in the cañons. Their site is marked by a low mound, but most distinctly by countless fragments of pottery scattered over the ground. Excavations were carried out in one of these burial places and a few skeletons found. Further details will be given below.

The ruins within the caves, the cliff-dwellings or rather cliff towns, are in several respects the most remarkable. Throughout the entire length of Mancos Cañon and in all its subdivisions fortress-like buildings have been erected of hewn blocks of sandstone on narrow ledges, often high up the cliffs in almost inaccessible situations. These structures, in consequence of their position under a sheltering vault of rock, are very well preserved, though they have been abandoned by their inhabitants for several centuries, so long that no tradition of them survives amongst the Ute Indians who lead a nomadic life in the neighbourhud. [1]

On account of their sheltered position not only the stone walls, but also in many cases the beams that support the floors between the different stories, are wonderfully well preserved. Among the fine, dry dust or the fallen blocks of sandstone that have filled the rooms, we find still in a wonderful state of preservation the household articles and other implements once used by the inhabitants of the cliff-dwellings. Even wooden articles, textile fabrics, bone implements, and the like are often exceedingly well preserved, although they have probably lain in the earth for more than five centuries.

It is no easy task to give even an approximate estimate of the number of ruins situated in the cañons of the Mesa Verde (Mancos Cañon and all its sub-divisions). According to RICHARD WETHERILL it exceeds 500. Merely in the cliffs on both sides of Mancos Cañon there are between 40 and 50 ruins, most of them, however, of inconsiderable size. The size of the cliff-dwellings is extremely variable. The Cliff Palace, according to R. WETHERILL, contains 125 rooms on the ground-floor. Many, on the other hand, consist merely of a single small, low room,

---

[1] BARBER, E. A. (On the Ancient and Modern Pueblo Tribes of the Pacific Slope of the United States. Am. Nat., Vol. XI, 1877, p. 593) says that the Ute Indians, when asked who had erected these buildings, always answered "Moquitch," meaning the agricultural Moki Indians of Arizona. RICHARD WETHERILL, who has long lived in these parts and is well acquainted with the Ute Indians, informs me, however, that they have borrowed this name from the whites, who used it because they supposed that the Moki Indians were related to the ancient inhabitants of the cliff-dwellings.

a regular den scarcely large enough for a human being to creep into. Every well-sheltered ledge of rock, every cave of sufficient depth has been taken advantage of by the builders. If we ever come across a cave suitable for building purposes, but where at a distance no ruins can be detected, we nearly always find on closer examination some remains of ruined walls or other traces of human habitation.

The cliff-dwellings are scattered throughout the Mesa Verde. The largest of them all, the Cliff Palace, lies in a branch of Cliff Cañon, which branch is named Cliff Palace Cañon from this ruin. In Cliff Cañon itself there are also several large ruins. The largest is Balcony House, remarkable as being the best preserved and possibly the most recently inhabited of all. Not far from the Cliff Palace, in a branch of Navajo Cañon, there lies in a deep cave imbedded among lofty sprucetrees a very handsome and well-preserved cliff-village, which has been named Sprucetree House. The ground floor contains 70—80 rooms. Many of the walls still rise to the roof of the cave. In several places the floors of an upper story are perfectly entire, and in others we find evident signs that three or four stories have formerly existed. In the same cañon where Sprucetree House lies there are several tiny ruins consisting of only one room.

Navajo Cañon with its extensive forks is richer in ruins than any other part of the Mesa Verde. The most important and largest of these ruins, exclusive of the Sprucetree House, lie in two cañons which surround a plateau to which I have given the name of *Wetherill's Mesa*. Most of the buildings are easily accessible from this mesa. I camped there with my workmen for several months, and made expeditions in different directions from the camping place. Wetherill's Mesa and its cañons were the strict field of my excavations.

In Ute Cañon only few and rather small ruins occur. Moccasin Cañon (N.E. of Cliff Cañon) is said to contain several cliff-dwellings of quite considerable size. On the other side of the Rio Mancos Johnson Cañon possesses the most numerous and most remarkable ruins. None of them, however, can rival those situated in Navajo and Cliff Cañons.

The ruins of the Mesa Verde were first explored and described [1] by W. H. Jackson, who in 1874 followed the Rio Mancos down its cañon and discovered several ruins, some at the bottom of the valley, some on its slopes. Most of these ruins, however, situated as they were in a position exposed to the action of the weather, were almost entirely levelled with the ground. Of the cliff-dwellings along the precipices only few were examined, and these with one exception of insignificant size. This larger ruin, Jackson's Cliff-house, lies in the upper part of Mancos Cañon, on its west side. The other cliff-dwellings described by Jackson also lay on the same side of the cañon. He expressly remarks that not the least trace of ruins was to be found in the east cliffs. This is a mistake. Mancos Cañon contains

[1] Jackson, W. H. Ancient Ruins in Southwestern Colorado. Rep. U. S. Geol. and Geogr. Survey of the Terr. 1874, p. 369.

no less than 50 cliff-dwellings distributed on both sides; but most of them are very small.

In the summers of 1875 and 1876 the ruins of South-western Colorado were explored by W. H. HOLMES.[1] HOLMES also made a journey through Mancos Cañon, and he describes several of its ruins, among these some remarkable towers at its bottom. Furthermore he gives figures and descriptions of some cliff-dwellings over-looked by JACKSON, two of them fairly important. A few figures and a plan are also given of Jackson's Cliff-house. HOLMES was fortunate enough to discover several earthenware vessels, some of them quite whole, and a few other objects, implements of stone, wood, etc., which he has figured and described.

The researches of HOLMES and JACKSON were until very recently the main sources of our information as to the ruins of South-western Colorado. The cliff-dwellings which they saw and described are, however, small and insignificant in comparison with those discovered in recent times. If they had only left Mancos Cañon and followed one of its northern lateral cañons for a few kilometres, they would have found ruins so magnificent that they surpass anything of the kind known in the United States. The honour of the discovery of these remarkable ruins belongs to RICHARD and ALFRED WETHERILL of Mancos. The family own large herds of cattle, which wander about on the Mesa Verde. The care of these herds often calls for long rides on the mesa and in its labyrinth of cañons. During these long excursions ruins, the one more magnificent than the other, have been discovered. The two largest were found by RICHARD WETHERILL and CHARLEY MASON one December day in 1888, as they were riding together through the piñon wood on the mesa, in search of a stray herd. They had penetrated through the dense scrub to the edge of a deep cañon. In the opposite cliff, sheltered by a huge, massive vault of rock, there lay before their astonished eyes a whole town with towers and walls, rising out of a heap of ruins. This grand monument of bygone ages seemed to them well deserving of the name of the Cliff Palace. Not far from this place, but in a different cañon, they discovered on the same day another very large cliff-dwelling; to this they gave the name of Sprucetree House, from a great spruce that jutted forth from the ruins. During the course of years RICHARD and ALFRED WETHERILL have explored the mesa and its cañons in all directions; they have thus gained a more thorough knowledge of its ruins than anyone. Together with their brothers JOHN, CLAYTON, and WYNN they have also carried out excavations, during which a number of extremely interesting finds have been made. A considerable collection of these objects, comprising skulls, pottery, implements of stone, bone, and wood, etc., has been sold to "The Historical Society of Colorado." A still larger collection is in the possession of the WETHERILL family. A brief catalogue of this collection forms the first printed notice of the remarkable finds made during

---

[1] HOLMES, W. H. Report on the Ancient Ruins of Southwestern Colorado, examined during the Summers of 1875 and 1876. Rep. U. S. Geol. and Geogr. Survey of the Terr. 1876, p. 383.

the excavations. F. H. CHAPIN, who visited the Mancos ruins in the summer of 1889, has since given an account[1] in a short paper in "Appalachia" partly of his own visits to the ruins and partly, in brief outline, of the information gained by the WETHERILLS' excavations. The best description yet published of the ruins of the Mesa Verde is a paper by W. R. BIRDSALL,[2] who visited the ruins in the capacity of a tourist. His stay in the neighbourhood lasted only a few days, and no excavations were undertaken, a circumstance which does not appear from the author's account. Though nothing is said of this, the objects described are principally such as were discovered during excavations instituted by me. Dr. BIRD-SALL visited my camp and watched the operations of the workmen for some days. I was absent during the first days of his visit on an exploration in the vicinity of Ute Cañon. My workmen were engaged in excavations on Wetherill's Mesa, and it is therefore that the ruins described belong principally to this neighbourhood. Besides the description of the ruins, which is accompanied by a few poor figures, a list is given of the most important objects found during our excavations. With the exception of a few immaterial errors, easily explained when we take into account the short time devoted to the visit, the paper contains a fairly good delineation of the most important facts touching a few of these remarkable ruins.

The above papers, if we except a few newspaper articles, for the most part worthless, compose the only literature that treats of the most imposing ruins of the United States. The archæological remains described are few, and the greater number of the figures defective. Still fewer are the figures and descriptions of the objects recovered by excavation, though during recent years so abundant material for such a description has been procured in several localities. It was these circumstances that induced me to devote a summer to explorations and excavations in the cliff-dwellings of the Mesa Verde. In the following chapters a description is given of the most remarkable ruins, the description being accompanied by figures for the most part directly reproduced from photographs taken by the author in person.

---

[1] CHAPIN, F. H. Cliff-dwellings of the Mancos Cañons. Appalachia, May 1890. Also in Am. Ant., Vol. XII, 1890, p. 193.
[2] BIRDSALL, W. R. The Cliff Dwellings of the Cañons of the Mesa Verde. Bull. Am. Geogr. Soc., Vol. XXIII, 1891, p. 584.

CHAPTER III.

Excavations in Cliff Cañon.

It had been my original intention to stay only about a week in the neighbourhood of Mancos, to which place I had come as a tourist in order to see the objects of interest in the vicinity. My first ride along Mancos Cañon, during which, with RICHARD WETHERILL as my guide, I visited some of the most remarkable and largest ruins, had already inspired me with a strong desire to examine them more closely. But before I determined upon the more extensive researches and excavations required to gain a thorough knowledge of the cliff-villages and their former inhabitants, I wished to undertake some preliminary work on a smaller scale. On the advice of RICHARD WETHERILL I began this work in a ruin in Cliff Cañon,[1] where only very little excavation had been carried out previously. The work of excavation was performed by R. and A. WETHERILL, whom I had engaged for this purpose, and occupied only two days.

There are two ways of reaching the ruin in Cliff Cañon which we proposed to examine. The first leads from Mancos straight up towards the Mesa Verde, which is ascended a little south of Point Lookout. From this point the trail, which is extremely hilly and difficult, follows the northern edge of the mesa across several cañons. Finally it bends to the left down into Cliff Cañon and follows its upper part for a distance of perhaps 8 kilom., right up to the ruin. The other route runs along Mancos Cañon to the mouth of Cliff Cañon, which it follows upwards over extremely rough ground to the place where the ruin is situated. A supply of water, an indispensable condition of long-continued work in a ruin, is afforded by a small spring in the upper part of Cliff Cañon; but the well is highly alkaline. The water of the same spring reappears further down Cliff Cañon, for a distance of several kilometres, in the form of small pools in the sand of the almost dry bed of the stream. A similar pool lay just below the ruin, but its water, concentrated as it was by evaporation, had a still more salt and nauseous taste than that of the spring itself. We camped here for a short time; but the water had an extremely injurious effect on the digestion, so that it would certainly have been impossible to use it for any lengthy period.

From the bottom of the cañon we force our way through dense thickets some hundreds of feet up the steep slope. Here we reach the sandstone cliffs, rising ledge upon ledge up to the mesa. The ruin lies upon one of the lowest ledges, and the climb, though troublesome, is attended with no serious difficulties.

---

[1] A map of a part of Cliff Cañon is given in one of the following chapters; this ruin is marked 9.

Among half-ruined walls and heaps of stones we can distinguish eleven different rooms, lying in an irregular row (see the plan,[1] fig. 5) along the narrow shelf, close to the edge of the precipice and sheltered by the overhanging rock. The way by which we have climbed has led us first into a circular room still in a fair state of preservation (fig. 5, *1*). The wall that lies nearest the precipice is for the most part in ruins; the rest of the room is well-preserved. After about half a metre of dust and rubbish had been removed, we were able to ascertain that the walls formed a cylinder 4.3 metres in diameter. The thickness of the wall is throughout considerable, and varies, the spaces between the points where the cylinder touches the walls of the adjoining rooms having been filled up with masonry. The height of the room is 2 m. The roof has long since fallen in, and only one or two beams are left among the rubbish. To a height of 1.2 m. from the floor the wall is perfectly even and has the form of a cylinder, or rather of a truncate cone, as it leans slightly inwards. The upper portion, on the other hand, is divided by

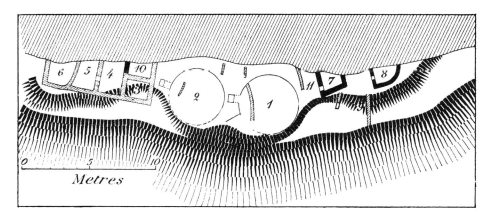

FIG. 5. PLAN OF A CLIFF HOUSE IN CLIFF CAÑON.

six deep niches into the same number of pillars (*a, a, a* in fig. 6). The floor (*b*) is of clay, hard and perfectly even. Near the centre is a round depression or hole (*c*), 0.5 m. deep and 0.8 m. in diameter. This hole was entirely full of white ashes. It was undoubtedly the hearth. Between the hearth and the outer wall stands a narrow, curved wall (*d*), 0.8 m. high. Behind this wall, in the same plane as the floor, a rectangular opening, 1 m. high and 0.6 m. broad, has been constructed in the outer wall. This opening forms the mouth of a narrow passage or tunnel (*e, e*) of rectangular shape, which runs 1.8 m. in a horizontal direction, and then goes straight upwards, out into the open air. The tunnel lies under one of the six niches, which is somewhat deeper than the others. The walls are built of carefully hewn blocks of sandstone, the inner surface being perfectly smooth and

---

[1] The shaded part at the top is the sandstone cliff. The walls that reach up to the roof of rock are given in black, a system followed in the other plans as well.

lined with a thin, yellowish plaster. On closer examination of this plaster it is found to consist of several thin layers, each of them black with soot. The plaster has evidently been repeatedly restored as the walls became blackened with smoke. A few smaller niches and holes in the walls (*f, f*), irregularly scattered here and there, have presumably served as places of deposit for different articles; a bundle of pieces of hide, tied with a string, was found in one of them. The lower part of the wall to a height of 0.4 metres is painted dark red round the whole room. This red paint projects upwards in triangular points, arranged in threes, and above them is a row of small round dots of red. This red design appears, though not quite

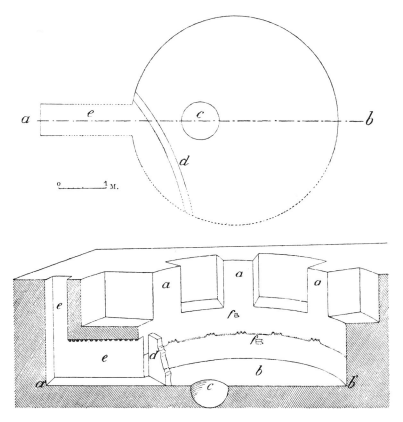

FIG. 6.   GROUND PLAN AND SECTION OF AN ESTUFA.

distinctly, in fig. 7. In fig. 6 the outlines are reproduced. It probably had some special significance, for it does not recur in any other room in the same ruin, and has only twice been observed in other ruins.

Circular rooms, built and arranged on exactly the same plan as that described above, reappear with exceedingly slight variations in size and structure in every cliff-dwelling except the very smallest ones. The other rooms show innumerable variations in form and size, but the round rooms are always alike. These round rooms undoubtedly correspond to those which among the Moki Indians of Arizona and the

Spruce Tree House, with its low cliff overhang, is one of the most photographed of the ruins. Photo not dated, but scene is essentially the same as it is in 1979. Photo courtesy MVNP.

A longer view of Spruce Tree House, showing in better detail the low overhang of the cave top. Photo not dated, but scene is essentially the same as it is in 1979. Photo courtesty MVNP.

Detail of Spruce Tree House to show architecture of doorways as reconstructed. No ruin in the Park has been reconstructed in its entirety. Photo not dated, but contemporary. Courtesy MVNP.

Notice the "T" shaped doorway at Spruce Tree House. Note also the difference where reconstruction commences from original structures. Photo not dated, but contemporary. Courtesy MVNP.

Vertical view of Balcony House ruin. Note cliff overhang at top right of photo. Reconstruction attempts to follow original structure as nearly as possible. Photo courtesy MVNP.

Balcony House gains its name from the balcony-type gangways, as here reconstructed. Vigas running atop and through walls support gangway. Photo courtesy MVNP.

A long view of Oak Tree House illustrates difficulty camera has in capturing ruins within a deep cave. Park literature describes how ruins got their names. Photo courtesy MVNP.

A closer view of Oak Tree House gives better idea of architectural detail, but narrows scope of the picture. Photo courtesy MV NP.

Pueblo Indians of New Mexico are known by the Spanish name of *estufa*,[1] and which serve as meeting-places for religious and political assemblies. This name is also applied to the round rooms in the ruins of the same regions. I shall hereafter employ it also to denote the round rooms in the cliff-houses.

The number of estufas varies in proportion to the size of the buildings and the number of rooms: sometimes we find only one; in the Cliff Palace, the largest of the cliff-dwellings of the Mesa Verde, more than twenty. The ruin which we were now engaged in excavating, contained two estufas and nine other rooms. The description of the first estufa applies in every respect to the second (*2* in the plan), with the single exception that the whole wall is coated with yellow plaster without any red painting. The wall between the hearth and the singular passage or tunnel de-

FIG. 7. PART OF AN ESTUFA. AT THE BOTTOM, SOMEWHAT TO THE RIGHT, THE HEARTH. BETWEEN THE HEARTH AND THE WALL A LOW PARTITION, AND BEHIND THIS THE ENTRANCE OF THE PASSAGE LEADING INTO THE OPEN AIR.
(From a photograph by the author.)

scribed above is replaced by a large slab of stone set on end. It is difficult to say for what purpose this tunnel has been constructed and the slab of stone or the wall erected in front of it. As I have mentioned above, this arrangement is found in all the estufas; I shall return to this question in a subsequent chapter.

North of the two estufas the walls of four more rooms may be distinguished. Three of them lie on a narrow upper ledge. A little room (*11*) is wedged in between the first estufa and the side of the cliff. The other two (*7* and *8*) are also

---

[1] Strictly = stove, and often used of sweat-houses. Sudorific baths are much in vogue among the Indian tribes of North America. This was not the purpose, however, of the estufas here in question.

very small, their walls are perfectly preserved and extend from the ledge right up to the low roof of rock. The northernmost room (*8*), which lies apart from the rest of the building, is particularly small and low; a man can neither stand nor lie at full length within it. Similar holes, often much smaller even than this, are common in the cliff-dwellings. Possibly they served as store-rooms for maize and other provisions.

On a lower ledge some feet below the three northernmost rooms we find two partly ruined walls (one of them is shown in fig. 8), which seem once to have belonged to a fourth and larger room (*9*). South of the two estufas lie five more rooms, the position of which is shown in the plan. *3* is a small, quadrangular cell, with one of its walls formed by the ledge on which *10* lies, about 2 metres higher up.

FIG. 8. NORTHERN PORTION OF RUIN 9 IN CLIFF CAÑON. TO THE LEFT ROOM 7, IN THE CENTRE *8*.
(From a photograph by the author.)

In *3*, below this ledge, is a natural hollow in the cliff, the size of the room being thus increased. *10* is a little, low room which runs deep in under the overhanging cliff. *3* has probably had an upper story on a level with *10*. The other three rooms (*4*, *5*, and *6*) lie in a row along the wall of rock. In this part of the building there has been ample space, and the rooms are therefore rectangular, of fairly regular form, and with almost right angles.

The walls, which are generally about 0.2 metres thick, are built of rough-hewn sandstone, the blocks being seldom too large to be lifted with ease in one hand. The surfaces of the walls are not so smooth as in the estufa, nor are they plastered. The stones are held together by mortar, which was probably prepared from clay, sand, and water. The entrances of the several rooms consist of rectangular openings in the walls, so small that it is only just possible to creep in; there is only one entrance to each room. The door sill consists of a flat slab of stone, the lintel of some small sticks across the opening. The entrance of the estufa was probably in the roof. It was impossible, however, in this ruin to arrive at any positive conclusion on this head. In estufa *1* it almost seemed as if a door had existed in the wall on the very brink of the precipice.

Our work began in estufa *1*, where WETHERILL had previously made some excavations, with fairly good results. Among the objects then discovered I shall mention: half of a bow, three or four arrows, a stone axe with handle, and a bone knife. Only a small part of the room had been examined, and the rubbish mixed with fine dust that had filled the room to a depth of nearly a metre, had nowhere been so thoroughly removed as to leave the floor bare. My two men worked hard; yet it took a day and a half completely to clear the estufa. The removal of the rubbish gave them little trouble; a single push of the spade sent it over the precipice. Great inconvenience was caused, on the other hand, by the fine dust, which rose in dense clouds at each blow of the spade. It was evident that not the least trace of moisture had been able to reach the rooms under the sheltering rock, and this explains how such things even as cotton cloth, wooden implements, string, pieces of hide, and the like were in a perfect state of preservation. The sun blazes with glowing heat during the greater part of the year, and the overhanging roof of rock affords an effectual shelter from the heavy showers of the short rainy season.

Having finished our excavation of estufa *1*, where we made a good number of finds, we continued the work in estufa *2*, which was filled to a depth of more than half a metre with rubble and a number of sandstone blocks from the dilapidated walls. But neither in this estufa nor in any of the other rooms subsequently examined, did we make any important find. This may possibly depend on the fact that the inhabitants, whose number had been reduced in some way before they finally left the building, had all moved into estufa *1* and deserted the rest of the house.

With respect to the result of the excavations I would remark, that in no other instance did we find in the same place so great a number of wooden and bone implements and so numerous fragments of hide and woven articles as in this estufa. My catalogue includes more than a hundred objects. Most of them were such as are found everywhere, in the other cliff-dwellings as well; but in order to procure as complete a collection as possible of everything that might illustrate the manners and customs of the former inhabitants, it was necessary at first to take care of even the most insignificant objects. Among the most common articles I shall mention:

Pieces of hide. Hide probably chiefly of deer and mountain-sheep also of smaller animals, was in general use for belts, moccassins, bags to contain salt and other substances, etc.

Pieces of cotton cloth. The cloth is well and evenly woven, rather coarse. Interwoven patterns are extremely rare.

Cords of yucca fibre. The yucca is a liliaceous plant with long, narrow, and sharp leaves, the tough fibres of which form the most excellent material for cord and rope.

Sandals plaited of fine strips of yucca leaf, sometimes of entire leaves or twisted string. They usually showed signs of long wear.

Pottery in fragments of several different types. Most of the vessels seem to have been well made and tastefully ornamented. Of the potter's art the cliff people were masters.

Maize. Partly entire ears, partly loose kernels, partly leaves and other refuse. It is evident that maize was the principal article of food among the cliff people and that they were industrious agriculturists. The seeds of several other plants are also found.

Implements of bone and wood. Awls and scrapers of the most primitive description, generally of deer or turkey bone. Pointed sticks, probably used in planting maize, etc.

Stone implements. Axes, sometimes with the handle attached. Arrow points and spear heads, knives, etc.

Of metal not a trace has been found.

Later on I shall give a detailed account, accompanied by figures, of all these objects and a number of others found during our excavations. The objects from different ruins lend themselves most easily to a continuous description, for they are all so similar that there is not the least doubt of their being the work of the same people. I have given this short list merely in order to show that the former inhabitants of the cliff-dwellings were *an agricultural people on the level of the Stone Age*, who had attained a very high rank in the art of making and ornamenting pottery and in the construction of stone buildings, but who at the same time stood comparatively low in other respects.

No human bones, which are otherwise of common occurrence in the cliff-dwellings, were found in this ruin. One is inclined to believe that the ruin has been abandoned voluntarily, and that the inhabitants took with them everything of value, leaving behind what they thought would not prove of any great service.

CHAPTER IV.

Wetherill's Mesa. Summary of the Excavations.

That part of the Mesa Verde the ruins of which formed the field of my researches and excavations during the greater part of the summer, was, as mentioned above, Wetherill's Mesa. Our route from the settlements at Mancos to this place follows Mancos Cañon all the way to the mouth of Navajo Cañon, a distance of about 45 kilometres. We then ride along this latter cañon in a nearly opposite direction for a distance of 9 kilometres, and here accurate knowledge of the locality is necessary to keep the right direction at each subdivision of the cañon. Then comes a difficult climb up the high slope of the cañon to the plateau — the height of the latter above the bottom of the cañon is here about 180 metres — and after a ride of a few kilometres more we reach that part of the mesa which I have named after the brothers WETHERILL, who have done so much service in the exploration of these regions, and whose knowledge of the Mesa Verde has given me such valuable assistance. A shorter way of reaching Wetherill's Mesa is to keep to the high road from Mancos to Montezuma Valley, to follow the latter for about 10 kilometres, then, turning to the left up a steep slope of 600 metres, to mount the plateau, and finally, after having crossed the upper part of several cañons, to follow the mesa between two of them in a southerly direction for about 6 kilometres. We generally chose the latter route. It was difficult to find, and a short time ago was known only to the Indians, who had shown it to WETHERILL.

The map in fig. 9, which has no pretensions to any great exactness, is intended to afford a survey of the position of the different ruins on Wetherill's Mesa. At the north of the mesa lies a fairly good spring; water is otherwise scarce in the neighbourhood. It was therefore that we pitched our camp first at this place. With JOHN WETHERILL as foreman and with two Mexican labourers, I now began my excavations on a larger scale. On WETHERILL's advice I determined to start work at Long House, a ruin situated about 3 kilometres south of the spring where we had our camp. It was my intention to excavate this ruin completely, but after the work had been carried on from the 14th of July to the 14th of August without any particularly good results, I decided to continue the excavations in another ruin. Great loss of time had been caused by the long distance between our camp at the spring and the field of our operations. I therefore had the camp removed to the ruin selected for our work, namely Kodak House [1] (22 in the map), where a scanty supply

----

[1] This cliff-dwelling is named after the well-known instantaneous camera "Kodak," as we kept one of these apparatuses hidden for some time in one of the rooms. The propriety of the name may be called in question, but as it has already gained ground, I have thought it best to retain it.

of water was found below the cliff house. From the 14th to the 28th of August we
camped on the mesa above this ruin, and simultaneously with our work here busied
ourselves with excavations in two smaller ruins (11 and 12) situated farther south. I had
engaged a third labourer. The results were now somewhat better than during the preceding month. Still they did not seem to me to repay the amount of labour expended
in the excavations, and I therefore resolved upon moving our camp a second time.
I had reason to suspect that in a ruin called Mug House (19), where the brothers WE-
THERILL had previously found a number of earthenware vessels and stone implements,
and where my labourers had also worked for one day with fair success, there was

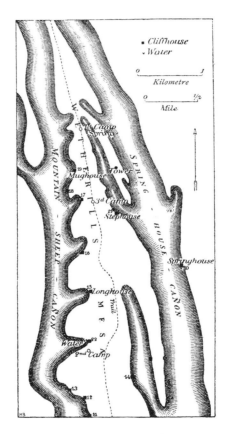

FIG. 9. MAP OF WETHERILL'S MESA.

still much to be found. I should have preferred to investigate places that had not
been touched before; but I finally came to the conclusion that this might not be
of much importance, the previous excavations having been far from complete, and
my limited resources not allowing of a thorough excavation of an untouched ruin.
In order to be as near Mug House as possible, and to be enabled to work at the
same time in some other ruins, situated near it and not yet examined, we pitched
camp on the 28th of August at about the middle of the mesa. There was no water
to be had, it is true; but the necessary quantity was conveyed thither on a pack-

horse from the spring, which was only one kilometre distant. Our work at Mug House was of no lengthy duration, for we found that another ruin, Step House (21), on the east side of the mesa, contained a number of graves deserving of investigation. Our find of pottery and skeletons in this ruin was very rich. When these graves had been thoroughly examined, I determined upon shifting the excavations from Wetherill's Mesa to another tract further west, namely to Sprucetree House and the ruins in its neighbourhood, where no important excavations had as yet been undertaken by WETHERILL. On the 14th of September I gave orders for the removal of the camp. While three of my men were thus employed, I conveyed, with the help of the other two (I had engaged one more labourer on the 5th of September), a portion of my collections on pack-horses to Mancos and thence to the railway station at Durango. There I was disagreeably surprised. Some slight difficulties which had previously been thrown in my way on the part of the authorities, but which I had imagined were already obviated, were now renewed in a more serious form. I was compelled after a fortnight again to return to Durango, where the complaints that had been lodged against my operations were, however, formally abandoned. Still I had already dismissed my men and given up the work in the ruins. The time had instead been employed in an exploration, on horseback and with two companions, of the whole of the Mesa Verde. During this expedition, which lasted a fortnight, we visited all the more important ruins for the purpose of photographing them, drawing plans, taking measurements, etc. The result was a collection of upwards of 150 photographs, which are in great part reproduced in this work. This was the end of my examinations of the cliff-dwellings of the Mesa Verde.

CHAPTER V.

Ruins in the West Cliffs of Wetherill's Mesa.

A narrow trail runs along about the middle of Wetherill's Mesa and throughout its whole length. Starting from our first camp at the spring, to reach Long House, the ruin where the first more comprehensive excavations were undertaken, we have to follow this trail for about 2 kilometres and then strike off to the right. After a ride of perhaps half a kilometre more, through dense woods of piñon and cedar, we suddenly find ourselves on the very brink of a cañon. Deep down at its bottom lies the dry bed of the stream, and on the other side we are faced by a long wall of steep cliffs of yellow sandstone. A keen eye may possibly detect in the distance, among these cliffs, the straight outlines of half-ruined walls, nestling in some small recess. But the largest ruins in the vicinity lie much nearer, though they are invisible from the mesa on the same side.   If we could cross to the other side of the cañon, which seems to be hardly a stone's throw distant, we should see in the cliff on whose brink we stood before, a long row of half dilapidated walls in a high-vaulted cave. It is this ruin that has received the name of Long House.   The descent to it from the mesa is not very difficult.   At a certain spot, known, however, only to those quite familiar with the tract, it is possible, by the help of some notches hewn in the sandstone, which formerly gave a foothold to the inhabitants of the cliff-dwellings, to clamber down the cliff for a distance of 50—60 metres to the point where the more gradual talus slope begins.   On following the sandstone cliff some hundred paces to the east, we reach a wide, semicircular hollow, a kind of gigantic niche, with high-vaulted roof.   Along the inner part thereof rises a row of partly

FIG. 10. LONG HOUSE IN NAVAJO CAÑON.   TO THE LEFT THE TOWER (3—5), IN THE MIDDLE THE ROOMS 18—25. TO THE RIGHT ON A HIGH NARROW LEDGE A LOW WALL WITH LOOPHOLES FOR ARROWS.

(From a photograph by the author.)

fallen walls out of mounds of sandstone blocks, from which a blackened rafter projects here and there.   Some rooms lie further in under the vault of rock, along an upper ledge; others, in general less preserved, further down the slope, which stretches, unbroken by any cliff, to the bottom of the cañon.   The figures (Plate II and fig. 10) and the plan (Plate III) give a better idea of the appearance of the ruin than any description could do.

If we follow the path described above, we first reach the westernmost part of the cliff-dwelling.   A triangular tower (3, 4, 5 in the plan), one wall of which is formed by the cliff, and which still stands to its full height of four stories, is the first object to attract our attention in this part of the ruin.   One cannot help

G. Nordenskiöld: The Cliff Dwellers of the Mesa Verde.

The west part of Long House.

From a photograph by the author.

At the top of the figure and at about the middle is shown the western of the two breast-works situated
above the ruins (see p. 28). This wall is not marked in the plan.

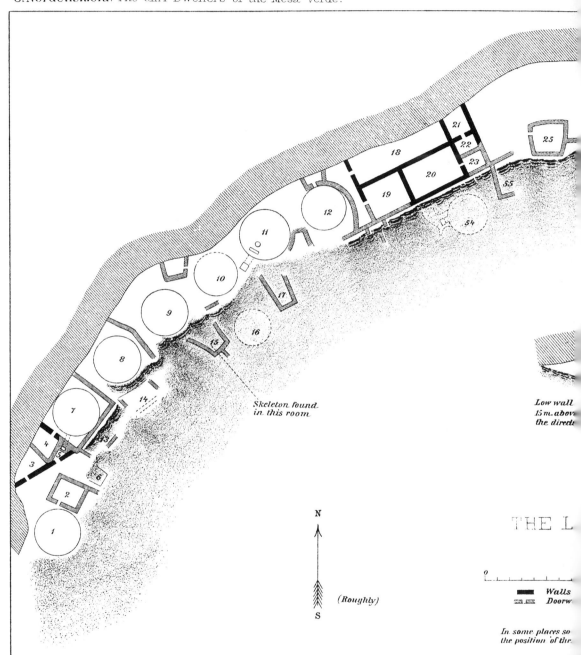

Skeleton found
in this room

N

S

(Roughly)

Low wall
15 m. above
the directi

THE L

Walls
Doorw

In some places so
the position of thr

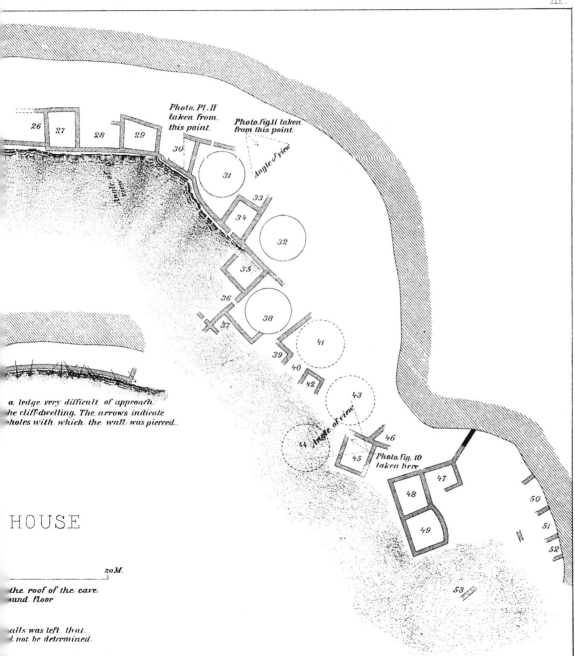

26 27 28 29

Photo, Pl. II taken from this point.

30

Photo. fig. 11 taken from this point.

31

Angle of view

33

34

32

35

36

38

37

41

39

40

42

43

a ledge very difficult of approach.
he cliff-dwelling. The arrows indicate
holes with which the wall was pierced.

44 *Angle of view*

46

45 *Photo. fig. 10 taken here*

47

48

49

50

51

52

HOUSE

_____ *20 M.*

the roof of the cave
und floor

alls was left that.
l not be determined.

53

admiring the skill with which it has been erected. The building material consists of the same soft sandstone as the vault of rock. The stones, generally a little larger than ordinary bricks (length 0.2—0.5 m.), seldom too large to be lifted without difficulty, are rough-hewn and cemented with mortar. The thickness of the walls is about 0.3 m. In order to give them additional stability, small chips of stone, fragments of broken earthenware, or the like have been wedged into the chinks between the stones. The east part of the second story is composed of a niche, the roof of which is formed of sticks laid across the opening, covered with twigs and with a layer of mortar at the top. The floor of the niche is pierced by a narrow passage, leading to an estufa (7) hard by. The room above the niche, the third story, is rather small, and the uppermost room is so tiny that it is impossible for a human being to gain entrance; it was no doubt employed merely as a storeroom for maize or other provisions. Ladders were probably never used to reach it, but only stones projecting from the wall or strong pegs driven into the latter. Nowhere among the ruins, either at Long House or at the other cliff-dwellings, do we find remnants of ladders,[1] though quantities of other wooden articles are still well preserved.

Outside the triangular tower stand a few more well preserved walls (2, 6). East of it lie in a continuous row six estufas (7—12), quite close to the cliff and on an upper ledge. The first of the latter (7) communicates with the above mentioned niche by means of a narrow, quadrangular passage of exactly the same construction as that described above (chap. III) in my account of an estufa in ruin 9 in Cliff Cañon. The niche has been built in the wall of the triangular tower in order to leave free space above the mouth of the passage leading from the estufa. On examining the interior of the estufas in Long House, we find even there exactly the same arrangement: a round hollow near the middle filled with ashes; between this hollow and the wall a low partition; behind the partition the entrance of the above-mentioned passage, which first runs a few metres in an horizontal direction and then straight up to the bottom of the niche or out into the open air; and lastly the six deep, broad niches in the circular wall, separated by the same number of pillars. The estufa itself is enclosed in a quadrangular room; the space between the inner cylindrical walls and the outer rectilinear ones is filled up to a level with the wall of the estufa, the cylindrical room being thus embedded in a solid cubical mass of masonry. In all the estufas the same construction is repeated, and the dimensions of the rooms are almost exactly similar.

Below this row of six estufas lies a series of rooms (13—17), for the most part buried under heaps of rubble and stones. I have endeavoured to represent in the plan as much of the walls as is still distinguishable. Further east, on the same ledge as the estufas, lies a block of rooms, the walls of which are still in a good state of preservation and extend quite up to the roof of rock. The innermost of these

---

[1] Only on one occasion did I find a part of a ladder, namely below Balcony House. But some marks of an edged tool sharper than a stone axe rendered its origin dubious.

rooms (*18*) is more than 6 metres long, but rather narrow and almost dark, the scanty light admitted through a narrow opening on the west side being too feeble to disperse the darkness. On the outer side of this room lie two others (*19—20*), which formerly possessed an upper story. The rafters are still in position, and project a foot or two on the outer side, where they probably afforded the cliff-dwellers a hold for the hands in passing the narrow ledge outside the wall. East of these two rooms lie three more (*21—23*); then, still on the same ledge, comes a long, open space (*24*) beneath the low roof of rock, and, in front of this, along the ledge, a long row of rooms, the walls of which, though well-preserved, fall short of the roof of rock. No rafters are left; whether these rooms ever had any, seems doubtful. The absence of any doorways in the outer walls suggests that the builders had thought of the possibility of hostile attacks. This inner part of the cliff-dwelling is reached by climbing to the upper shelf between rooms *23* and *25*, where there is a breach in the wall. A few holes hewn by the cliff-dwellers in the sandstone give a foothold and make the ascent less difficult. Behind the long row of rooms it is possible to follow the free inner part of the cave all the way to the eastern extremity of the ruin.

In the innermost part of the cave a sparse growth of moss betrays the presence of water, of which at our first visit we found a small pool in a little hollow in the sand. We tried by digging a deeper hole to procure a sufficient quantity to be of service to us, but in vain. There is no doubt, however, that by making suitable arrangements a considerable supply of water might be gained from this spring. Similar aquiferous strata are of frequent occurrence in the depths of the caves in which the cliff-dwellers built their houses. Fig. 11 gives an idea of the appearance of this innermost part of Long House.

East of the last-mentioned series of rooms lie two estufas (*31, 32*), and between them two other rooms. The outer wall in front of the eastern estufa still rises at one point almost to the roof of rock. Below this estufa, to the south, lies a series of rooms on a lower level. The roof of rock extends even over these rooms, but not so far as to prevent the wind from sometimes driving a shower of rain against the walls, which are therefore more dilapidated here than in the rest of Long House. The mortar has been washed away, and the stones are somewhat worn. The upper ledge ends above these rooms, and the fairly steep talus reaches the innermost part of the cave. This eastern part of the building once consisted of a number of rooms; but now only isolated walls rise out of great heaps of stones. Here and there one can distinguish the outlines of a circular estufa. At the extreme end, however, the walls of three or four rooms are still in a fairly good state of preservation. Some paces farther east the cave ends, and the sandstone cliff again rises vertically upwards. It is only seldom that the cliff-dwellings extend beyond the sheltering roof of rock, and when this is the case, the mortar is always completely washed away, while in most of such instances the walls have also fallen, their site being marked merely by the much worn stones of which they were constructed. These circumstances may possibly indicate the great age of the buildings.

The walls of the other rooms in Long House are constructed in the same manner as in the tower first described; their thickness is also the same, or on an average 0.3 m. The dimensions of the rooms are shown in the plan. Their average size may be estimated at 2.2 × 2.5 m., with a height of about 2 m. All the doorways are small, measuring 0.5 × 0.7 m., and have served as windows as well. They resemble the doorways of the other cliff-dwellings, and their appearance will be given more minutely in a description of a better preserved ruin. The estufas are of similar form and almost the same size everywhere. They never have an upper story, and they generally lie, when the nature of the ground permits, with the floor sunk

FIG. 11. THE INTERIOR OF THE LONG HOUSE CAVE.
(From a photograph by the author.)

lower than that of the adjoining rooms of the ordinary type. The arrangement of the other rooms shows an almost entire want of system. It seems as though the building had been extended by the erection of new rooms as they were called for by the increasing population of the village.

Among the ruins we remark at several spots in the sandstone rock oblong marks about 2 dm. in length. They occur in most of the cliff-dwellings (fig. 12), and are the places where the stone axes were ground. Long, straight, and narrow grooves, crossing each other in all directions, are the spots where other implements, such as bone awls etc., were sharpened.

I have still to describe one part of Long House, and this not the least remarkable. About 15 metres above the ruins just described, in the overhanging vault,

are two long, narrow, horizontal shelves, separated by the smooth rock. Along the
edge of these shelves run low walls, pierced with small loopholes. The west shelf
had already been scaled, with the help of a long joist raised against the cliff, by
WETHERILL, who had there found an earthenware lamp and a few other objects. The
east shelf nobody had yet succeeded in reaching. The ascent seemed to offer insurmountable difficulties; the shelf lay 17 metres above the lower ledge, and the longest
pole available measured only a little over 9 metres. After two days' work, however,
we succeeded in erecting a scaffolding (fig. 13), by which we could climb up at the
risk of breaking our necks. The reward of all our trouble was, however, but scanty,
for, though we found indications to show that human beings had once dwelt behind
these walls, no object of any great interest was discovered. The ledge itself was
quite narrow, the rock above it so low that one had to creep on hands and knees.
The wall along the ledge was only 1 m. high and 14 m. long. In the wall we found
fifteen small apertures, only a few inches wide. These apertures must undoubtedly

FIG. 12. MARKS LEFT BY THE GRINDING OF STONE AXES. FROM A RUIN IN JOHNSON CAÑON.
(From a photograph by the author.)

have been loopholes for arrows (see the plan Plate III, where the course of the
loopholes is indicated), and were skilfully arranged in all directions, so that the
archers were able to command all the approaches to the cliff-dwelling, and could
discharge a formidable shower of arrows upon an advancing enemy. As I have
already mentioned in the above description, Long House lies at the top of the slope
extending from the bottom of the cañon to the perpendicular sandstone cliff. The
site of the building has thus not been such as to render it impregnable. It is therefore
that the two breastworks for archers have been raised on the ledges above the cliff-
dwelling. It is difficult to conjecture in what way the inhabitants ascended to and
descended from the eastern of these fortifications. Possibly the high wall which is
seen in fig. 10 below the fort, reached right up to it; or perhaps ladders of yucca
rope were employed. But no fragments which might be supposed to be remains of
these ladders have been found.

A long view of Sun Temple ruin and Mummy House ruin, taken from viewpoint across canyon. Note that cliff is almost totally vertical. Photo courtesy MVNP.

A long view of Mummy House; relative smallness of the ruin by comparison with the cliff gives an idea of immensity of the canyon walls. Photo courtesy MVNP.

Long House: view is of reconstructed kiva structure showing portion of bench within. Terrace walls follow original structure as nearly as possible. Photo courtesy MVNP.

Looking down into Long House ruin, where reconstruction shows faithful reproduction or original structure. Note cliff overhang at left. Photo courtesy MVNP.

This long photo shot is of the Long House ruin, giving a good idea of how the original structures were built within eroded caves in the canyon walls. Photo courtesy MVNP.

An overall view of Long House ruin with cliff overhang allows better idea of size and extent of this complex. Compare with photos of Long House taken by author. Photo courtesy MVNP.

Repetitive views of Long House from different viewpoints allows visitors and students to better evaluate these aboriginal dwellings; each viewpoint is unique. Photo courtesy MVNP.

Water apparently was plentiful when cliff dwellings were begun; not so now. This is a picture of Seep Spring, near Long House; the water is potable today. Photo courtesy MVNP.

Though the inhabitants of Long House, as may be gathered from the above, were admirably prepared for defence, still there are indications to suggest that they eventually succumbed to their enemies. Human bones — ribs, vertebræ, etc. — are strewn in numbers here and there among the ruins.

As I have mentioned in the preceding chapter, we worked about a month in Long House without making many finds of special interest. While we were engaged in room *16*, the wall of the adjoining room (*15*) gave way, exposing a perfect human skeleton. It had undoubtedly been buried in the room. Similar cases of burial in a room within the building itself, in the midst of the living, the entrance of the improvised tomb having been simply walled up, are not uncommon in the cliff-

FIG. 13. THE ASCENT TO THE FORTIFIED LEDGE.
(From a photograph by the author.)

dwellings. The most remarkable instance of this was observed by JOHN WETHERILL, and I shall give a more detailed account thereof in the following chapter.

The reason of the disappointing results of our excavations in Long House is possibly to be found in the fact that the walls were often so dilapidated, and the rooms so full of rubble and stones, that long labour was necessary to reach the floors, where we might first expect to find the most numerous objects. Perhaps too the place had been entirely plundered of any articles of special value by victorious enemies.

A hundred and fifty paces south of Long House lie the ruined walls of two rooms. There we found fragments of human skeletons, probably the remains of four individuals, and a quantity of yucca cord.

About 1 kilometre south of Long House lies another ruin, *Kodak House*, which, although smaller, in many respects resembles the former. A short lateral cañon, running from Mountain Sheep Cañon,[1] cuts into the mesa and ends in a cliff divided by horizontal hollows into several ledges (Plate I). The deepest of these hollows forms a semicircular cave, in the shelter of which the buildings have been erected. On an upper shelf, very difficult of access, lies another long row of rooms. In order to descend to the ruin from our camp, which during our work here lay on the mesa just east of the ruin, we had set up a long notched tree-trunk, to serve as a ladder, at a spot a little east of the ruins which are represented in Plate I. From this point we could follow the ledge all the way to the buildings. It was not so easy, however, to reach the upper portion of the ruin. We only once visited this part. Almost vertically above the extreme west of the ruins on the upper ledge, there lie on a still higher ledge two huge blocks of stone; we climbed down to this ledge from the mesa and crept along it to the east, till we reached a spot where a small, dry cedar afforded a treacherous hold for a rope (to the extreme right in Plate I). John Wetherill clambered down the rope, while I supported the tree. Having reached the ledge below, he followed it to the ruins, which he hurriedly examined, without finding any object worthy of remark, and then returned the same way. When the houses were inhabited, it is evident that the inhabitants did not take this round-about way. The most easterly part of the buildings on the lower ledge, where some walls still rise to a height of three stories (6.₅ metres), probably extended right up to the rooms above.

I shall not enter into any minute description of this ruin, which would only be a repetition of what I have said above of Long House; but I may refer the reader to the photograph (Plate I). The cliff-dwelling consists of 30—40 rooms, including 5 or 6 estufas.

Some hundreds of feet from the ruins, at the bottom of the cañon, there is a fairly good spring, which, after it had been partly cleaned, supplied our camp with water. Beyond doubt it also afforded a sufficient supply to the inhabitants of the cliff village.

The circumstance that induced me to remove the work to this ruin, was the discovery of a grave quite near it. Together with John Wetherill I had made an excursion to the ruin from our former camp, and we had then discovered, 30—40 metres below the lower inhabited ledge, under a low jutting rock, half of an earthen-ware bowl and the top of a skull projecting from the sand (fig. 14). The corpse lay with its face turned towards the rock; the legs were drawn up, with the knees close to the chin. A row of stones, the remains of a low wall, were piled on the outer side of the grave. With the aid of some sticks we dug out the skeleton and the bowl. The former was not very complete, but the skull was in a good state of

---

[1] So named because in this cañon we had seen, at very close range, a mountain sheep, an animal extremely rare in these regions. John Wetherill had not seen one for six years.

preservation. It belonged to a person of great age, for the teeth and their sockets were entirely wanting. In the bowl lay a small ladle, also of earthenware. That this grave really dated from the time of the cliff people, is shown by the ornament of the bowl, which exactly corresponds to the designs on the pottery found in the cliff-dwellings. I supposed that we might possibly find some other graves in the vicinity, but I was disappointed. The results of the excavations within the ruins themselves were not much better than in Long House.

Kodak House lies, as I have mentioned above, in a short subdivision of Mountain Sheep Cañon, a long branch of Navajo Cañon. The same cañon contains many smaller ruins, several of which lie in the cliff opposite Wetherill's Mesa. On the same side as Long House and Kodak House and south of them, we find the ruins of three cliff villages smaller than these, but still very interesting. The first of them, reckoning from the north (13 in the map, fig. 9), lies about a kilometre south of Kodak House. The rooms lie on two ledges, the upper one rather difficult of access. On the lower ledge the walls are much dilapidated. We did but very little work at this spot. A handsome vase of earthenware was the best find.

FIG. 14. GRAVE BELOW KODAK HOUSE.
(From a photograph by the author.)

On following the lower ledge from the last-mentioned ruin (*13*) a few hundred paces farther south along the sandstone cliff, we soon find ourselves again below a row of half ruined walls (see fig. 15), the remains of a cliff village which I have marked 12 in the map.

Ruin 12 is distinguished from the ruins previously mentioned in this chapter by the difficulty of approaching it. The whole cliff-dwelling lies on a ledge at the brink of the cliff, being thus rendered almost impregnable merely by its site. On going a little way past the ruin, however, we find a place where it is possible to climb, without great difficulty, up to the ledge, along which the approach to the ruin is easy. I here give a plan of the ruin (Plate IV: 1). The walls reach in several places to the roof of rock. The long outer wall on the north-west side of the ruin

is constructed with especially great skill and in a line with the precipice. To
find a foundation for a wall so high on the steeply sloping rocks, was a task
involved with great difficulties, which have, however, been skilfully overcome. The
wall, firmly fixed on its sloping foundation, now rises in the form of an immediate
continuation of the perpendicular cliff. Three estufas lie in the north part of the
building. Both their dimensions and their construction are the same as elsewhere.
The third estufa, reckoning from the north-west, contains within the narrow, walled
passage described above, and leading from the interior of the room out into the open
air, two crossbars as thick as one's finger, built diagonally into the walls near the top.
We are thus compelled to reject the explanation which HOLMES seems to have been
inclined to adopt in his description of another ruin, namely that the passage was used

FIG. 15. CLIFF-DWELLING 12 IN THE WEST CLIFF OF WETHERILL'S MESA.
(From a photograph by the author.)

as an entrance to the estufa, for even without the crossbars it is scarcely large
enough to let a man through. There is not the least trace of soot on these bars
or on the stone walls of the passage either in this estufa or in any other that I
have seen. It cannot therefore be a chimney leading from the hearth. A further
proof of this is given by the wall between the fireplace and the mouth of the passage.
That it played an important part in some respect, is indubitable, for it recurs in
exactly the same form in every estufa. Its purpose is a mystery to me. Perhaps it
served simply as a ventilator, so that the smoke might pass out more freely through
some aperture in the roof, though I confess that even this explanation seems highly
improbable. — The entrance of the estufa, an opening which also served as an outlet
for the smoke, was certainly constructed in the roof, as in the similar rooms

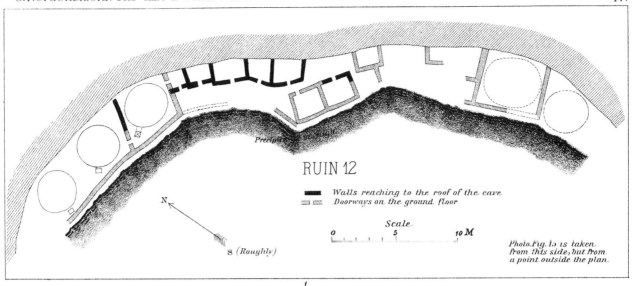

RUIN 12

▬▬▬ Walls reaching to the roof of the cave
▨▨ Doorways on the ground floor

Scale

0   5   10 M

N

S (Roughly)

Precipi...

Photo. Fig. 15 is taken
from this side, but from
a point outside the plan.

1

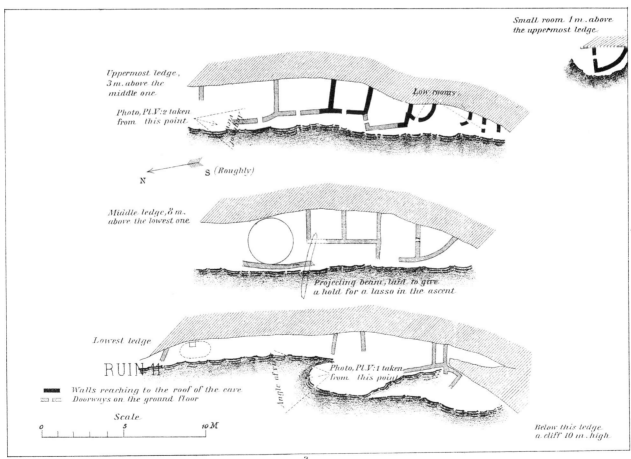

Small room 1 m. above
the uppermost ledge

Uppermost ledge,
3 m. above the
middle one

Photo, Pl. V: 2 taken
from this point

Low rooms

N   S (Roughly)

Middle ledge, 8 m.
above the lowest one

Projecting beam, laid to give
a hold for a lasso in the ascent

Lowest ledge

RUIN 11

Photo, Pl. V: 1 taken
from this point

Angle of r...

▬▬▬ Walls reaching to the roof of the cave
▨▨ Doorways on the ground floor

Scale

0   5   10 M

Below this ledge
a cliff 10 m. high

2

2

1

RUIN 11, MOUNTAIN SHEEP CAÑON

among the Mokis. In all the estufas I have visited the roof had fallen in, with one single exception, of which I shall give a fuller account below. Our excavations in ruin 12 were not very extensive. The most numerous objects were found in the third estufa, reckoning from the north-west. A few woven belts (Pl. XLIX: 1 and 2), with warp of cotton and woof of yucca fibre, probably used in carrying burdens, were in the best state of preservation.

Just south of the ruin described above (12) there is a spot where it is possible, though with some difficulty, to climb up the sandstone cliff to the mesa. Farther south the rocks are again quite precipitous and inaccessible. A few hundred paces from ruin 12 along the slope below these rocks lead us to another cliff-dwelling,

FIG. 16. STEPS LEADING TO A CLIFF-DWELLING.
(From a photograph by the author.)

which lies on three different ledges in the cliff. The appearance of the ruins is shown in Plate V: 2. The ascent is illustrated by the same plate: 1. My companion succeeded, by the help of his skilled practice in the use of the lasso, in casting a rope from below round the pole projecting from the wall as shown in the figure. By this means the break-neck ascent was rendered easier. The first visitor to the ruin had made the climb without any such assistance, a very venturesome undertaking. Since then a piece of old floor-timber had been laid across the outer wall to serve as a hold for a rope. In spite of this one of my Mexican labourers preferred, while engaged in the upper part of the ruin, going without his dinner to risking the climb twice a day.

The original photograph of Plate V: 2 is taken from the north end of the shelf on which the upper part of the ruin is situated, and shows the different ledges on which the buildings are erected. In Plate IV: 2 plans of the ruin are given. The narrow ledges at the very edge of the precipice have not afforded space for any extensive constructions. The rooms are small and generally almost rectangular; but often the surrounding rocks have determined the position of the walls. Many of the rooms are narrow cells, in which it would be impossible to turn, even if one had succeeded in slipping in through the tiny doorway. The latter is quadrangular, usually somewhat narrower at the top, the dimensions being about 0.4×0.7 m. One doorway in this ruin has a form approaching that of a cross, two stones opposite each other having been removed, one on each side of the doorway. — Generally speaking, all the ruins

FIG. 17. CLIFF-DWELLING (16) IN THE WEST CLIFF OF WETHERILL'S MESA.
(From a photograph by the author.)

on Wetherill's Mesa are so like one another in the size and structure of the rooms that a description of one of them applies to most of the rest. The only variations appear in their situation — in the inaccessible precipice or on the talus slope at its foot — and in the size, according to the nature of the place chosen for their erection.

North of Long House, still on the west side of Wetherill's Mesa, lie two extensive ruins. The first of them (16 in the map, fig. 9) is reached from the mesa above it by steps cut in the rock (fig. 16). Similar steps, once used by the cliff people, occur in several places among the ruins. It is evident that a lively intercourse existed between the inhabitants of the different cliff-dwellings. Ruin 16 contains little of any special interest. A mummy was found there by WETHERILL. It had not been buried, but lay in an estufa, half within the tunnel which I have spoken of above. It was the body of a man, probably one of the ancient inhabitants of the cliff-dwelling who had fallen in defence of his hearth and home. The position seemed to indicate that he had tried to escape from the estufa by the said passage.

Still farther north lies another large ruin, named *Mug House* from the quantity of pottery, especially mugs, which has been found there. These mugs, which have the form of a cylinder or truncate cone, are perhaps the most singular specimens

FIG. 18. FIREPLACE IN MUG HOUSE.
(From a photograph by the author.)

of the cliff-dwellers' pottery. Figures and description of them are given in Pl. XXIX.

At Mug House rather considerable portions of the ruin have been buried under large blocks that have fallen from the roof of rock. This may possibly be an indication of the great age of the ruin. In a room under one of these blocks we found a quantity of perforated shells (Pl. LI: 2), which had probably composed a necklace, and two well preserved and handsomely ornamented earthenware vessels. Neither in Mug House nor in ruin 16 were our excavations very extensive.

The rooms of the cliff-dwellings are almost invariably destitute of any fittings. Mug House contains the only example of a fireplace that I have observed in any cliff-dwelling, except the hearths which always occupy the centre of the estufas. This fireplace consists of a curved elevation of masonry in a corner of one of the rooms (fig. 18).

Between Mug House and ruin 16 lie some smaller cliff-dwellings. Two of them are marked in the map (fig. 9). The southern one (17), which I have seen only at a distance, has nothing of special interest to offer. The other deserves mention on account of its singular position. A few hundred paces north of ruin 17 the cliff may be descended from the mesa by a break-neck climb. On following the lower part of the cliff in a northerly direction, we come after a while to a small crack, open towards the north. On the sand and stones that have filled the bottom of this fissure, we follow a steep ascent for a few dozen paces, and then turn off, almost in the opposite direction, into another very narrow crack (Pl. VI: 1). In the upper part of this lies the ruin (Pl. VI: 2), which is of insignificant size. I cannot tell what freak of chance led to the discovery of this little eyrie. No place of refuge could be better hidden from an advancing enemy. The ruin itself consists merely of a few low walls, roughly put together on an extremely narrow ledge to one side of the chasm. There is a great difference in architecture between these humble dwellings and such magnificent buildings as the Cliff Palace, Long House, etc.

The chasm that affords the only way of reaching this ruin, branches off into another, still narrower cleft, through which a man of ordinary build can force his way to a small and narrow ledge in the open. From this ledge one may climb, clinging fast with tooth and nail, round an extremely dangerous corner of the cliff, and thus reach another shelf with a second ruin, which consists of a few rooms, and probably belonged to the same community as the dwelling just described. Here we found a large and handsome black jar of a type — the so-called *coiled ware* — fragments of which are very common, but which, as it is extremely fragile, is only seldom found entire. The jar turned out, however, to be too large for conveyance through the cleft, through which we had ourselves forced a passage only with difficulty. Still we succeeded after great exertions in carrying it down the cliff and then up again to the mesa, where we, however, had to leave it, as on this occasion we had no means of transporting it farther.

I have now given descriptions and figures of the most important ruins on the west side of Wetherill's Mesa, and shall pass in the next chapter to the cliff-villages situated on the east side thereof.

G Nordenskiöld: The Cliff Dwellers of Mesa Verde

RUIN 18 MOUNTAIN SHEEP CAÑON

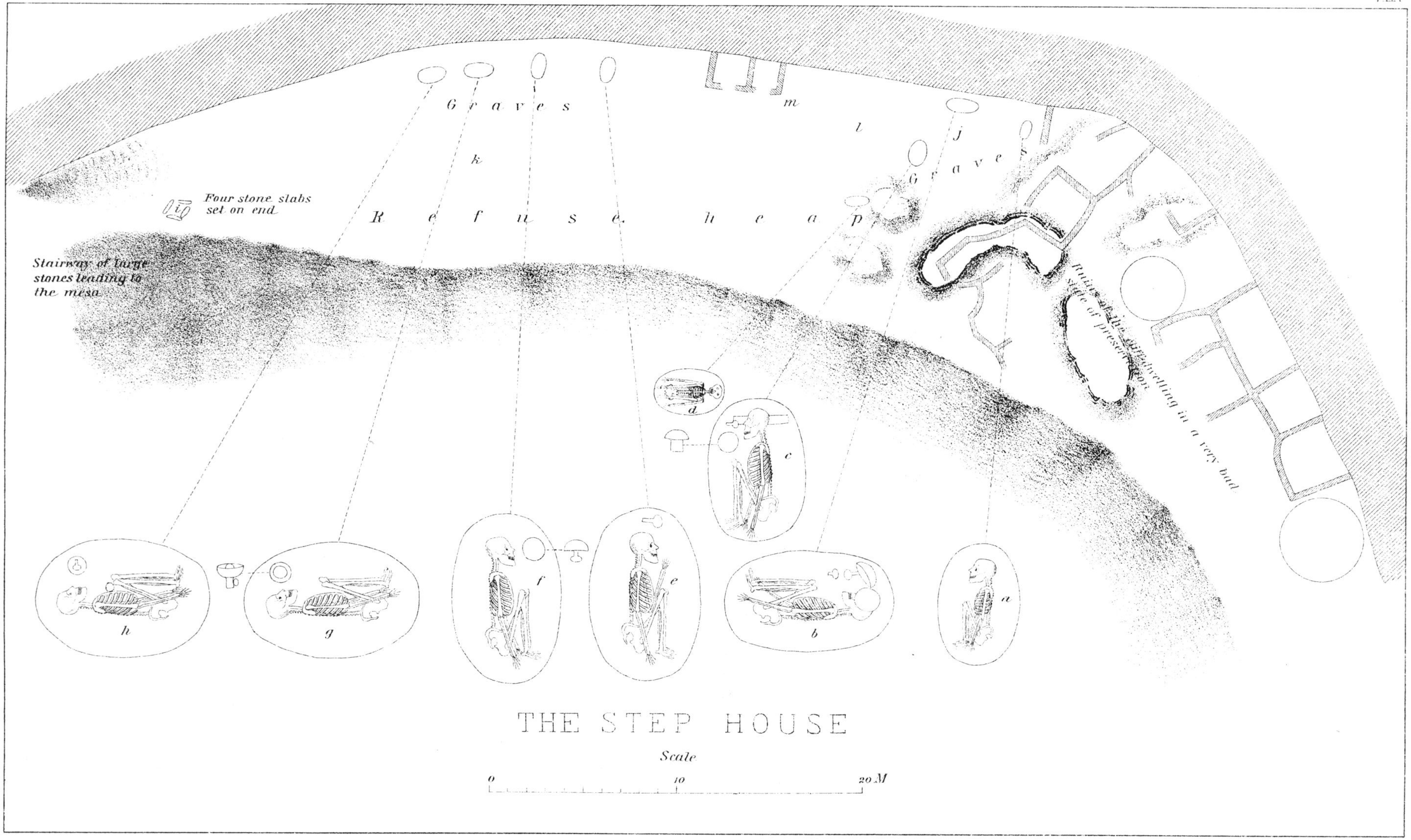

G. Nordenskiöld: The Cliff Dwellers of the Mesa Verde

Ruins of the cliff-dwelling in a very bad
side of preservation

Graves

Refuse heaps

Four stone slabs
set on end

Stairway of large
stones leading to
the mesa

THE STEP HOUSE

Scale

0   10   20 M

CHAPTER VI.

Ruins in the East Cliffs of Wetherill's Mesa.

Wetherill's Mesa is bounded to the east by a fork of Navajo Cañon, to which fork I have given the name of Spring House Cañon, from a ruin, Spring House, situated in the same. From this cañon several short subdivisions jut into Wetherill's Mesa. Both in Spring House Cañon and in these subdivisions lie several ruins, some of them fairly extensive and interesting.

FIG. 19. THE STEP HOUSE CAVE. THE MUCH DILAPIDATED RUINS OF THE CLIFF-DWELLING ARE SHOWN AT ABOUT THE MIDDLE OF THE FIGURE.
(From a photograph by the author.)

After completing our work in the neighbourhood of Kodak House, I had the camp removed to about the middle of Wetherill's Mesa (3rd camp, fig. 9). A few hundred paces eastwards from this camping place bring us to the edge of Spring House Cañon, and here, in a very short subdivision of the same, lies a ruin of insignificant appearance, which proved, however, to be of exceedingly great interest. It has received the name of *Step House*, from a stairway, built of large blocks of stone, that leads to the ruin. Both to the north and south of the ruin there is a practicable descent to the same from the mesa. To the north steps have been hewn at several spots in the sandstone cliff to facilitate the descent. Along a shelf of rock

we reach a high, vaulted cave (fig. 19), open to the east. Its length is about 70
metres, its depth 15 metres. At one end lie the much dilapidated ruins of a considerable cliff-village. A plan thereof is given in Plate VII. The ruins occupy only
the north end of the cave. The remainder is an open space 40 metres in length
and roofed in by the high vault of rock. Throughout almost the whole of this open
space the ground consists of refuse, bird droppings, probably of the turkey, leaves
and cobs of maize, mixed with rubbish and dust. To the south of this space is a
slope covered with large blocks of sandstone, which have been arranged to form a
stairway (fig. 20) of about 60 steps, leading almost up to the mesa. The cave is
adjoined below by a rather steep slope, densely overgrown with bushes, which extends
to the very bottom of the cañon.

FIG. 20. STAIRWAY LEADING TO STEP HOUSE.
(From a photograph by the author.)

We excavated partly in the ruins themselves, partly in the refuse south of them.
Our finds in the ruins were rather few. Previous excavations of a less thorough
description, made on the open space south of the ruins, had not yielded any results
worthy of mention. Now, however, we found several graves and a hiding-place
where it was evident that on some occasion of imminent danger jars and other objects
of value had been buried. The plan shows the site of the different graves, and the
places where the various finds were made. I shall first give an account of the former.

Quite close to the ruins, between them and the cliff, at the foot of a dilapidated wall, we found the body of a child (Pl. XIX: 3; *a* in the plan, Pl. VII).
It was half mummified. One hand and the feet were in such a good state of preservation that even the nails were partly left. The head showed signs of strong,

artificial depression; this was the case with all the skulls we dug up in the cliff-dwellings (Pl. XVIII). The corpse had been shrouded, in a crouching position, with the legs drawn up to the breast, in a kind of cloth made of cords wrapped in feathers, the manufacture of which fabric I shall describe more fully below.

Near the child-mummy and also quite close to the wall of rock, we found a second grave (*b*); this contained an adult. The body had been wrapped, in the customary position, with the knees drawn up to the chin, in a kind of mat made of osiers. This mat was composed of long, narrow withes, which had been split in two and pierced, at intervals of about 10 cm., with fine holes, through which long cords of yucca had been passed to tie them together (a similar mat is represented in Pl. XLVIII: 1). The body was only partly mummified. The left ribs, shoulder-blade, and thigh-bone, a part of the spine, and both pelvic bones were still united in one piece. One hand was also perfectly mummified; even the nails were preserved. Of the rest of the body only the skeleton was left. The skull was in excellent condition, and all the teeth still remained. Four earthen vessels had been buried with the corpse. A bowl (Pl. XXVI: 5) had been turned over the head, another, somewhat larger bowl (Pl. XXVI: 4) lay on the top of the first, a small mug (Pl. XXIX: 1) and a smaller bowl (Pl. XXVII: 3) had been set in front of the face. The face was turned towards the cliff.

Not far from this last grave, a little to the north and 2.4 metres from the back of the cave, we found the body of an adult (*c*), completely mummified (Pl. XIX: 2). This seemed to have been the grave of a person of importance, to judge by the care with which the body had been buried. The head had been covered with a skin cap, the feet with moccasins or shoes of the same material. The position of the body was the same as in all the other graves. The corpse was wrapped in a kind of net of cords, spirally wound with strips of hide, on which the hair was still partly preserved. These cords were further held together by strips of yucca leaf, under which thick bunches of cedar bast had been inserted. The entire absence of moisture had presumably been enough without further preparation to transform the corpse to a mummy. All the soft parts were completely dried; the hair, which was black and rather coarse, still hung to the head. Under the mummy lay a mat of withes, similar to that described in the account of the preceding grave. The head rested on a short, rounded block of wood. A mat of the same kind as the one under the corpse had finally been spread over it. Thus enveloped, it had been buried in the ground, a couple of feet below the surface, close to the ruins. The body had been laid in this grave with the head turned towards the cliff and facing the south-east. Care had been taken not only to prepare a comfortable resting-place, but also to provide the deceased with the necessaries of life. In front of the head stood a basket (Pl. XLIV: 3), half full of maize meal and covered with a handsome bowl (Pl. XXVI: 3) turned upside down. Beside the basket lay a small ladle or spoon (Pl. XXX: 3), and between the two a maize cob. Both the basket and the meal were well preserved. The latter was of a slightly yellowish colour and rather coarse.

Farther out from the cliff, at the foot of a large block of stone, a child had been buried (*d*). The position was the usual one, with the knees drawn up, but the corpse lay on its back. The body with its shroud of feather cloth had dried into a lump. The anterior part of the skull, which had not been sufficiently ossified during life, was entirely decayed. Quite near the mummy we found a long stick, flattened towards one end and pointed, probably an implement for the planting of maize (Pl. XLIII: 12). Whether it had been laid there at the same time as the corpse, is a question that I shall leave open. Between this grave and the ruined buildings we found an incomplete skeleton; even the skull was wanting.

The four graves next described (*e*, *f*, *g*, *h*, Plate VII) lay in a row close up to the cliff and about half-way between the ruins and the stairway at the opposite end of the cave. In the first of them, reckoning from the ruins (*e*), the body had been laid in a hole of oval shape, dug in the rather hard ground, and large enough comfortably to contain the corpse in a crouching attitude. The hole had then been covered with a roof of short poles, and over these, to prevent the soil from falling on the corpse, with a mat of withes, like that described above. The mat had been covered with a large flat slab of stone, and the whole grave had finally been buried under a layer of earth, scarcely a foot in depth. The lower half of the corpse, had undergone the process of decomposition, this being due to the dampness of the ground on which it rested. The upper half was partly mummified. Above the head lay a small ladle of earthenware (Pl. XXX: 6). To judge from the skull this was probably the grave of a woman. Pl. XIX: 1 represents the body.

The next grave (*f*) was situated only a few paces from the preceding one and was constructed in the same manner. Even the skeleton was here entirely decayed; the skull, remarkable as being very much flattened, was all that was worth saving; it unfortunately fell to pieces in course of transportation. Two earthen vessels were found in the grave: a small jar (Pl. XXIX: 2), which stood upright, and a bowl (Pl. XXVI: 2) turned over the jar.

Near the stairway we found another grave (*g*). Here too the same care had been bestowed on the arrangement of the resting-place for the body. A hole had been dug in the ground, and precaution had been taken, by covering the hole with thick crossbars and a mat of withes on the top, to prevent the soil from coming in immediate contact with the corpse. Close in front of the face lay three earthenware vessels: a mug, on which stood a large bowl, and a smaller bowl within the latter (Pl. XXIX: 6, Pl. XXV: 4, Pl. XXVII: 6). Immediately above the crossbars forming the roof of the grave lay a long, round pole of oak, similar to the stick found in the grave *d*. In this grave too the soft parts were decomposed, but the skeleton was well preserved. The appearance of the grave and the position occupied by the skeleton are shown in fig. 21.

Step House got its name from ancient steps leading from valley floor to site, courtesy G. Nordenskiold. This photo shows terracing supporting some higher structures. Courtesy MVNP.

The kiva at Step House (in this photo) shows a built-in altar structure. Ruin has been here stabilized, rather than reconstructed. A very interesting ruin. Photo courtesy MVNP.

The cave in which Step House was built is truly enormous, and its size can best be gauged by this long view. Growth of coniferous trees on mesa top is clearly visible. Courtesy MVNP.

Another long view of Step House, here showing very nicely the relative size of the ruin complex and the overhanging roof of the cave. Photo courtesy MVNP.

This is a petroglyph carved into the stone at Step House. Some students of aboriginal art believe the carvings like this are "doodles". Photo courtesy MVNP.

Another petroglyph at Step House. Most scholars believe the petroglyph carvings have a definite meaning, and were not done to just ". . . while away time". Photo courtesy MVNP.

A difficult frontal view of Mug House, which got its name from the huge quantity of mugs found by excavators working in the ruin. Note restored wall. Photo courtesy MVNP.

A long view of Mug House, showing the rounded natural erosion of the cave roof. Note how top of walls reach very nearly to the ceiling of the cave. Photo courtesy MVNP.

Quite near this grave we found another (*h*). The arrangement of the cross-bars and of the mat of withes above them was the same; but the roof had fallen in, and the grave was full of earth. Close beside the knees of the corpse lay the fragments of a black jar of coiled ware. In front of the face a bowl (Pl. XXVII: 7) had been set, and within it was a small ladle. On the top of the body we found half of another bowl (Pl. XXVII: 2). This skeleton was that of a man. It was well-preserved, though denuded of all the soft parts.

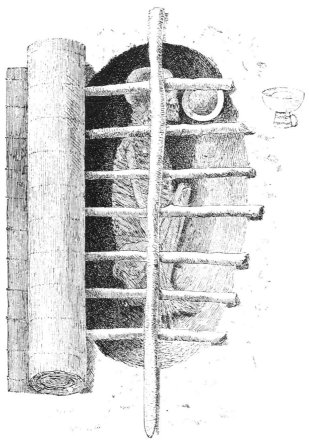

FIG. 21. GRAVE (*g*) AT STEP HOUSE, SEEN FROM ABOVE.

In all the four graves last described the dead occupied the usual squatting position. They lay on the left side; the two nearest to the ruins had the face turned to the north, the others to the west, towards the cliff. None of them was buried more than some decimetres under the surface. The skull was artificially flattened in each case.

An oblong chamber (*i* in the plan), 1.5 m. long and 1 m. broad, situated close to the stairway and built of some flat slabs of stone set on end, should possibly be also explained as a grave. Within it we found some fragments of a coarse earthenware vessel, some charred maize cobs, and a little charcoal and ashes. The ashes contain phosphoric acid, and may thus possibly be the remains of bones. Close to these slabs we discovered a small spherical earthen vessel of coarse execution (Pl. XXIV: 10) and a large *metate stone*,[1] with two small, rounded stones, which had presumably been employed in the crushing of maize. If we are right in the assumption that this chamber is a grave, an assumption which cannot be regarded as anything more than a mere surmise, we have here an instance of cremation.

The ground within the vault of rock, from the ruins almost to the stairway, was composed, as I have mentioned above, of refuse, consisting of bird droppings mixed with sand, fragments of maize, and miscellaneous rubbish. This accumulation of refuse was 40 m. long and 13 m. broad. The depth was measured at a few spots, and varied between 0.6 and 2 m. The contents of this mass of rubbish were probably between 200 and 300 cubic m. All the graves were situated in this refuse heap, where we also found a number of other objects, some of which, as mentioned above, had evidently been buried designedly, perhaps on some occasion of hurried flight from an approaching enemy.

Among these latter objects I shall mention the following, which were found almost at the same spot (*j* in the plan):

Several earthenware vessels: among them a large white jar with black design (Pl. XXXI). That it had been hidden purposely, is suggested partly by the position, partly by the mouth's having been furnished with a temporary lid, consisting of a lump of clay, to prevent the soil from falling into the jar. A large black jar (Pl. XXI: 1), which had been hidden hard by, had been closed by laying across the mouth some small sticks and above these tangled yucca fibre.

A bundle of reeds, probably intended to be made into arrows.

A large piece of flint of the kind often used in the manufacture of arrow heads.

A quantity of well-preserved maize ears.

A piece of cotton cloth.

Some woven baskets of yucca (Pl. XLIV: 4, 5).

Pieces of a white, kaoline-like substance, wrapped in maize leaves and lying at the bottom of a large jar. This substance was probably employed, as I shall show later on, in the manufacture of pottery.

The entire shell of a pumpkin with lid, the latter fastened with a string (Pl. XLV: 4). All the cracks were carefully stopped with clay. The pumpkin contained materials for the manufacture of feather cloth, together with some cloth already finished.

In another place (*k*) we found two earthenware vessels (Pl. XXIII: 1, Pl. XXIV: 2) of a rather unusual type. At *l* we discovered three earthenware vessels (Pl. XXV: 5, Pl. XXVIII: 4, Pl. XXVII: 5) of a common type, decorated in black and white, at *m* an excellently preserved pouch (Pl. XLIX: 3) made of the skin of a

---

[1] *Metate stone* (from Mex. *metlatl*) is the name applied to a flat, somewhat concave disk of stone (about 50 × 40 cm.), which seems to have been used in the grinding of maize among the greater part of the aborigines of North America. I shall give below a figure of a metate stone from a cliff-dwelling.

prairie dog and full of common salt. Here and there among the refuse a number of other articles were found.

Our excavations in the rooms within the ruin itself were not very productive. The few objects found there were of no especial interest.

On following the edge of Wetherill's Mesa from Step House a few hundred paces to the south or south-east, we descry in the opposite wall of the cañon an extensive cliff-dwelling, *Spring House* (marked 20 in the map). What a striking view these ruins present at a distance! The explorer pictures to himself a whole town in miniature under the lofty vault of rock in the cliff before him. But the town is a deserted one: not a sound breaks the silence, and not a movement meets the eye, among those gloomy, half ruined walls, whose contours stand off sharply from the darkness of the inner cave. — Spring House is situated high up the wall of the cañon, and both below and above the ruin the rocks are very steep. The rooms of the building lie on two ledges within the same cave. On the lower and larger shelf the walls are much dilapidated; many rooms are entirely buried in rubble. The upper part of the ruin is smaller, but, on the other hand, in a complete state of preservation (see Pl. VIII), in consequence of its more sheltered site. It consists of a long row of rooms, some of which are divided into two stories. The rafters project, as is often the case, a foot or two beyond the wall. The entrances both of the upper and lower stories are shown in Pl. VIII to the right, in the upper corner. A flat slab of stone projecting from the wall forms a kind of platform in front of the door of the upper story. As in most of the ruins previously described, there are no doorways in the outer wall, which stands close to the edge of the shelf and reaches up to the roof of rock.

This ruin has been called Spring House from a spring situated at the back of the cave. In fig. 22 a representation is given of the part of the cave that lies nearest to the cliff, and in which the spring is situated. Two slender, quadrangular pillars of sandstone have been erected here to support an extensive roof. It seems to have been customary in the construction of these buildings always to leave an open space behind the whole cliff-dwelling. In order to provide support for the floor of an upper story, without having to encroach upon this space by building walls, the builders have erected these pillars.

I carried out only quite superficial excavations in a few of the rooms on the lower ledge in Spring House. Still, several objects of interest were found. The most remarkable of them was a bowl (Pl. XXXIII) of a variety, ornamented in red, white, and black, small fragments of which are often seen strewn on the ground, both among the ruins and on the plateau, but which is very rare in entire specimens or large fragments. The bowl was not entire, and in spite of the offer of a high reward not all the pieces were found; but what we secured, was sufficient to enable me to give a restored figure. Two other earthenware bowls (Pl. XXV: 1 and 3) were found in an estufa filled to the roof with rubble and stones. Both the earthenware and the timber in this estufa showed evident traces of the action of fire. The place seems to have been ravaged by a violent conflagration.

Spring House is fairly well protected from attack by its site. From the bottom of the cañon the buildings can be reached only by a difficult and dangerous climb from ledge to ledge; and a very circuitous route, either up or down the cañon, must be taken to scale the mesa from the ruin. This cliff-dwelling does not belong to Wetherill's Mesa, it is true; but I have mentioned it in connexion with the

FIG. 22. THE INTERIOR OF SPRING HOUSE.
(From a photograph by the author.)

ruins of the said tract, because our visits to the ruin were made with the camp at the middle of Wetherill's Mesa as the starting-point.

Before concluding this chapter I have still to mention one more cliff-dwelling of some considerable size, which is marked 14 in the map (fig. 9), and situated in a small cañon that runs from Spring House Cañon into Wetherill's Mesa. Fig. 23 is a representation of this ruin, seen at a distance. It is rather far from the ruin to a place which offers a practicable ascent to the mesa, and the climb is attended

THE SPRING HOUSE

with great difficulties. Most of the rooms in the cliff-dwelling lie between the sandstone cliff and the lower slope of the cañon. The upper part of the ruin is situated on several ledges separated by the perpendicular cliff and in part very difficult of access. The ledge visible to the left of the figure seemed at first sight completely inaccessible. The cliffs leant outwards, and there was no spot where any inequalities might afford a footing. But from one of the walls two beams projected, and round one of these CLAYTON WETHERILL succeeded by a skilful cast in fastening his lasso. He then clambered up the slender rope to the ledge. None of the lower buildings had apparently been high enough to reach up to this ledge. The communication had presumably been kept up by means of ladders of yucca rope attached to the beams, which had probably been

FIG. 23. CLIFF-DWELLING (14) IN SPRING HOUSE CAÑON.
(From a photograph by the author.)

placed there for this very purpose, or possibly by the aid of logs set on end and lashed fast. What can have induced a people to have recourse to dwelling-places so incommodious? This is a question that has undoubtedly suggested itself many times already to the reader. The answer must be, that nothing short of the ever imminent attacks of a hostile people, can have driven the cliff-dwellers to these impregnable mountain fastnesses, which afforded a safe refuge, so long as food and water held out.

On the opposite side of the cañon in which the cliff-dwelling just described is situated, lies a very small ruin, where we found a skeleton, the condition of which was, however, such that only the skull was worth saving. By the customary artificial flattening of the head, a singular form had been given to the skull (Pl. XVIII: 1).

On the other side of the narrow strip of mesa that separates the cañon in which the last mentioned ruins are situated, from Spring House Cañon, of which the former cañon is a fork, lie a few more, small ruins, which do not appear in the map. In one of them we found a handsome and well-preserved jar (Pl. XXII: 1).

I have now described most of the important ruins in the vicinity of Wetherill's Mesa. I have omitted to mention several smaller ones; but they do not possess any special interest.

As this chapter contains the account of most of the graves discovered, I have thought it appropriate here to append a summary of the various modes of burial observed during my investigations among the ruins of the Mesa Verde. According to the site of the graves they may be classified as follows:

I.   *Graves in the ruins within the caves:*
    a) *in a room, usually walled up, within the building itself;*
    b) *in the refuse heap at the back of the cave, behind the ruins or close beside them.*
II. *Graves under a jutting rock or in a small hollow of the cliff, generally in the neighbourhood of a ruin.*
III. *Graves on the mesa.*

Graves in a room within the cliff-dwelling itself.

Often the dead were buried within the building itself, perhaps in the very room where they had died. Similar customs prevail among several Indian tribes of North America.[1]

An example of the mode of burial in question has been given above in the description of Long House (p. 29). At Sprucetree House, a ruin which I shall describe in the following chapter, we found far in under the vault of rock, in a little room, the doorway of which did not seem to have been walled up, the corpses of three children. The most remarkable instance of a living-room having been changed to a sepulchre was observed by JOHN WETHERILL in a ruin situated in a subdivision of Johnson Cañon, on the mesa east of the Rio Mancos. The following description is taken from his own notes:

"We (CHARLEY MASON and JOHN WETHERILL) dug a while in a room we had worked in before dinner; but finding nothing I began shovelling in a room Captain BAKER's men had nearly cleared. Glancing up I noticed a door that had been sealed up. I removed a rock and saw that it was the only entrance. I told CHARLEY of this, and he said I would find a skeleton. I removed the rocks down to the

---

[1] YARROW, H. C. A further Contribution to the Study of the Mortuary Customs of the North American Indians. First. Ann. Rep. Bur. Ethn., p. 122.

floor and noticed some wrappings, the same that they bury the dead in. While clearing away the rubbish I found a piece of a cinch. It was three-coloured, red, white, and black. I then broke through the wall on another side. As soon as I dug to the floor I uncovered more matting. I removed some dirt and found an arrow with an agate point on it, the first ever found in a Cliff-house in Mancos Cañon. I took it to where CHARLEY was, and he concluded to help me dig. CHARLEY removed two or three shovelfuls of dirt and dug out a basket; it was 12 inches across the top and 6 inches deep. Henceforward our finds came fast and close together. We found 17 arrows lying across the heads of five bodies. Between the skulls were four bowls. One large skeleton lay on the top of the mat with a bow on one side, a mug and a basket on the other. He had nothing over him; a pair of moccasins on his feet and some feather cloth under his head. Near him lay a hollow stick with both ends wrapped with sinew and with a bone-point at the end about six inches long. The stick was about twenty inches long. Lying alongside of this body were the skeletons of three babies. The rats had eaten them so much that they were not worth saving. Two of them had pieces of buckskin with them. After taking them up we found a large mat covering the whole floor. We removed this and found another skeleton and a stick with a loop at the end, that we took for a medicine stick, also two prairie-dog skin pouches. The skeleton was covered with a willow mat. Under the mat were two more made of grass. Under the grass mat was one of feather cloth, after that a buckskin-jacket with fringes. We found also two awls and a walnut, and in the same room two or three buckskin bags. The three baby skeletons were lying on the skeleton with the buckskin jacket. A large mug lay at the head of one of the babies. The three baby skeletons and the one on the top lay with their heads up the cañon, while the other had its head down the cañon."

Graves in the refuse heap within or beside the cliff-dwelling.

The open space or inner court which is often to be found within the cave behind the rooms of the more extensive cliff-villages, has generally been employed as a burial ground. Here, in the soil, which consists of bird droppings — tame turkeys were probably kept in this place — and miscellaneous refuse, graves are very often found. At Step House this burial ground is situated beside the buildings, but still within the same cave. The resting-places of the dead were prepared with great care, as I have described in the preceding part of this chapter.

Graves in hollows of the rock.

Often, too, we find graves beneath some sheltering projection of rock, or in some small hollow worn by water in the sandstone cliff. In places of this nature the dead were probably buried very often, though it is not so easy to discover these graves, from their being scattered over a comparatively wide extent of ground. That these graves also date from the period of the cliff-dwellers, appears partly

FIG. 24.   GRAVE IN POOL CAÑON.
(From a photograph by the author.)

from their proximity to the ruins, partly from the pottery found in them, which resembles that discovered in the ruins themselves.   The grave which we found below Kodak House, and which is described on p. 30, is an example of this mode of burial.

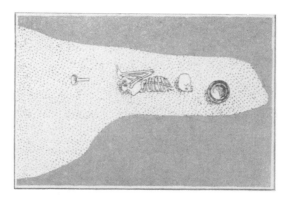

FIG. 25.   PLAN OF A GRAVE IN POOL CAÑON.

We found another similar grave in Pool Cañon, a branch of Navajo Cañon. The grave was situated 35 paces south of the ruins of a small cliff-dwelling, between the sandstone cliff and the talus at its foot.   Fig. 24 shows the mouth of the hole, which was 2 or 3 metres deep; the skeleton, together with two bowls and a ladle found beside it, is removed from the grave and laid at the mouth thereof. A plan showing their original position is given in fig. 25. The skull had somehow or other been disturbed. The lower jaw was found loose among the rubbish that had been removed from the cave. The covering wrapped round the body was in a bad state of preservation. It seemed that the corpse had been laid in a wrapping of feathercloth, and over this rush matting. The skeleton rested upon a layer of soft cedar bark. At the head lay the two earthenware bowls (Pl. XXV: 6 and XXVI: 1), in another part of the grave a small ladle similar to the one figured on Pl. XXIV: 11.

Graves on the Mesa.

I have last to mention the graves on the mesa. As I have stated above, the burial places situated there are very numerous. It is not quite certain whether they are really the graves of the people who inhabited the cliff-villages. I shall return to them in a subsequent chapter.

The grave situated near the stairway at Step House and mentioned on p. 42, is omitted from the above summary of the different modes of burial, it being a mere conjecture that we have here a case of the burning of the corpse previous to its interment. That cremation, however, was sometimes practised by the cliff-dwellers, seems probable from the fact that RICHARD WETHERILL observed in the same ruin where the above-mentioned burial chamber was found, bodies which had apparently been burnt together with the pottery belonging to the dead.

CHAPTER VII.

Ruins in the Cliffs of Chapin's Mesa.

This chapter will be devoted to a description of some ruins which I visited on several occasions, but where, with two exceptions, no excavations were carried out during my stay. Two of these ruins are not only the largest on the Mesa Verde, but also, considering their size and the excellent state of preservation they show, certainly the most important in the whole of the United States. In these great ruins even excavations of relative insignificance would have involved far too heavy expenses. Still I examined some rooms in Sprucetree House as well as in another ruin not far away, and made some good finds.

These ruins lie on a plateau bounded to the east by Cliff Cañon, to the west by a fork of Navajo Cañon, and indented at the sides by numerous small cañons. I call this plateau *Chapin's Mesa* after F. H. CHAPIN, who was the first to publish

any description of the more important ruins of the Mesa Verde. The route from
Mancos to this locality passes Point Lookout (see the map, fig. 1). From this place
it follows the north edge of the Mesa Verde across several cañons. Between two
of them, the westernmost fork of Cliff Cañon and the most eastern branch of Navajo
Cañon, the trail bends to the south. No stranger to the tract could find his way
among the labyrinth of trails that here intersects the vast piñon forest in every direction.

  During the short period occupied by my excavations in this neighbourhood
my camp lay on the west side of Chapin's Mesa, beside Sprucetree Cañon, a name

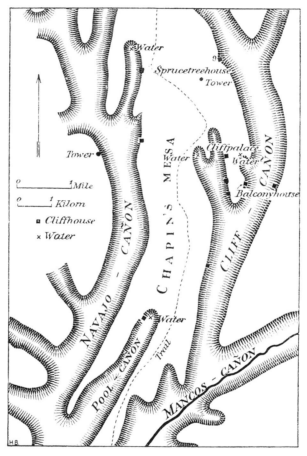

FIG. 26. OUTLINE MAP OF CHAPIN'S MESA.

which I gave to a branch of Navajo Cañon. From the valley, which is shut in
by a semicircle of precipitous cliffs, a whole forest of huge sprucetrees raise their
majestic heads, here and there towering to a level with the mesa. Not far from
the beginning of the last-mentioned cañon is a place where the descent of the cliff
is possible. A few hundred paces to the north along the cliff lead to a large cave,
in the shadow of which lie the ruins of a whole village, *Sprucetree House*. This cave
is 70 m. broad and 28 m. in depth. The height is small in comparison with the depth,

the interior of the cave thus being rather dark. The ground is fairly even and lies almost on a level, which has considerably facilitated the building operations. A plan of the ruins is given in Pl. IX. A great part of the house, or rather village, is in an excellent state of preservation, both the walls, which at some places are several stories high and rise to the roof of rock, and the floors between the different stories still remaining. The architecture is the same as that described in the ruins on Wetherill's Mesa. In some parts more care is perhaps displayed in the shape of the blocks and in the joints between them. The walls, here as in other cliff-dwellings, are about 0.₃ m. thick, seldom more. A point which immediately strikes the eye in Pl. IX, is that no premeditated design has been followed in the erection of

FIG. 27. SPRUCETREE HOUSE FROM THE MESA. A GREAT PART OF THE RUIN IS HIDDEN BY THE TREES. TO THE LEFT A VERY SMALL CLIFF-DWELLING.

(From a photograph by the author.)

the buildings. It seems as if only a few rooms had first been built, additions having subsequently been made to meet the requirements of the increasing population. This circumstance, which I have already touched upon when describing other ruins, may be observed in most of the cliff-dwellings. There is further evidence to show that the whole village was not erected at the same time. At several places it may be seen that new walls have been added to the old, though the stones of both walls do not fit into each other, as is the case when two adjacent walls have been constructed simultaneously. The arrangement of the rooms has been determined by the surrounding cliff, the walls being generally built either at right angles or parallel to it. At some places the walls of several adjoining apartments of about equal size have been consistently erected in the same direction, some blocks of rooms thus possessing a regularity which is wanting in the cliff-village as a whole. This is perhaps the first stage in the development of the cliff-dwellings to the villages whose ruins are common in the valleys and on the mesa, and which are constructed according to a fixed design.

In the plan (Pl. IX) it may be seen that the cave contains two distinct groups of rooms. At about the middle of the cliff-village a kind of passage (*23*), uninterrupted by any wall, runs through the whole ruin. We found the remains, however, of a cross wall projecting from an elliptical room (*14* in the plan) in the south part of the village. Each of these two divisions of the ruin contains an open space (*16* and *28*) at the back of the cave, the ground in both these places being covered with bird droppings. It is probable that this was the place where tame turkeys were kept, though it cannot have been a very pleasant abode for them, for at least in the north of the ruin this part of the cave is almost pitch dark, the walls of the inner court (*28*), rising up to the roof of rock. In each of the two divisions of the cliff-village a number of estufas were built, in the north at least five, in the south at least two; while several more are, no doubt, buried in the heaps of ruins. These estufas preserve to the least detail the ordinary type (diam. 4—5 metres) fully described above. They are generally situated in front of the other rooms, with their foundations sunk deeper in the ground, and have never had an upper story. Even their site suggests that they were used for some special purpose, probably as assembly-rooms at religious festivities held by those members of the tribe who lived in the adjacent rooms. In all the estufas without exception the roof has fallen in. It is probable, as I have mentioned before, that the entrance of these rooms, as is still the case among the Pueblo Indians, was constructed in the roof. The other rooms were entered by narrow doorways (breadth 40—55 cm., height 65—80 cm.). These doorways are generally rectangular, often somewhat narrower at the top; the sill consists, as already described, of a long stone slab, the lintel of a few sticks a couple of centimetres in thickness, laid across the opening to support the wall above them. The arch was unknown to the builders of these villages, even in the form common among the ruins of Central America, and constructed by carrying the walls on both sides of the doorway nearer to each other as each course of stones was laid, until they could be joined by a stone slab placed across them. Along both sides of the doorway and under the lintel a narrow frame of thin sticks covered with plaster was built (see fig. 28 to the left). This frame, which leant inwards, served to support the door, a thin, flat, rectangular stone slab of suitable size. Through two loops on the outside of the wall, made of osiers inserted in the chinks between the stones, and placed one on each side of the doorway, a thin stick was passed, thus forming a kind of bolt. Besides this type of door most cliff-villages contain examples of another.

G. Nordenskiöld: The Cliff Dwellers of the Mesa Verde.

THE SPRUCETREE HOUSE

Walls reaching to the roof of the cave
Doorways on the ground floor

Scale
0   40   20 M.

N

S (Roughly)

Refuse heap

Refuse heap

Photo. Pl. X: 2 taken from this point

Wall two high

1

2

THE SPRUCE TREE HOUSE

Nordenskiold named this ruin the Spring House, because of a nearby spring of sweet water. The ruin is situated so deeply under the cliff it is difficult to photograph. Photo courtesy MVNP.

Another rather dim view of a structure at the Spring House site. Some restoration has been done, and is visible in the picture. Photo courtesy MVNP.

An Anasazi (ancient ones) basket, with artistic pattern woven in skillfully. Still could be useful, after passage of centuries. Photo courtesy MVNP.

Another Anasazi basket. Note the colors in the pattern. The basketmakers preceded the Cliff Dwellers; apparently they had an artistic eye for geometric patterns. Photo courtesy MVNP.

Some doorways present the appearance shown in fig. 28 to the right (height 90 cm., breadth at the top 45 cm., at the bottom 30 cm.). They were not closed with a stone slab. They probably belonged to the rooms most frequented in daily life, and were therefore fashioned so as to admit of more convenient ingress and egress. The other doorways, through which it is by no means easy to enter, probably belonged in general to storerooms or other chambers not so often visited and requiring for some reason or other a door to close them. It should be mentioned that the large, **T**-shaped doors described above are rare in the ruins on Wetherill's Mesa, which both in architecture and in other respects bear traces of less care and skill on the part of the builders, and are also in a more advanced stage of decay, thus giving the impression of greater age than the ruins treated of in the present chapter, though without showing any essential differences.

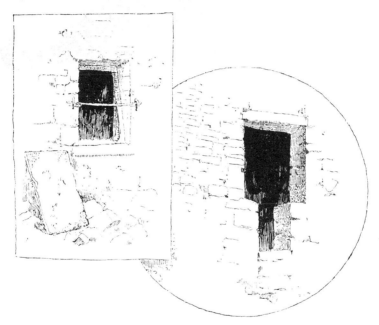

FIG. 28. DOORWAYS OF DIFFERENT FORM.
(From photographs by the author.)

The rooms, with the exception of the estufas, are nearly always rectangular, the sides measuring seldom more than 2 or 3 metres. North of the passage (*23*) which divides the ruin into two parts, a whole series of rooms (*26, 29—33*) still extends outwards from the back of the cave, their walls reaching up to the roof of rock, and the floors between the upper and lower stories being in a perfect state of preservation. The lower rooms are generally entered by small doors opening directly on the "street." In the interior the darkness is almost complete, especially in room *34*, which has no direct communication with the passage. It must be approached either through *35*, which is a narrow room with the short side towards the "street" entirely open, or through *33*. We used *34* as a dark room for photographic purposes.

The walls and roof of some rooms are thick with soot. The inhabitants must have had no great pretensions as regards light and air. The doorways served also as windows, though at one or two places small, quadrangular loop-holes have been constructed in the walls for the passage of light. Entrance to the upper story is generally gained by a small quadrangular hole in the roof at a corner of the lower room, a foothold being afforded merely by some stones projecting from the walls. This hole was probably covered with a stone slab, like the doors. Thick beams of cedar or piñon and across them thin poles, laid close together, form the floors between the stories. In some cases long sticks were laid in pairs across the cedar beams at a distance of some decimetres between the pairs, a layer of twigs and cedar bast was placed over these sticks, and the whole was covered with clay, which was smoothed and dried.

In several other parts of the ruin besides this the walls still reach the roof of the cave. These walls are marked in the plan. In all the estufas and in some of the other rooms, perhaps the apartments of chiefs or families of rank, the walls are covered with a thin coat of yellow plaster. In one instance they are even decorated with a painting, representing two birds, which is reproduced in one of the following chapters. Pl. X: 2 shows a part of the ruin, situated in the north of the cave. The spot from which the photograph was taken, as well as the approximate angle of view, is marked in the plan. The left half of the photograph is occupied by a wall with doorways, rising to a height of three stories and up to the roof of the cave; within the wall lies a series of five rooms on the ground floor; behind these rooms the large open space mentioned above (*28*) occupies the depths of the cavern. Here the beams are all that remains of the floors of the upper stories, their ends projecting a foot or two beyond the wall between the second and third stories, where support was probably afforded in this manner to a balcony, as an easier means of communication between the rooms of the upper stories. In front of this part of the building, but not visible in the photograph, lie two estufas, and outside the latter is a long wall. To judge by the ruins, the roofs of these estufas once lay on a level with the floors of the adjoining rooms, so that over the estufas, which were sunk in the ground, only the roofs being left visible, the inhabitants had an open space, bounded on the outside by the said long wall, which formed a rampart at the edge of the talus. The same method of construction is employed by the Moki Indians in their estufas; but these latter rooms are rectangular in form. — Farther north lies another estufa. Its site, nearest to the cliff wall, would seem to indicate that it is the oldest. The walls in the north of the ruin still rise to a height of 6 metres.

The south part of the ruin is similar in all respects to the north. Its only singularity is a room of elliptical shape (axes 3.6 and 2.9 m.); from this room a wall runs south, enclosing a small open space (*16*), where, as at the corresponding place in the north of the ruin, the ground is covered with bird droppings mixed with dust and refuse. At one end there are two semicircular enclosures (*17, 18*) of loose stones forming low walls. In a pentagonal room (*8*) south of this open space one corner contains a kind of closet (height 1.2 m., length and breadth 0.9 m.) composed of two large upright slabs of stone, with a third slab laid across them in a sloping position and cemented fast (see fig. 29). Of the use to which this "closet" was put, I am ignorant. Farther south some of the rooms are situated on a narrow ledge, along which a wall has been erected, probably for purposes of defence.

Plate X: 1 is a photograph of Sprucetree House from the opposite side of the cañon. The illustrations give a better idea of the ruin's appearance than any description could do.

Our excavations in Sprucetree House lasted only a few days. This ruin will certainly prove a rich field for future researches.[1] Some handsome baskets and pieces of pottery were the best finds made during the short period of our excavations.

FIG. 29.   THE INTERIOR OF A ROOM IN SPRUCETREE HOUSE.
(From a sketch by the author.)

In a room (*69*) belonging to the north part of the ruin we found the skeletons of three children who had been buried there.

A circumstance which deserves mention, and which was undoubtedly of great importance to the inhabitants of Sprucetree House, is the presence at the bottom of the cañon, a few hundred paces from the ruin, of a fairly good spring.

Near Sprucetree House there are a number of very small, isolated rooms, situated on ledges most difficult of access. One of these tiny cliff-dwellings may be seen to the left in fig. 27. It is improbable that these cells, which are sometimes so small that one can hardly turn in them, were really dwelling-places; their object is unknown to me, unless it was one of defence, archers being posted there when

---

[1] Since this was written, a well-preserved mummy has been found by WETHERILL in the open space (*28*) at the very back of the cave. This is a further example of the burial of the dead in the open space between the village and the cliff wall behind it (see p. 47).

danger threatened, so that the enemy might have to face a volley of arrows from several points at once. In such a position a few men could defend themselves, even against an enemy of superior force, for an assailant could reach the ledge only by climbing with hands and feet. Another explanation, perhaps better, was suggested to me by Mr. FEWKES. He thinks that these small rooms were shrines where offerings to the gods were deposited. No object has, however, been found to confirm this suggestion.

To the right of fig. 27 a huge spruce may be seen. Its roots lie within the ruins of Sprucetree House, the trunk projecting from the wall of an estufa. In Pl. X: 1 the tree is wanting. I had it cut down in order to ascertain its age. We counted the rings, which were very distinct, twice over, the results being respectively

FIG. 30. SQUARE-TOWER HOUSE.
(From a photograph by the author.)

167 and 169. I had supposed from the thickness of the tree that the number of the rings was much greater.

In the cliff bounding Chapin's Mesa from Navajo Cañon several more ruins are situated, none of which, however, can rival Sprucetree House in size. Some of them deserve brief mention.

The name of *Square-tower House* (fig. 30) is derived from a tower, four stories high, which in its construction bears undeniable witness to the great skill of the builders, especially when we remember the rude implements with which their work was executed. The ruin contains numerous other rooms. A description of them, however, would only be a repetition of what has previously been said of other buildings. Two estufas, the roofs of which are partly preserved, are of interest, for, to the best of my knowledge, this is the only cliff-dwelling where these rooms retain their roofs. The remnants of the roofs threaten at each moment to give way. In spite of this, I crept into one of the estufas, the nearer to the cliff. The floor was covered with rubbish to a depth of several feet. The roof rested on the six stone pillars between the niches, and was built in two parts, the lower consisting, as shown in fig. 31, of five courses of poles, laid horizontally in a circle, and thus increasing the height of the estufa by some feet. These poles supported a flat roof of beams 15 centimetres in diameter, which covered about half the surface of the estufa. The beams lay close together in two groups, on one side 6—8 parallel beams close together,

FIG. 31.   ROOFED ESTUFA IN SQUARE-TOWER HOUSE.
(From a photograph by the author.)

then a space of 0.6 metres, covered with thin sticks laid crosswise, then again three beams parallel to the first ones. The remaining half of the roof consisted of more slender poles, placed at right angles to the latter group of beams, on which they rested at one end, the other end being supported on the lower framework of the roof. The walls contained no doorway, and the entrance must therefore have been constructed in that part of the roof which has now fallen in. The above-described type of roof is of interest, as closely resembling the method employed by some of the nomadic Indians in erecting their houses. On my way through the Navajo Indian

Reservation I observed a *hogan* — the name given by these Indians to a house — constructed in exactly the same manner as the roof of the estufa in Square-tower House, or of horizontal poles laid in a ring. The simplest way of roofing an estufa, an example of which was observed in another estufa at Square-tower House, is to lay poles horizontally across the room — poles of sufficient length may easily be procured either of piñon or cedar. This form of roof is also the general one in all the quadrilateral rooms. It is probable that the type of roof described first, as well as the round shape of the estufas, is a reminiscence of the time when the cliff-dwellers were a nomadic people. I shall perhaps have an opportunity below of returning to this interesting question.

FIG. 32. A NARROW STAIRCASE.
(From a photograph by the author.)

The cave in which this ruin lies is very high. In a cleft of the rock at the back of the cave it is possible to climb up to one or two small rooms, perched on the steepest part of the cliff. Here as in so many of the ruins already described, it is evident that the defence and fortification of the dwelling were uppermost in the mind of its builders.

Another ruin, interesting on account of its site, is represented in fig. 33. To descend thither, especially when encumbered with our camera, was a matter of no little difficulty; the most troublesome part of the climb is shown in fig. 32. The descent would probably have been impossible, had not the same route been employed in former times, and notches therefore been hewn in the rock to afford a footing. This rude stairway was probably the best means of communication between the inhabitants of this cliff-dwelling and their neighbours. By the aid of these steps, weather-worn as they were, we succeeded in letting ourselves and our photographic appliances down the cliff. To reach a suitable point to the north of the ruin, from which to photograph the place, was also a difficult task. We climbed up at the south of the ledge where the ruin lay. But a good view was possible only from the north, and we were therefore compelled to creep a long distance on hands and knees within the walls, which were built on the very edge of the precipice, to the north end of the ledge.

I photographed a few other ruins in Pool Cañon, a fork of Navajo Cañon running into Chapin's Mesa. But a description or figure of them would only be a tedious repetition of what the reader has seen above.

I have still to mention some ruins situated on the Cliff Cañon side of Chapin's Mesa. For the reasons just mentioned I will not enter into any greatly detailed description of them, but only point out their characteristic or singular features.

In a long, but not very deep branch of Cliff Cañon, a wild and gloomy gorge named Cliff Palace Cañon, lies the largest of the ruins on the Mesa Verde, the Cliff Palace. Strange and indescribable is the impression on the traveller, when, after a long and tiring ride through the boundless, monotonous piñon forest, he suddenly halts on the brink of the precipice, and in the opposite cliff beholds the

FIG. 33. A CLIFF FASTNESS.
(From a photograph by the author.)

ruins of the Cliff Palace, framed in the massive vault of rock above and in a bed of sunlit cedar and piñon trees below (Pl. XII). This ruin well deserves its name, for with its round towers and high walls rising out of the heaps of stones deep in the mysterious twilight of the cavern, and defying in their sheltered site the ravages of time, it resembles at a distance an enchanted castle. It is not surprising that the Cliff Palace so long remained undiscovered. An attempt to follow Cliff Palace Cañon upwards from Cliff Cañon meets with almost insurmountable obstacles in the shape of huge blocks of stone which have fallen from the cliffs and formed a barrier across the narrow wate course, in most parts of this cañon the only practicable path between the steep walls of rock. Through the piñon forest, which renders the mesa a perfect labyrinth to the uninitiated, chance alone can guide the explorer to the exact spot from which a view of the Cliff Palace is possible.

The descent to the ruin may be made from the mesa either on the opposite side of the cañon, or on the same side a few hundred paces north or south of the cliff-dwelling. The Cliff Palace is probably the largest ruin of its kind known in the United States. I here give a plan of the ruin (Pl. XI) together with a photograph thereof, taken from the south end of the cave (Pl. XIII). In the plan, which represents the ground floor, over a hundred rooms are shown. About twenty of them are estufas. Among the rubbish and stones in front of the ruin a few more walls, not marked in the plan, may possibly be distinguished.

Plate XIII, as I have just mentioned, is a photograph of the Cliff Palace from the south. To the extreme left of the plate a number of much dilapidated walls may be seen. They correspond to rooms *1—12* in the plan. To the right of these walls lies a whole block of rooms (*13—18*), several stories high and built on a huge rock which has fallen from the roof of the cave. The outermost room (*14* in the plan; to the left in Pl. XIII) is bounded on the outside by a high wall, the outlines of which stand off sharply from the dark background of the cave. The wall is built in a quadrant at the edge of the rock just mentioned, which has been carefully dressed, the wall thus forming apparently an immediate continuation of the rock. The latter is coursed by a fissure which also extends through the wall. This crevice must therefore have appeared subsequent to the building operations. To the right of this curved wall (still in Pl. XIII) lie four rooms (*15—18* in the plan), and in front of them two terraces (*21—22*) connected by a step. One of the rooms is surrounded by walls three stories high and reaching up to the roof of the cave. The terraces are bounded to the north (the left in Pl. XIII) by a rather high wall, standing apart from the remainder of the building. Not far from the rooms just mentioned, but a little farther back, lie two cylindrical chambers (*21 a, 23*). The wall of *21 a* is shown in Pl. XIII, with a beam resting against it. The beam had been placed there by one of the WETHERILLS to assist him in climbing to an upper ledge, where low walls, resembling the fortress at Long House (p. 28), rise almost to the roof of the cave. The round room *23* is joined by a wall to a long series of chambers (*26—41*), which are very low, though their walls extend to the rock above them. They probably served as storerooms. These chambers front on a "street," on the opposite side of which lie a number of apartments[1] (*42—50*), among them a remarkable estufa (*44*) described at greater length below. In front of *44* lies another estufa (*51*), and not far from the latter a third (*52*).

The "street" leads to an open space. Here lie three estufas (*54, 55, 56*), partly sunk in the ground. Much lower down is situated another estufa (*57*) of the same

[1] The room marked *48* in the plan is visible in Pl. XIII. Almost in the centre of the plate, but a little to the right, two small loopholes may be seen, and to their right a doorway, all of which belong to room *48;* the walls of *49* and *50* are much lower than those of *48*. Behind *48* the high walls of *43* may be distinguished.

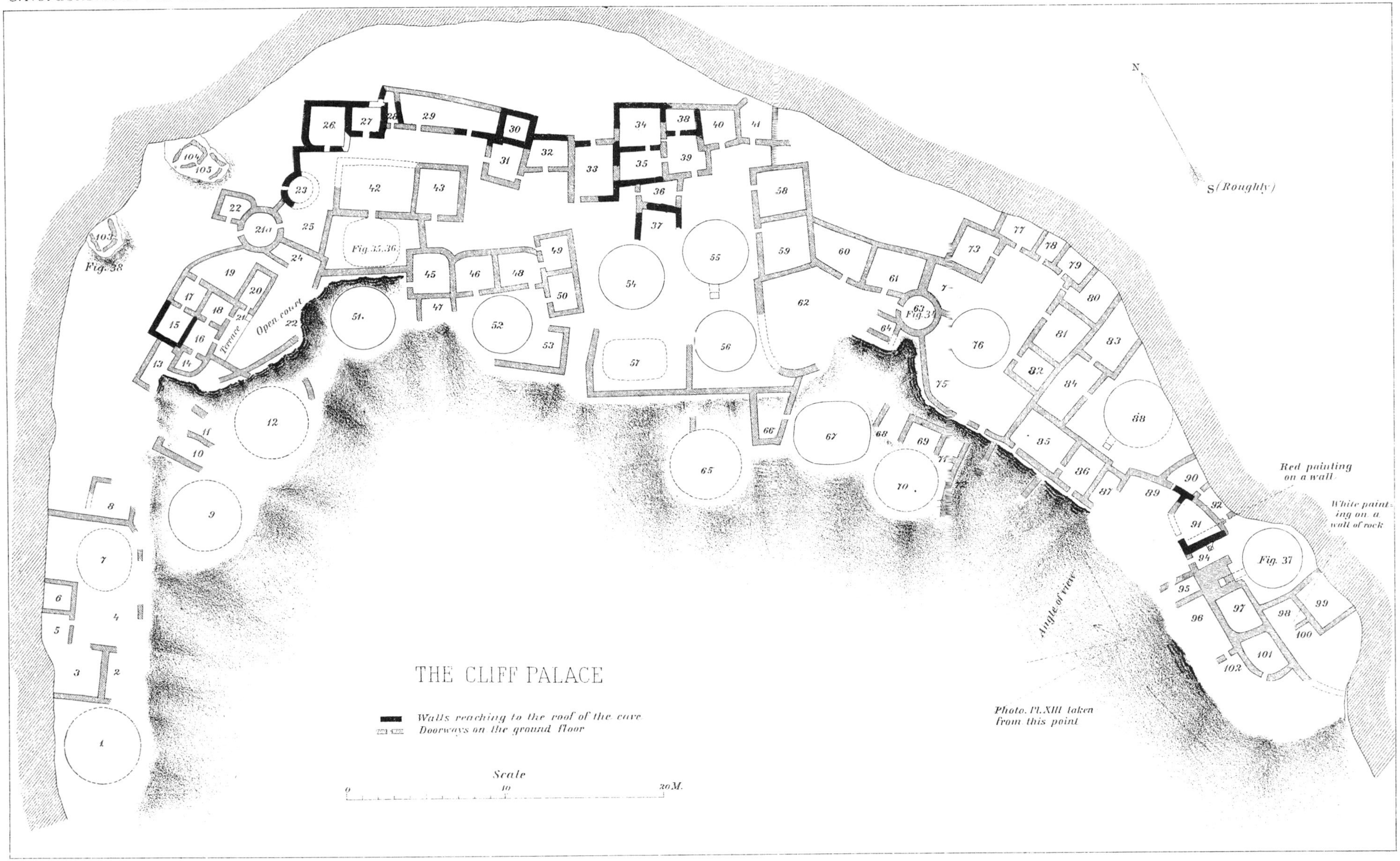

G. Nordenskiöld: The Cliff Dwellers of the Mesa Verde.

THE CLIFF PALACE

Walls reaching to the roof of the cave
Doorways on the ground floor

Scale

0   10   20 M.

S. (Roughly)

N

Red painting on a wall

White painting on a wall of rock

Angle of view

Photo. Pl. XIII taken from this point

Open court

Terrace

Fig. 37

Fig. 35, 36

Fig. 33

THE CLIFF PALACE

type as *44*. It is surrounded by high walls.[1] South of the open space lie a few large rooms (*58—61*). A tower (*63* in the plan; the large tower to the right in

FIG. 34. TOWER (*63*) IN THE CLIFF PALACE.
(From a photograph by the author.)

Pl. XIII) is situated still farther south, beside a steep ledge. This ledge, north

[1] They are shown in the plate just to the left of the fold at its middle, rather low down.

of the tower (to the left in the plate), once formed a free terrace (*62*), bounded on the outside by a low wall along the margin. South of the tower is an estufa (*76*) surrounded by an open space, southeast of which are a number of rooms (*80—87*). In most of them, even in the outermost ones, the walls are in an excellent state of preservation. The wall nearest to the talus slope is 6 metres high and built with great care and skill.[1] South of these rooms and close to the cliff lies a well-preserved estufa (*88*), and south of the latter four rooms are situated, two of them (*90, 92*) very small. The walls of the third (*91*) are very high and rise to the roof of the cave. At one corner the walls have fallen in. This room is figured in a subsequent chapter in order to show a painting found on one of its walls. Near the cliff lies the last estufa (*93*), in an excellent state of preservation. The rooms south of this

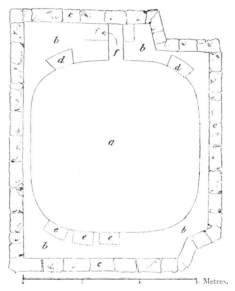

FIG. 35.   PLAN OF A SINGULAR ESTUFA IN THE CLIFF PALACE.

estufa are bounded on the outer side by a high wall rising to the rock above it. An excellent defence was thus provided against attack in this quarter.

Two of the estufas in the Cliff Palace deviate from the normal type. This is the only instance where I have observed estufas differing in construction from the ordinary form described in Chapter III. The northern estufa (*44* in the plan) is the better preserved of the two. To a height of 1 metre from the floor it is square in form (3 × 3 m.), with rounded corners (see figs. 35 and 36). Above it is wider and bounded by the walls of the surrounding rooms, a ledge (*b, b*) of irregular shape being thus formed a few feet from the floor. In two of the rounded corners on a level with this ledge (a little to the right in fig. 36) niches or hollows (*d, d*; breadth 48 cm., depth 45 cm.) have been constructed, and between them, at the

---

[1] A part of this wall may be seen to the extreme right of Pl. XIII, and also in fig. 34 behind and to the right of the tower.

middle of the south-east wall, a narrow passage (breadth 40 cm.), open at the top. At the bottom of one side of this passage a continuation thereof was found, corresponding probably to the tunnel in estufas of the ordinary type. At the north corner of the room the wall is broken by three small niches (*e, e, e*) quite close together, each of them occupying a space about equal to that left by the removal of two stones from the wall. The sandstone blocks of which the walls are built are carefully hewn, as in the ordinary cylindrical estufas. Whether the usual hearth in form of a basin, and the wall beside it, had been constructed here, I was unfortunately unable to determine, more than half of the room being filled with rubbish. I give the name of estufas to these square rooms with rounded corners, built as described above, because they are furnished with the passage characteristic

FIG. 36. ESTUFA OF SINGULAR CONSTRUCTION. THE PASSAGE (*f*) AND THE NICHES (*d, d*) ARE SHOWN A LITTLE TO THE RIGHT.
(From a photograph by the author.)

of the round estufas in the cliff-dwellings. Perhaps they mark the transition to the rectangular estufa of the Moki Indians. Besides the estufas there are some other round rooms or towers (*21 a, 23, 63*), which evidently belonged to the fortifications of the village. They differ from the estufas in the absence of the characteristic passage and also of the six niches. Furthermore, they often contain several stories, and in every respect but the form resemble the rectangular rooms. The long wall just mentioned, built on a narrow ledge above the other ruins, and visible at the top of Pl. XIII was probably another part of the village fortifications. The ledge is situated so near the roof of the cave that the wall, though quite low, touches the latter, and the only way of advancing behind it is to creep on hands and knees.

A comparison between Pl. VIII and Pl. XIII shows at once that the inhabitants of the Cliff Palace were further advanced in architecture than their more western kinsfolk on the Mesa Verde. The stones are carefully dressed and often laid in regular courses; the walls are perpendicular, sometimes leaning slightly inwards at the same angle all round the room — this being part of the design. All the corners form almost perfect right angles, when the surroundings have permitted the builders to observe this rule. This remark also applies to the doorways, the sides of which are true and even. The lintel often consists of a large stone slab, extending right across the opening. On closer observation we find that in the Cliff Palace we may discriminate two slightly different methods of building. The lower walls, where the stones are only rough-hewn and laid without order, are often surmounted by walls of carefully dressed blocks in regular courses. This circumstance suggests that the cave was inhabited during two different periods. I shall have occasion below to return to this question.

The rooms of the Cliff Palace seem to have been better provided with light and air than the cliff-dwellings in general, small peep-holes appearing at several places in the walls. The doorways, as in other cliff-dwellings, are either rectangular or **T**-shaped. Some of the latter are of unusual size, in one instance $1._{05}$ m. high and $0._{81}$ m. broad at the top. The thickness of the walls is generally about $0._3$ m., sometimes, in the outer walls, as much as $0._6$ m. As a rule they are not painted, but in some rooms covered with a thin coat of yellow plaster. At the south end of the ruin lies an estufa (*93*) which is well-preserved (fig. 37). This estufa is entered by a doorway in the wall, one of the few instances where I have observed this arrangement. In most cases, as I have already mentioned, the entrance was probably constructed in the roof. The dimensions of this estufa were as follows: diameter $3._9$ m., distance from the floor to the bottom of the niches $1._2$ m., height of the niches $0._9$ m., breadth of the same $1._3$ m., depth of the same $0._5$—$1._3$ m., height of the passage at its mouth $0._{75}$ m., breadth of the same $0._{45}$ m. Five small quadrangular holes or niches were scattered here and there in the lower part of the wall.

I cannot refrain from once more laying stress on the skill to which the walls of the Cliff Palace in general bear witness, and the stability and strength which has been supplied to them by the careful dressing of the blocks and the chinking of the interstices with small chips of stone. A point remarked by JACKSON in his description of the ruins of Southwestern Colorado, is that the finger marks of the masons may still be traced in the mortar, and that these marks are so small as to suggest that the work of building was performed by women. This conclusion seems too hasty, for within the range of my observations the size of the finger marks varied not a little.

Like Sprucetree House and other large ruins the Cliff Palace contains at the back of the cave extensive open spaces where tame turkeys were probably kept. In this part of the village three small rooms, isolated from the rest of the building,

ALACE

occupy a position close to the cliff; two of them (*103, 104*), built of large flat slabs of stone, lie close together, the third (*105*), of unhewn sandstone (fig. 38), is situated farther north. These rooms may serve as examples of the most primitive form of architecture among the cliff people.

In the Cliff Palace, the rooms lie on different levels, the ground occupied by them being very rough. In several places terraces have been constructed in order to procure a level foundation, and here as in their other architectural labours the cliff-dwellers have displayed considerable skill.

One very remarkable circumstance in the Cliff Palace is that all the pieces of timber, all the large rafters, have disappeared. The holes where they passed into the walls may still be seen, but throughout the great block of ruins two or three

FIG. 37. ESTUFA (93) IN THE CLIFF PALACE.
(From a photograph by the author.)

large beams are all that remain. This is the reason why none of the rooms is completely closed. At Sprucetree House there were a number of rooms where the placing of the door stone in position was enough to throw the room into perfect darkness, no little aid to the execution of photographic work. It is difficult to explain the above state of things. I observed the same want of timber in parts of other ruins (at Long House for example). In several of the cliff-dwellings it appears as if the beams had purposely been removed from the walls to be applied to some other use. Seldom, however, have all the rafters disappeared, as in the Cliff Palace. There are no traces of the ravages of fire. Perhaps the inhabitants were forced, during the course of a siege, to use the timber as fuel; but in that case it is difficult to understand how a proportionate supply of provisions and water was obtained. This is one of the numerous circumstances which are probably connected with the extinction or migration of the former inhabitants, but from which our still scanty information of the cliff-dwellers cannot lift the veil of obscurity.

The ruins on the Cliff Cañon side of Chapin's Mesa also include the building (ruin 9) described in Chapter III, where our first excavations were carried out. One or two kilometres from this ruin, about four kilometres from the mouth of Cliff Cañon, lies another remarkable and extensive cliff-dwelling, *Balcony House*. A few hundred paces north of the ruin we descend about 30 metres from the mesa. We then follow the cliff to a point below the ruin, whence it may be reached by a break-neck climb.

FIG. 38. SMALL ROOM AT THE BACK OF THE CLIFF PALACE.
(From a photograph by the author.)

Balcony House cannot rival Sprucetree House or the Cliff Palace in size. I have not had the opportunity of executing any plan of the ruin. This cliff-dwelling is the best preserved of all the ruins on the Mesa Verde. It also seems as if the architecture of the cliff-people had here reached its culminating point. Still more care has been bestowed on the erection of the walls in general than in the Cliff Palace. The stones are hewn and fitted together with the utmost care, the surface of the walls is perfectly smooth, and the corners are turned at perfect right angles. Plates XIV and XV show these points with distinctness.

Balcony House occupies a better position for purposes of defence than the other large ruins described in this chapter. A handful of men, posted in this cliff-house, could repel the attacks of a numerous force. At the south end of the ruin additional precautions have been taken for the strengthening of its defences. A very narrow cleft, which forms the only means of reaching the south part of the ledge, has been walled up to a height of nearly five metres. The lower part of the wall closing the cleft is pierced by a narrow tunnel. Its mouth is shown in fig. 39. Through this tunnel a man may creep on hands and knees from the cliff-dwelling to the south part of the ledge. The latter affords a footing, with the precipice to the left and the cliff to the right, for about a hundred paces, the ledge being here terminated by the perpendicular wall of the cañon. The ruined walls of a strong tower, built to cut off approach on this side, may still be traced.

At the north end of the ruin the ground has given the builders great trouble, but the difficulties have skilfully been overcome. A supporting wall (to the right in Pl. XIV) has been erected on a lower ledge, to form a stable foundation for the outer wall of the upper rooms, where the higher ledge was too narrow or too rough for building purposes. The total height of the wall has thus been raised to 6.₅ metres. South of the rooms fronted by this wall is a small open court, bounded at the back by a few very regular and well-preserved walls, which rise to the roof of the cave. On the outer side the court is enclosed within a low, thick wall, built on the edge of the precipice (see Pl. XV). The second story is furnished, along the wall just mentioned, with a balcony; the joists between the two stories project a couple of feet, long poles lie across them parallel to the walls, the poles are covered with a layer of cedar bast and, finally, with dried clay. This balcony was used as a means of communication between the rooms in the upper story. The roof of the rooms just north of this point (see Pl. XV, a little to the right) is constructed in the same manner as the balcony just described. It projects a few feet beyond the walls on two sides, forming a spacious platform. In most of the cliff-dwellings the roofs probably consisted of similar platforms, and it was presumably here that the cliff-dwellers spent most of their time and performed their household duties, as the custom is to the present day among the Moki Indians of Arizona. Near the cliff, between the platform and the balcony, is a deep hole forming a small passage through which it is possible to descend, by the aid of some pegs driven into the walls, to a lower, very narrow ledge. Ladders seem, as mentioned above, to have been seldom employed by the cliff people. The perilous climbs that formed a part of their daily life, had inured them to difficult pathways. A few pegs in the walls, or a few projecting stones, were certainly enough to satisfy their primitive wants in this respect. On one single occasion, just below Balcony House, I found one of the side-pieces of a ladder. A strong cedar pole and a slender oak prop had been bound together with bands of yucca fibre. The bands were placed at regular intervals, answering to the distance between two rungs: the rungs had then been inserted between the two poles, each rung resting on a yucca band. A cut, made apparently with some metal implement, gave me reason, however, to doubt whether the ladder was really the work of the cliff people.

FIG. 39. FORTIFIED CLEFT, OPENING INTO BALCONY HOUSE.
(From a photograph by the author.)

XIV

Just north of Balcony House a fork of Cliff Cañon runs about half a kilometre into the plateau. At the head of this fork are a few cliff-dwellings of insignificant size, perched on quite inaccessible ledges.

I have now described all the more important ruins situated in that part of the Mesa Verde which lies north-west of the Rio Mancos. The system of cañons south-

FIG. 40. CLIFF-DWELLING IN JOHNSON CAÑON.
(From a photograph by the author).

east of this river also contains numerous cliff-dwellings of considerable size. I did not carry out any excavations there, but only photographed a number of the most important ruins, namely those in Johnson Cañon. A figure of one of them is given here (fig. 40) as an example of an inaccessible or at least almost inaccessible cliff-dwelling. As appears from the figure, the building lies high up the cliff, on a ledge or shelf. As far as I could ascertain by a hurried investigation, the ruins in Johnson Cañon differ in no essential respect from the other cliff-dwellings on the Mesa Verde. Estufas are present in all the larger ruins, and preserve in all respects the ordinary type. I observed one single exception, which affected only an unimportant detail. In one estufa the low wall (*d* in fig. 6) consisted, not of stone, as is usually the case, but of thick stakes, driven into the ground close to each other, and fastened together at the top with osiers. On the side nearest to the hearth this wooden screen was covered with a thick layer of mortar, probably to protect the timber from the heat.

I did not undertake any excavations in the ruins in Mancos Cañon. They are described at length in the works to which references are given in Chapter II. These cliff-dwellings also resemble those described above, but are of no considerable size. Whether the estufa was of similar construction to those of which an account is given in the present work, I cannot say, for no estufa from a cliff-dwelling has ever been described before, although this room is so singular in its arrangement. Personally I have not been able to ascertain anything on this head, for I paid only a single visit, and that a very hurried one, to one of the ruins in Mancos Cañon. There is no reason, however, to believe that these estufas differ from the corresponding chambers in the ruins to the east and west of this cañon.

CHAPTER VIII.

Ruins on the Mesa.

As I have mentioned in a previous chapter, the mesa is also dotted with numerous ruins of prehistoric erection. Much may be said in favour of the opinion that the villages on the mesa and the cliff-dwellings are the work of the same people, though no positive proof of this can be given. The fragments of pottery which are found everywhere near the ruins on the mesa correspond in every respect to the earthenware of the cliff-dwellers. As far as can be gathered from the heaps of ruins that now mark the site of these villages, the walls were constructed in the same manner as the best built parts of the Cliff Palace or Balcony House, of hewn stone in regular courses. The arrangement of the rooms, the plan of the building, etc. cannot be ascertained without extensive excavations, for the execution of which I had no time. The far more advanced stage of decay attained by these ruins may possibly be adduced as evidence of their greater age. For although those parts of the cliff-dwellings which lie outside the shelter of the cave are much dilapidated, the mortar having disappeared, and the stones having suffered greatly from the action of the weather, yet the walls are often standing, sometimes to a height of several metres. On the other hand, there are a few ruins on the mesa where the walls still rise to a considerable height. Besides, the more exposed parts of a cliff-dwelling are better sheltered than a building on the mesa, the cliff shielding them on one side from many storms which wreak their violence unchecked on the ruins in the open. For reasons which I shall give in a subsequent chapter, I am inclined to believe that the cliff-dwellings were erected at an earlier period than the buildings on the mesa.

FIG. 41. RUIN ON THE MESA.
(From a photograph by the author.)

As I was prevented from carrying out the extensive excavations without which any thorough study of the ruins on the mesa was impossible, I cannot describe them in detail. I shall only give a short notice of two towers which I visited, and which were in a state of preservation good enough to render it possible to examine them without undertaking any excavations.

From the mesa near Square-tower House a keen eye can detect on the opposite side of the cañon the ruins of something not unlike a stone monument raised on a conical, isolated rock. A descent of 200 m., followed by an upward climb to the same height on the other side of the cañon, brings the explorer to the place. Pl. XVI is a photograph of the tower, taken from the mesa on the same side. The wall stands on the top of a sandstone cone about 9 m. high, and is perfectly

cylindrical, 0.6 m. thick, and 2.7 m. in height at the highest point.   The interior is
full of stones and rubbish.   We found a stone axe there.   On one side lies the mere
remnant of an outer wall, which probably did not surround the rock, but only
formed a rampart on the mesa side.   By the aid of some much worn steps carved
in the sandstone it is possible to climb to the tower and even to walk round it.
This building probably served as a look-out, from which warning might be given of
an enemy's advance.   It affords a fairly extensive view down the cañon.   At some
other places, as for example on the tongue of Wetherill's Mesa opposite Step House,
similar towers occur, and some of these structures, situated in Mancos Cañon, have
been described by Jackson.

FIG. 42.   RUINS OF A RESERVOIR.
(From a photograph by the author.)

Fig. 41 is a reproduction of another ruin, hidden in the piñon forest on the
mesa, about half a kilometre west of ruin 9 (see chapter III).   The tower, only
half of which remains, was once of rectangular form (4.6 × 3.6 m.).   The corners are
rounded; the greatest height of the wall is 3.3 m., its thickness 0.75 m.   It is difficult
to conjecture the purpose for which this tower was erected.   Placed, as it is, in the
centre of the mesa, it cannot have commanded any wide view of the country, even
assuming that it overtopped the piñon trees.   Perhaps it should be regarded as a
religious edifice.

It is easier to explain the low walls (fig. 42) whose remains may be seen in
several parts of the mesa, crossing the shallow depressions that lead the water from
the plateau down to the cañons.   The site of these walls distinctly shows that they

Ruins of a tower in Navajo Cañon.

From a photograph by the author.

are the ruins of reservoirs where water was collected after the melting of the snow or the brief downpour of the rainy season, in anticipation of the long period of drought. Owing to their site these walls have of course been very much exposed to the ravages of running water; and consequently only fragmentary remains of them are now to be found.

The dam represented in fig. 42 at present consists of a few stones heaped in a row. It is situated above Kodak House. Near the same ruin lies another dam; and above Long House there are three, one of them circular in form. In the neighbourhood of all the large ruins we generally find one or more reservoirs, destroyed to a greater or less extent. Besides these artificial receptacles for water

FIG. 43. RUINS OF A RESERVOIR.
(From a photograph by the author.)

there are in many places natural tanks, worn in the rock, from which the cliff people drew their supply. One of these is situated on the mesa near Square-tower House in Navajo Cañon, and is surrounded by rather steep ledges of sandstone, some metres in height. The difficulty of the descent has been overcome by means of seven deep steps hewn in the rock and affording a safe and convenient pathway down to the water. It is interesting to observe these circumstances, for they seem to me conclusive evidence that the cliff-dwellers had to contend with the same dry climate and the same scarcity of water as now obtain in these regions. The assertion made by HOLMES, that it is absurd to suppose that a dense agricultural population could have inhabited these regions under the same climatic conditions as we now find there, is thus probably groundless. The most convincing proof of the erroneousness of this opinion is the rapid revival of agriculture in these tracts by the building of canals and ditches for irrigation in modern times. It is not at all improbable that irrigation by artificial means was in use even among the prehistoric inhabitants of the Mesa Verde. In Northern Arizona the ruins of ancient irrigation works are still to be seen, and I have been told that similar ruins have been observed on several occasions in South-western Colorado.

A structure of considerable size, which was probably utilised for purposes of irrigation, lies on Chapin's Mesa, some kilometres above the great ruins, and not very far from the slope into Montezuma Valley. A large shallow depression

FIG. 44. TERRACES ON A TALUS SLOPE.
(From a photograph by the author.)

30 m. in diameter is surrounded by a low, circular wall 4.5 m. thick. Water was probably conducted to this reservoir from some neighbouring gulch. Traces of a ditch which formed the connexion have been observed north of the reservoir by RICHARD WETHERILL. A view of the reservoir is given in fig. 43, which however shows only a part of a low, ring-shaped mound overgrown with bushes, all that is left of the thick wall. Quite near the reservoir we find the ruins of a con-siderable village, but the walls are now levelled with the ground, leaving only huge heaps of stones to mark the site.

Pictured upside down, this is a basket (Anasazi) for carrying loads upon the back; similiar "carry baskets" can be seen among the Indians of Mexico and Central America today. Courtesy MVNP.

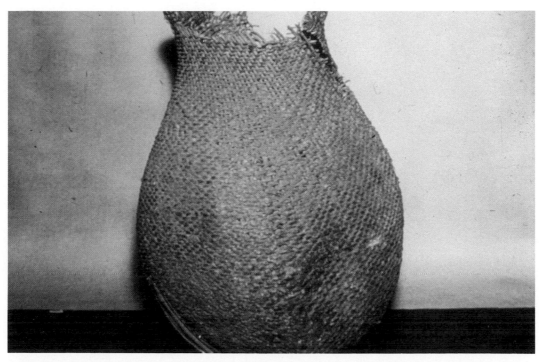

This is an Anasazi basket found by Nordenskiold and now cataloged in the Nordenskiold collection in Helsinki. It is probably a "storage basket". Photo courtesy MVNP.

Aboriginal pottery is almost entirely utilitarian; as often as not, by the time it was finished, the bottom had lost its flatness and thus needed a "pot ring". Photo courtesy MVNP.

Pot rings like the above were also used on the head to balance pottery containing weight. Made of reeds and grasses, these two photos are superb examples. Photo courtesy MVNP.

There is no doubt that agriculture was widely practised among the cliff people. This is shown not only by the quantity of maize found in the ruins, but also by some agricultural works which I discovered below and a little south of Step House. The talus slope, which is not very steep at this point, had been divided by low stone walls, built one above another and still in a fair state of preservation, into several level terraces, much as the hillsides in the wine-producing districts of Southern Europe. Fig. 44 is drawn from a photograph of two of these terraces.

In addition to the ruins already described in this chapter I will mention the burial places, often of considerable extent, which are common on the mesa. Their site is indicated as a rule by a slight elevation, but most infallibly by numerous fragments of pottery and chips of flint strewn on the ground. On one occasion we counted as many as 31 bits of earthenware to a square foot, and to judge by their appearance, most of them were pieces of different vessels. In two such mounds

FIG. 45. GRAVE ON THE MESA, SEEN FROM ABOVE.
(From a photograph by the author.)

on Wetherill's Mesa excavations were instituted. We found in them a few objects, among these bone awls of the same type as in the cliff-dwellings, stone axes, also similar to those discovered in the ruins, and a little plain bowl of earthenware with handle. Human bones were always to be found in quantities, but most of them were decayed. In one of the barrows, not far from Long House, we found a skeleton, almost complete and in a good state of preservation, some decimetres below the surface. The position of the skeleton was not the usual flexed one, but that shown in fig. 45. Quite close to this skeleton lay another, not so well preserved, and in the same mound parts of several more. No pottery seemed here to have been buried together with the dead. Perhaps it was the custom to smash the vessels on the grave where the corpse had been interred. The quantities of such fragments found on these mounds suggest that this was the case. The same custom seems, according to FEWKES, to have prevailed in earlier times among the Moki Indians. The pottery from the Mesa Verde mounds is of the same sort as that found in the cliff-dwellings. The skulls from these two localities are also similar; and there can thus be hardly any doubt that these burial places belonged to the cliff-dwellers, or to a people nearly akin to them, who inhabited the villages on the mesa. RICHARD WETHERILL, however, states that there is a difference in the mode of flattening the head. In the skulls of the mesa dwellers the artificial depression of the posterior part of the cranium has been applied obliquely from above, so that it principally affects the parieto-occipital region; the skulls from the cliff-dwellings have been flattened straight from behind, the occipital region being most affected.

CHAPTER IX.

Pottery from the Cliff-dwellings of the Mesa Verde.

In the preceding chapters I have described the most important cliff-dwellings of the Mesa Verde. The study of these ruins in themselves gives some idea of the life of the people who once inhabited this now depopulated tract. It is evident that, at the period when the stone buildings in the caves were erected, this people ranked higher in some points of culture than the nomadic Indians. From the above description of the cliff-dwellings we gather that their inhabitants were a people who had permanent domiciles which they constructed with great skill of sandstone, generally in roughly dressed blocks sometimes laid in regular courses. In architecture they had achieved great proficiency. Other archæological remains indicate that the prehistoric population of the Mesa Verde practised agriculture on no insignificant scale. We have still to decide what degree of development the cliff-dwellers had attained in other respects; and this we are enabled to do by examination of the objects still found buried in the ruins of their habitations or deposited in the graves with the dead. Among these objects there are none which bear witness to the attainment of proficiency in a fixed industry so clearly as the specimens of pottery. The ornamentation of the earthenware also betokens a certain sense of beauty, a quality which we have no opportunity of observing in other productions of the cliff-people's industry. In the present chapter I shall give a description of the pottery of the Mesa Verde, and in the next pass to an account of the other objects, implements, textile fabrics, etc., found during my excavations in the cliff-dwellings.

The numerous fragments of pottery scattered on the ground in countless places both on the Mesa Verde and along its cañons, show that the prehistoric inhabitants were diligent in their exercise of the potter's art. Near a barrow not far from Step House I once counted, as mentioned above, no less than 31 pieces to a square foot. Holmes[1] states that in the neighbourhood of Mancos he found an area 10 feet square to contain fragments from which he could determine with certainty that they belonged to 55 different vessels. In Arizona, the north-west of New Mexico, and parts of the two neighbouring states to the north, in a word throughout the region formerly inhabited by tribes kindred with the cliff people, the ground is strewn in many places with bits of earthenware, sometimes in such numbers that it is impossible to take a step without treading on them. But, though fragments are so plentiful, whole vessels are rather rare. During my excavations, however, about sixty perfect or nearly perfect specimens were collected among the ruins of the Mesa Verde. Most of them were found in graves. One or more bowls were almost always buried with the dead. Many earthenware vessels were also found in the rooms within the cliff-dwellings.

The ancient pottery of Arizona and the neighbouring states has been considered at length in an excellent work by Holmes.[2] He describes numerous vessels of different types, principally from two localities, a burial place in Southern Utah, and the Province of Tusayan or Moki district of North-eastern Arizona. A number of pieces are also described from the San Juan-basin, a region which embraces South-eastern Utah, South-western Colorado, and portions of the adjoining territories. The pottery of these various regions on comparison shows great similarity both in *technique* and ornamentation. Holmes is, however, inclined to believe that the specimens from the neighbourhood of the Rio San Juan represent the most ancient type. This region includes the country round Mancos and the Mesa Verde. My collections bear out the assumption made by Holmes, and should therefore possess special interest, only few specimens of pottery having as yet been described from this tract, and most of these specimens being merely fragmentary. Further interest is given to my collection, as compared with those previously described, by the fact that all the vessels are from cliff-dwellings situated within a narrow area, and thus represent in all probability the same stage of development in the ceramic art of the cliff people. Furthermore, all the details of their discovery are known, whereas the other collections of pottery from the South-western States have consisted in great

---

[1] Holmes, Ruins of S. W. Colorado, p. 403.

[2] Holmes, W. H. Pottery of the Ancient Pueblos. Fourth Ann. Rep. Bur. Ethn., p. 257.

part of specimens purchased from Indians or presented by farmers, which of course must often have rendered their actual place of origin uncertain.

HOLMES distributes the antique pottery of the South-western States among three main groups:

    I.   Coiled ware;

   II.   Plain ware;

  III.   Painted ware.

The pottery of the Mesa Verde I consider it most convenient to divide into two main groups:

    I.   Coiled and indented ware;

   II.   Coiled ware or ware of ordinary manufacture, with the surface made quite smooth.[1]

The latter group may be distributed among four subdivisions:

   1.   Plain ware, undecorated;

   2.   Plain ware, with indented or incised ornament;

   3.   Ware painted in black or black and white;

   4.   Ware painted in red, black, and white.

I. Coiled and indented ware.

The details of the methods employed by the potters of prehistoric tribes are indeed unknown; but much information may be gained as to the materials used and the mode in which the vessels were shaped, baked, decorated, etc., by close examination of those specimens of ancient pottery which have been preserved to the present day. The body of the vessels belonging to this group consists of clay mixed with rather coarse sand, but not the quartz sand formed by the weathering of the mesa sandstone.[2] The fine clay which occurs in many places along the beds of the cañons, was seemingly mixed with the grit left by the erosion of some volcanic rock, probably the basalt of which dikes are quite common on the Mesa Verde. The minerals of which this stone is composed correspond to those contained in the pottery. Perhaps the rock was also crushed for use. From the plastic mass thus prepared long strips of the thickness of coarse string were kneaded. One end of the strip was then rolled in spiral coils, thus forming a disk to compose the bottom of the

---

[1] A division into ware coiled and not coiled would be the most correct, but cannot be adopted, for all the depressions are often effaced, and it is then impossible to determine how the vessel was made. Many of the large vessels decorated in black and white are probably coiled ware.

[2] A section of the body, examined under the microscope, proved to contain but little quartz and only small grains (0.2—0.4 mm.). The coarser grains (0.8—2.0 mm.) were composed in great part of plagioclase. There was besides a little pyroxene, mica, and olivine. Between the mineral grains, which lay rather densely, was a dark brown mass, probably coloured with soot.

vase. Coil by coil the size of this disk was increased, a concave shape being given to it at the same time. Gradually the coils rose higher and higher, and a bowl was shaped; the diameter of the coils being slowly reduced the bowl was transformed by degrees to a jar. This group is made up chiefly of large jars with wide mouth (see Pl. XXI and XXII). As the work advanced, all inequalities on the inside were effaced either with the fingers, the marks of which may sometimes be seen in the fired clay, or with some suitable implement, the inner surface being thus rendered perfectly smooth. The outer surface of the bottom is sometimes also smooth, this being perhaps caused inadvertently, the jar having rested on some support in process of manufacture. Otherwise the corrugations formed by the spirally coiled strip of clay have been carefully retained. These corrugations have even been employed for purposes of ornamentation. As the work progressed, the potter kept making with his finger small dents in the topmost coil, close to each other. On careful examination we may often trace fine lines, the impression left by the skin of the fingers.

The task of shaping an earthenware vessel according to the method described above must certainly have required great experience, especially when we bear in

FIG. 46.   FRAGMENT OF A JAR WITH RELIEF ORNAMENT.

mind that the large jars, 35 cm. deep, which are very common in this group, are seldom more than 3 or 4 mm. thick. Both in the even thickness of the ware and the regularity and graceful proportions of the form, the potter has generally succeeded in attaining a high degree of excellence. When the shaping of the vessel was completed, it was well baked, the surface being often so hard that it cannot be scratched with steel, and thus acquired the requisite durability.

A corrugated ornament was produced, as I have just described, as the vessel was coiled, of the narrow strips of clay. Variety was attained by different arrangements of the impressions made with the fingers on different vessels. In the jar figured in Pl. XXI: 1, the potter has alternated 4 or 5 plain coils with about twice as many decorated in the ordinary manner. On another jar in my collection, of the same size and shape (Pl. XXII: 2), a handsome ornament has been produced by arranging the small dents in triangles.[1] Patterns executed in relief on the surface of the vessel also occur. Fig. 46, a fragment of a jar of

---

[1] A similar vessel is figured by HOLMES (Pottery, p. 297).

the same type as those already described, is the only specimen of this style in my collection. The outer surface bears a double spiral in relief. HOLMES describes several other designs of this sort. He also gives examples of animal forms modelled in clay; but such ornaments are extremely rare.

Most of the utensils belonging to this group are of the same size (cubical contents about 25 litres) and shape as the jars represented in Pl. XXI and XXII: 2; and the ware is very thin. Their chief use was probably the storage of water. When cracked, or in some other way incapacitated for this purpose, they were employed as receptacles for maize. On several occasions I found these jars sunk in the masonry at the bottom of a niche within the cliff-dwelling. In most cases they have been smashed, owing to their fragility, by the falling walls. They were sometimes set on the fire for culinary or other purposes. The outside, especially the under surface, is sometimes coated with a layer of soot deposited in the small depressions. For the transportation of water they were probably too fragile. The jar represented in Pl. XXI: 2 is bound with narrow strips of yucca, probably because the bottom was cracked, and perhaps too for the attachment of a ring of yucca leaf as a stand under the round bottom.

Jars of this group are found throughout the Mesa Verde, and a considerable percentage of the fragments on the ground always belong to the same. Yet it is very seldom that entire specimens are met with, this being due, as already mentioned, to the ware being generally very thin and brittle. My collection contains only a few perfect vessels of this type (Pl. XXI and XXII).

The above described method of manufacturing pottery has been practised by many of the Indian tribes both in North and South America. To the few North American tribes that still make pottery it seems, however, to be now unknown. In South America, on the other hand, it is in general use. Quite unique, however, is the skill with which the prehistoric tribes of the South-western States of North America utilised the art of coiling for the production of a handsome and singular ornament.[1]

II. Ware with smooth surface.

To this group I refer all the vessels the surface of which has been smoothed during manufacture, rendering it in most cases impossible to decide how they were made. The large vessels in general were probably of coiled ware. Ladles, spoons, and small bowls were presumably moulded with the hand from a lump of clay.

The body of the vessels belonging to this group differs both in colour and texture from that of the pottery of which the preceding group is composed. The

---

[1] HOLMES, Pottery, p. 297, describes bowls of coiled ware, corrugated externally, smoothed and painted inside. I have fragments of such bowls from the Mesa Verde. They form the transition to the following group.

grain is much finer, and the material consists probably of clay mixed with fine quartz sand[1] and crushed bits of pottery. The surface of fracture often shows at the middle, a darker, sharply defined zone; nearer the surface the body is light gray. This difference in colour is due to the more powerful heat to which the outer layers have been subjected, all organic substances being thus destroyed. After the body had been prepared, the vessels were shaped without the aid of a potter's wheel. When the clay was dry, the surface was generally smoothed with care, by rubbing it with a round stone or the like. This is indicated in most cases by the appearance of the surface. In Ruin 13 I found some round pebbles (Pl. XXXVII: 9), much worn and polished on the two flatter surfaces. They had perhaps been used for this purpose. When the vessel had thus been moulded to the shape desired, it was baked, with varying success in different cases. As a rule the baking was suffi-ciently thorough to render the surface so hard that it cannot be scratched with steel. Sometimes the heat has been so powerful as to vitrify the superficial layer into a sort of glaze, the surface thus acquiring a fairly strong lustre and additional hardness. Only seldom has the baking succeeded so well that the ring of the vessels when struck is metallic.

The moulding of the ware was probably accomplished, as I have just said, without the aid of any mechanical appliances. In spite of this it is in most cases admirably executed. Bowls and jars are almost perfectly circular, the diameter in different directions varying hardly more than a few millimetres. The symmetry in other respects is faultless to the eye. In many cases not even the most searching examination can detect any flaw. There is a great variety of shapes, different vessels being intended for different uses. As I have already mentioned, the group may be distributed among four subdivisions.

1. *Plain ware, undecorated.*

In general only small vessels have been left entirely without ornament. The composition of the body of these vessels is the same as above described. Perhaps the baking has generally been carried out with less care, and the surface is therefore often softer. Vessels of this description are shown in Pl. XXIV: 1—3 and 5—11; Pl. XXIII: 2.

---

[1] The material is light gray, and in microscopical section appears almost colourless. In a mass which shows hardly any structure, lie scattered mineral grains. Plagioclase is rare, and occurs only in fine grains (0.1—0.2 mm.). Quartz, on the other hand, is plentiful, but chiefly in minute grains (0.05—0.1 mm.). Small pieces of the same appearance as the body in general, but with de-fined limits, are probably the crushed fragments of other vessels. The other minerals are mica, sometimes rather plentiful, pyroxene, in small quantities, and possibly magnetite. These last minerals are possibly the remains of crushed bits of pottery from the preceding group. To the same source we should probably ascribe the fine grains of basalt which sometimes occur. A few vessels are of coarser material, more like that used for the vessels of group I. The body of the red pottery is different in composition.

2. *Plain ware, with indented or incised ornament.*

This subdivision is represented in my collection by only two vessels, figured in Pl. XXIII: 1 and Pl. XXIV: 4. One of them is a large, flat bowl. The material is rather coarse clay, moulded without particular care, so that the surface is uneven. The baking has been very imperfect, for the surface is friable to the nail. The bowl was moulded within a flat basket, the traces of the plaited basketwork being still distinctly visible on the under surface. The edge of the bowl extended, however, some centimetres beyond the basket, which appears from the absence of such traces on this part. Perhaps it was these undesigned marks that suggested the idea of the singular ornament on the corrugated jars, as it was probably the spirally plaited basket that taught the potter to roll out the plastic clay in a long strip, and then lay this strip in a spiral, like the osier in the wickerwork.

On the upper surface of the bowl, which is represented in Pl. XXIII: 1, a singular ornament has been executed, consisting of small indentations set in double straight lines radiating in four directions from a circle in the centre and twice bent at an angle. At the middle section of two of these pairs of lines four double triangles have been set symmetrically opposite to each other. On the outside of the bowl are two rough handles. Both in form and ornament this utensil differs from the rest of the pottery found in the cliff-dwellings. It was discovered in the refuse heap at Step House, in the part of the cave most remote from the ruin, and was buried 0.6 m. below the surface of the ground. A ladle (Pl. XXIV: 2) was found at the same spot, and with respect to the material resembles the bowl. It is possible that both these vessels are older than the rest of the pottery from the cliff-dwellings. Perhaps they are the work of a people who inhabited the Step House cave before the erection of the cliff village.

The other vessel in my collection belonging to this subdivision, is figured on Pl. XXIV: 4. The soft surface is scratched with a simple ornament, composed of two systems of equilateral triangles lying within each other. This vessel was procured from a Ute Indian, who stated that he had found it in a ruin on the Mesa Verde.

3. *Ware painted in black or black and white.*

Most of the vessels which I found in the cliff-dwellings of the Mesa Verde, belong to this subdivision. With respect to the material there is hardly any difference between this subdivision and 1. The moulding of the vessel and the smoothing of the surface also seem to have been performed in the same manner, but more care has generally been taken in the baking, a harder and more durable ware being thus produced. The surface often has a faint lustre, as if glazed, which was attained partly by intensified heat in the baking and partly, it is probable, by previously coating the surface, before the black ornament was applied, with a layer of some easily fusible substance. In a large jar (Pl. XXI: 2) which had been buried in the refuse heap at Step House, I found lumps (about 160 grammes) of a white kaoline-like substance tied in a maize husk (fig. 47). These lumps were easily crushed to a fine white powder, which proved on analysis to be of the following composition:

Silica	63.77
Alumina	16.95
Ferric oxide	2.13
Magnesia	2.87
Potash	2.84
Soda	1.77
Water (140°)	4.67
Ign	5.52
	100.52.

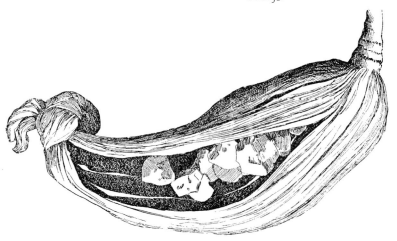

FIG. 47. KAOLINIC SUBSTANCE PRESERVED IN A MAIZE HUSK. STEP HOUSE. ($^1/_2$.)

A substance similar in appearance to that described here was found at Ruin 9 in Cliff Cañon, wrapped in a piece of cloth. It seems highly probable to me that it was this very substance with which the surface of the vessel was coated before the black ornament was executed.[1] Owing to the high percentage of alkali (4.61) and the low percentage of alumina (16.95) this powder is comparatively easy of fusion. On being heated, for example, at a blast-lamp in a small crucible of platinum it melts into a porcelaineous mass. When diluted with a little water, it forms a tenacious slip, excellently suited for application, with a brush of yucca fibre for example, to the surface of the earthenware.

---

[1] According to BARBER (BARBER, E. A. The Ancient Pottery of Colorado, Utah, Arizona, and New Mexico. Am. Nat., Vol. X, 1876, p. 458) Captain JOHN MOSS had been told by the Moki Indians that, according to a tradition which survived among them, the ancient pottery was manufactured of a kind of white stone, which was pulverized and diluted with water to a thin paste; but the Mokis had never been able to discover from what source this material was procured. Perhaps this tradition refers to the very substance found by me. Tales of such traditions should, however, be received with caution.

Sometimes the black ornament was painted directly on the gray clay. As a rule, however, the surface of the vessel was first coated with a white substance, which also served as a glaze, and the black design was drawn on this white surface. In one case I have succeeded in ascertaining the composition of the black pigment. On one jar the colour was so thick that it was possible to scrape off a quantity sufficient for chemical examination. The result showed that the substance was principally composed of iron. It is probable that the colouring matter was the magnetic oxide (Fe_3O_4). This is also indicated by the reddish brown tint sometimes given by weathering to the black ornament. The substance for the preparation of this paint might be procured in Grass Cañon, where I observed a bed of brown powder consisting of ferruginous ochre. In Ruin 9 I found a small splinter of wood some inches long (Pl. LI: 1). To one end of it was attached a lump of some reddish substance, which proved on analysis to be resin mixed with ferruginous ochre. This was perhaps paint ready for use and intended for the ornamentation of pottery. The resin probably had a reductive influence on the red oxide of iron, whereby the latter was converted into black magnetic oxide.

In the same part of Grass Cañon there was a rich deposit of a white substance closely resembling the white lumps of which I have spoken above.

Of the cliff people's decorative art, as it is displayed in this painted pottery, I shall give a more detailed account at the end of this chapter. In Pl. XXV—XXXII representations are given of most of the vessels belonging to this subdivision which were found during my excavations.

4. *Ware painted in red, black and white.*

I have still to deal with the last of the divisions among which I have distributed the pottery of the Mesa Verde. This may be done in a few words, for though small fragments of vessels belonging to this subdivision are fairly common, I only once succeeded in finding so many pieces of the same vessel as to enable me to give a complete figure. This vessel was a bowl, which is reproduced in Pl. XXXIII. If this bowl be really the work of the cliff-dwellers, we have here the most perfect specimen of their pottery. But it is not impossible that the vessel was obtained by barter from some other people, perhaps from the inhabitants of the more southern pueblos, for in the composition of the body [1] it differs widely from the pottery of the preceding subdivisions. It seems as if the material consisted principally of clay, with a slight admixture of crushed potsherds, but with hardly any other additions. The ornament reminds us of the preceding subdivision, but is somewhat more intricate here than

---

[1] In a microscopical section the outside proves to be made up of a narrow (0.6—0.12 mm.) red margin answering to the superficial layer containing the red pigment. The body is brownish gray and opaque. Grains of quartz (0.3—0.5 mm.) lie here and there, but are much more scattered than in the ware of the other subdivisions. Crushed fragments of pottery, on the other hand, are common. The grains of quartz are often sharp-edged. There are no other minerals. The red colouring matter proved on qualitative analysis to consist of sesquioxide of iron.

there. The shape deviates from the normal type, the sides of the bowl slightly approaching each other at the top. The baking has been carried out with great care, and the surface is very hard. The rarity of the red pottery and its elaborate execution render it probable that these vessels were intended for some special purpose, perhaps connected with the rites of religion.

I have now given a description of the different sorts of pottery found in the cliff-dwellings of the Mesa Verde. This description is based, with very few exceptions, on the materials collected during my excavations in the ruins of this region. Compared with the ancient pottery from more southern ruins, in the north-east of Arizona, as described by HOLMES in his excellent work, these vessels show great similarity both in *technique* and ornamentation. Still the comparison confirms the assumption already made by HOLMES, who had a few specimens from the region of the Mesa Verde at his disposal, namely that the pottery from this region represents a comparatively ancient type. On the ware from more southern localities we find the same ornament — stepped figures and meanders with many variations. But these ornaments are generally combined into complicated patterns, whereas in the pottery from the Mesa Verde and the neighbouring tracts they are seen in their simplest form.

The ornaments on the ware from the Mesa Verde form the first link in a long chain of development the more perfect types of which are found in the ruins farther south. Special interest is given to the ornamentation of the Mesa Verde by the fact that these first series in the evolution of ornament, as represented by the vessels found in this region, are almost entire. Between the most simple ornament, copied directly from the productions of the textile industry, and the most complicated pattern on the pottery from the cliff-dwellings of the Mesa Verde, we have a succession of transitions. To prove this will be my task in the remaining portion of the chapter on the pottery.

Unless the above circumstance had attached special interest to the ornamentation of the cliff-dwellers, I should not have trespassed upon a subject which has already been treated in so masterly a fashion by HOLMES in several papers.[1] HOLMES argues in these writings that the ornament on the ancient pottery of the south-western regions was developed from textile patterns. But he considers[2] that in the evolution of ornament, as in that of natural forms, the intermediate forms have disappeared, leaving only solitary links of the chain, and that it is thus "impossible to show that any particular design of the highly constituted kind was derived through a certain

[1] HOLMES, W. H.   Origin and Development of Form and Ornament in Ceramic Art.   Fourth Ann. Rep. Bur. Ethn., p. 437.
A Study of the Textile Art in its Relation to the Development of Form and Ornament.   Sixth Ann. Rep. Bur. Ethn., p. 189.
On the Evolution of Ornament — an American Lesson.   Am. Anthr., Vol. III, 1890, p. 137.
[2] Evolution of Ornament, p. 141.

identifiable series of progressive steps." The possibility of this demonstration appears
from the following account of the decorative art of the cliff-dwellers.

Among the cliff people, as I have already mentioned, the *motifs* of the first
patterns executed in colours must be sought among the productions of the textile
industry, where the ornament is often the necessary result of a method of weaving
or plaiting, or at least is evolved therefrom by some simple device, first suggested

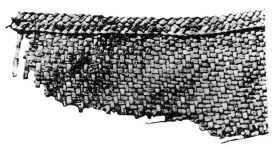

FIG. 48.   FRAGMENT OF A RUSH-MAT.   ($^1/_4$.)

perhaps by chance. There is, for example, a very common method of plaiting which
was employed partly in the working of rush-mats, partly in the making of sandals.
Fig. 48 shows a fragment of one such mat. If the straws in a horizontal as well as
in a vertical direction are alternately light and dark, we have the pattern shown in
fig. 49, *a*. It is true that I never observed this very pattern, a circumstance which
is perhaps due to the small number of plaited mats in my possession. My collection
contains some baskets of more complicated patterns, and it is far from improbable
that the pattern in fig. 49, *a*, which is produced by so simple a process, was known.

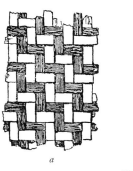

a   *b*

FIG. 49.

A similar pattern is shown in fig. 49, *b*. It is produced by taking the straws lying
in one direction darker than those at right angles to them. A fragment of a mat
of this description was found by HOLMES [1] in a ruin in Mancos Cañon.

The former of these two patterns, reproduced in colours, reappears, for example,
on the mug Pl. XXIX: 3 and on many other vessels in my collection; it is on the

---

[1] HOLMES, Ruins of S. W. Colorado, Pl. XLVI.

whole one of the most common ornaments used by the Mesa Verde potters. The other pattern (fig. 49, *b*), which in the main differs but slightly from fig. 49, *a*, is also copied on several vessels fragments of which I have examined. Many other designs of the simplest character, the fine, parallel lines, the rows of dots, etc., as well as

FIG. 50.

the arrangement of the design in a belt round the most prominent part of the vessel, were presumably suggested by plaited baskets. The more complicated patterns were almost invariably evolved by a series of gradual modifications from the plaited designs in fig. 49. The first of these designs is represented in fig. 50: 1, and shown as painted on an earthenware vessel in fig. 50: 2 and in fig. 52. In fig. 50: 3—7 we see the further development of this pattern. By joining the extremities of the white, grady lines with straight white lines the potter has produced the pattern shown in fig. 50: 3. A tendency, also derived from the textile art, to divide a band into equal compartments, was perhaps the first origin of this alteration. Both this pattern and the preceding one are very common, and were drawn with the grady line obliquely ascending from the left, or obliquely descending from the same quarter. Fig. 50: 4 shows the same pattern, but with a still further change, the straight white line being intersected by a black line. This pattern appears

FIG. 51.

on the bowl represented in Pl. XXV: 1, and like the preceding one is an ornament of frequent occurrence. In fig. 50: 5 the direction of the oblique, grady line is altered. Another way of expressing this alteration is that instead of standing on its broader base, the black "stairway" is inverted and set on the narrower end. The same alteration applied to fig. 50: 3 produces the pattern fig. 51: 2, from which a series of more and more intricate meanders is evolved. That this change is less violent than one is perhaps inclined at first to believe, appears from a specimen of the Tusayan pottery figured by HOLMES.[1] On this vessel the potter had purposed to execute a series of figures similar in appearance to fig. 50: 5, and has also per-

[1] HOLMES, Pottery, p. 353.

formed his task with perfect accuracy; only in one compartment has he failed in his design, and instead reproduced the ornament shown in fig. 50: 4. — The pattern of fig. 50: 5 was observed on a mug in WETHERILL's collection from the Mesa Verde. In fig. 50: 6 all the "steps" but one have disappeared. This pattern is seen on the bowl Pl. XXVIII: 5. Finally the last "step" was removed, and in the middle of each compartment the ends of the **L**-shaped black lines were joined. In this way the potter produced the handsome meander fig. 50: 7, which reappears on the bowl Pl. XXVI: 3.

FIG. 52.

It is probable that among the cliff-dwellers the meander originated in various ways. Of the almost innumerable combinations of lines from which the meander may be developed by the repetition of slight modifications, several were probably in actual use. I have above cited an example indicating an evolution of the meander different from that represented in fig. 50. I refer to the passage in which I showed how, by the same alteration as distinguishes fig. 50: 4 and fig. 50: 5, the pattern

FIG. 53.

fig. 51: 2 was developed from 50: 3. When once the development had taken this course, it advanced in the same direction, giving birth to more and more intricate meanders (fig. 51: 3). I might give further examples, illustrating meanders more or less fully developed; but I should then be compelled too often to have recourse to materials which have not been collected on the Mesa Verde, though in close proximity to this tract. The three patterns shown in fig. 51 are borrowed from fragments of pottery figured by JACKSON[1] and found in South-western Colorado not far from the Mesa Verde. With the exception of these designs and the patterns figs. 52 and 55, my arguments are based exclusively on materials from the Mesa Verde.

The pattern represented in fig. 50: 1 is, as mentioned above, one of the commonest. It was sometimes applied in parallel bands, obliquely crossing the broad zone which usually formed the ornament (see fig. 52).[2] On the outside of the bowl which on its inner surface affords us an example of this ornament, the same pattern

FIG. 54.

is repeated, but in a single straight band. In the same manner more complex ornaments were often executed in oblique compartments, and origin was given to new figures. Fig. 53, a pattern which I observed in WETHERILL's collection, shows how a fairly complex meander (differing but slightly from fig. 51: 3) was drawn diagonally in this way. In order to fill the triangular spaces left by this distribution of the square compartments, the potter was compelled to modify the design, and thus give it a new appearance. This modified pattern was afterwards employed *minus* the

FIG. 55.

square compartments, thus producing the ornament shown in fig. 54 and to be seen on a bowl in my collection. The connexion between this type of ornament and the grady lines is also suggested by fig. 55, a pattern observed on a small jar from the Rio San Juan.[3]

---

[1] JACKSON, W. H. A Notice of the Ancient Ruins in Arizona and Utah lying about the Rio San Juan. Bull. U. S. Geol. and Geogr. Survey of the Terr., Vol. II: No. 1, Wash. 1876, Pl. 21. The paper is identical with that quoted from another publication on p. 11, the only difference being in the plates.

[2] This pattern was observed on a bowl from the Rio San Juan (HOLMES, Pottery, p. 317).

[3] HOLMES, Pottery, p. 320.

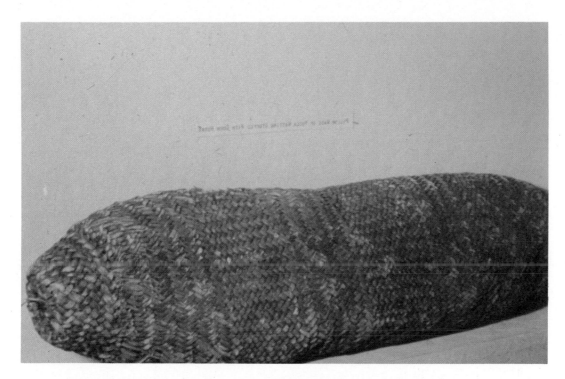

Some of the Cliff Dwellers liked their comfort; above is a pillow almost entire, made of yucca fibers throughout. Yucca is a long-bladed cactus, familiar all over the west. Courtesy MVNP.

This is a Cliff Dweller snowshoe now in the Nordenskiold collection in Helsinki. Bandelier writes that when this kind of shoe was worn backward, it fooled enemies because they thought the victim was going in the opposite direction. Photo courtesy MVNP.

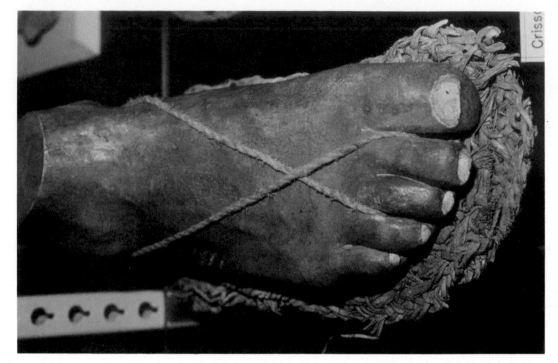

This shows how the Cliff Dwellers wore a sandal, presumably in warm weather. Even aboriginal feet needed some kind of protection from the rough and thorny land. Courtesy MVNP.

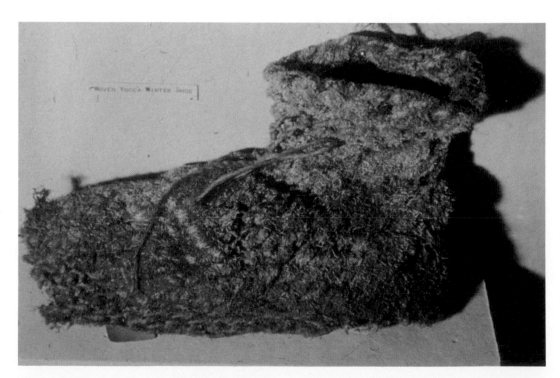

This is a Cliff Dweller boot made of reeds, grass and fibers with feathers woven into the interstices for warmth. Feathers might keep out the cold, but not water or mud. Photo courtesy MVNP.

This is a curious piece of woven tapestry. It is made of grass fibers, into which was woven a rabbit fur "yarn" and turkey feathers — perhaps a shoulder cloak. Photo courtesy MVNP.

A closeup detail of weaving using rabbit fur. Such ingenuity may have been forced upon the Cliff Dweller; after all, necessity is the mother of invention. Photo courtesy MVNP.

The Cliff Dwellers knew and raised cotton, and they also found out what they could do with it. This is a sample of woven cotton cloth in the Nordenskiold collection in Helsinki. Photo courtesy MVNP.

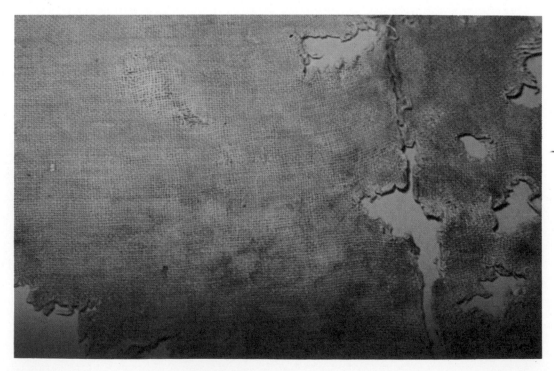

Another sample of woven cotton cloth on display at the MVNP Museum. This ancient material has stood the test of time better than some modern materials will. Photo courtesy MVNP.

Of the very common ornament fig. 50: 4 several modifications are found. On a mug in WETHERILL's collection this pattern is drawn in two rows, one above the other, and the outermost white lines in each compartment are produced upwards and downwards (fig. 56: 1; the ornament is so arranged that the left side of the figure is turned upwards in the original). The same pattern, modified as in fig. 56: 2, recurs on a vessel (Pl. XXIX: 5) in my collection. Some white lines have been added, enclosing the first pattern within a meander.

I may perhaps be permitted to give another series of patterns, starting from fig. 50: 5. The singular and handsome zigzag design (fig. 57: 3) which appears on a bowl in my collection, I was at first unable to trace through any intermediate forms in existence to the typical grady ornament. Then my attention was drawn to a bowl in WETHERILL's collection from the Mesa Verde, with an ornament (fig. 57: 2)

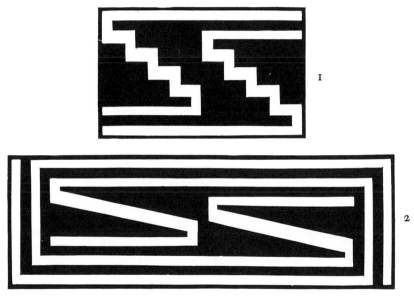

FIG. 56.

closely resembling the zigzag pattern, but with the "steps" still preserved. This ornament again may easily be derived from fig. 57: 1, a pattern which occurs on a fragment of a bowl in my collection, and is simply a modification of fig. 50: 5.

In the same manner as that illustrated by the above examples, all the ornaments on the cliff-dwellers' pottery, to judge by the materials at my disposal, may be traced through intermediate forms to patterns derived from textile fabrics, and the great majority of them, meanders and similar designs, are evolved from the first four patterns in fig. 50.

A more searching analysis of the causes which gradually raised the decorative art of the cliff-dwellers from a lower stage of development to a higher one, is a task impossible of accomplishment, at least with the materials now available. Even in the case of an aboriginal people surviving to the present day, it is difficult to trace the causes of and the course followed by the evolution of ornament. How much more intricate is the problem, when we have to deal with a people long extinct, of whose history and culture we possess no records save the scattered remains of household utensils, implements, and weapons, to be brought to light only by careful search among the ruins of its long deserted habitations. Still I may be allowed to point out one circumstance touching this development. As I have already intimated, the simpler types of ornament recur in identically the same form on numbers of different vessels, and even the more intricate patterns are often copied

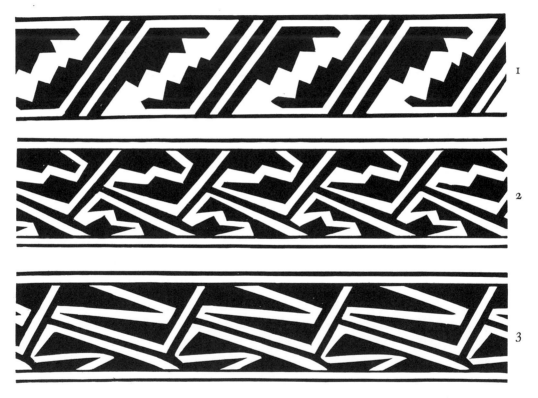

FIG. 57.

in detail. This observation, and the fact that, taking them on the whole, so complete series of patterns have been deduced from materials so scanty as those at my disposal, show that the same pattern was repeated many times, that a long period elapsed before this pattern was further modified, and that, even when decorative art had reached a comparatively high point, the designs in use among the cliff-dwellers of the Mesa Verde were relatively few. The evolution of ornament was therefore extremely slow, for it was probably but seldom that the potter deviated intentionally from established patterns.

CHAPTER X.

Weapons, implements, woven and wicker articles, and other objects found in the cliff-dwellings of the Mesa Verde.

If we should base our judgment of the prehistoric culture of the Mesa Verde on the above account of the architectural and ceramic productions of the cliff-dwellers, we should arrive at entirely erroneous conclusions. For among the objects which I discovered during my excavations in the cliff-dwellings, there are, with the exception of the pottery, extremely few that bear witness to the advanced development of any special industry. The woven and plaited articles are indeed excellently made, but are surpassed by the best work of modern Indian tribes in the same regions, and with the exception of a few baskets and a single fragment of woven cloth, are entirely destitute of ornament. This contrast between a development so high in one respect and a standpoint, comparatively speaking, so low in another, invests the cliff people with special interest. The explanation thereof may be found in the extraordinary conditions under which this nation struggled for existence. Constantly menaced, as an agricultural people, by their warlike neighbours, the nomad Indians, they turned their attention principally to the improvement and perfection of the cliff-dwellings and the adequate fortification of their homes. The scarcity of running water, the lack of springs, necessitated the transportation of water from great distances, and often rendered a considerable stock indispensable. Suitable vessels were required for this purpose; hence the proficiency attained in the potter's art.

Though in some respects the implements, weapons, and textile fabrics found in the cliff-dwellings are thus a less interesting subject of description than the pottery, they are still of great importance. Only by their aid we can picture to ourselves the life of a people who probably inhabited the South-western States long before the discovery of America, and every contribution to our knowledge of the population of the New World, when it was as yet entirely uninfluenced by European culture, is naturally of weight, especially when it bears upon a nation so singular in their manner of life as the cliff-dwellers.

The staple industry of the cliff people was the cultivation of *maize*. This may be gathered from the plentiful remains of this cereal to be seen everywhere in the cliff-dwellings and their neighbourhood. Well-preserved ears of maize (Pl. XLV: 6—9) are sometimes found in the ruins. They belong to several varieties, and are yellow or reddish brown. I never found an ear similar in colour to the blue maize of the

Moki Indians. As a rule the maize is smaller in ear than that cultivated by the Indians of the present day. On various occasions I procured from the cliff-dwellings perfect ears of maize, loose kernels, stripped cobs, husks, and pieces of the stem and leaves. These last fragments are very common in the refuse heap behind or beside the cliff-dwelling. I once found some maize flour; this was contained in a large basket discovered in a grave at Step House. The maize was probably grown partly on the mesa, partly on the more gradual talus slopes, which were sometimes terraced for this purpose. The ground was probably irrigated in some places by means of ditches. After the harvest the corn was stored in rooms set apart for this use in the bottom story of the cliff-dwelling. It was ground on a large slab of stone, a description of which will be given below.

Besides maize the cliff-dwellers cultivated *beans* of a brown variety, solitary specimens of which I found in some ruins, and probably some species of *gourds*. The stalks of the latter are common; bits of the rind are also found, and, more seldom, the seeds. Of the rind vessels of different shapes were made. My collection contains a cup (Pl. XLV: 5) made of the top of a pumpkin; the very tip, which was cracked, had been bound with yucca string and the crack stopped with pitch. Of a smaller species of gourd I discovered a whole shell (Pl. XLV: 3), pierced with two small holes near the scar, and quite empty. It had probably been filled with small stones and used as a rattle. Rattles made in the same way are employed by the Mokis and other Indians in their dances.

Cotton was used by the cliff-dwellers as the raw material of superior textile fabrics. Numerous fragments of cotton cloth have been found. The cotton shrub was probably cultivated by the cliff people, at least in some localities, for in the cliff-dwellings of Southern Utah the seeds of this shrub have been observed.[1] On the Mesa Verde no such find has been made.

The *yucca* plant (fig. 58) afforded an excellent raw material for rope, cord, and coarse woven fabrics. This plant, which is extremely common both on the mesa and in the beds of the cañons, has long, narrow, sharp leaves, composed of long and very tough fibres. The cliff-dwellers were not slow to discover its utility, and it constituted, we may say, the most important material employed in the textile industry. The leaves were cut, harvested and dried, and stored in large bundles (Pl. XLVIII: 3). They were used whole in the plaiting of sandals. Narrower strips were made partly into sandals, partly into baskets. Finally the fibres were separated by pounding and twisted into cord, of which coarser ropes were braided, or net-like fabrics tied. In the ruins I found bundles of leaves, prepared fibre, cord ready twisted, and fabrics knotted, or made in some other way, of the cord. Even the fruit of the yucca plant (Pl. XLV: 10) was used for some purpose; in one cliff-dwelling I discovered a quantity of this fruit threaded on a stalk to dry.

---

[1] According to the statement of a person living at Durango.

Besides yucca and cotton other vegetable substances were employed in the manufacture of various articles. Of willow osiers mats were knotted, and baskets braided. Several species of bushes and trees afforded materials for various weapons and implements of wood.

The animal kingdom too was laid under contribution for miscellaneous purposes. Several circumstances lead us to the conclusion that the cliff-dwellers kept some bird, probably the turkey, in a domesticated state. Huge layers of excrement occur in the open space already mentioned on several occasions, which lies at the back of the cave in the more extensive cliff-dwellings. At Step House, where these deposits lay beside the ruin, their depth was 0.6—2 m., their breadth 13 m., and their length 40 m. In this instance the entire mass of turkey droppings mixed with all kinds of refuse probably contains between 200 and 300 cubic m., a quantity which must have taken a long time to collect. The brothers WETHERILL, who are experienced ranchers, consider these excrements, which are in a very good state of

FIG. 58. YUCCA PLANTS.
(From a photograph by the author.)

preservation, to be turkey droppings. That this bird occupied an important place in the domestic economy of the cliff-dwellers, is shown by the fact that most of the bone awls are made of turkey bones.[1] This bird probably supplied the down of which the so-called feather cloth, or rather down cloth, was made, for the material consists of the humeral quill-coverts of a gallinaceous bird. In CASTAÑEDA's description of the first meeting of the Spaniards with the Pueblo Indians we are told that the latter had indigenous fowls,[2] by which the turkey is probably meant. The turkey is still kept in a state of domestication among the same Indian tribes.

[1] The bones of birds and mammals found during my excavations in the cliff-dwellings have been determined by Dr. JÄGERSKIÖLD, whenever the collections of our museums, with their somewhat scanty materials of North American origin, were sufficiently comprehensive.

[2] PEDRO DE CASTAÑEDA DE NAGERA. Relation du Voyage de Cibola. TERNAUX-COMPANS, Sér. I: T. IX, Paris 1838, p. 171. "Il y avait dans cette province une grande quantité de poules du pays et de *gallos de papada* (littéralement, coq à gosier)."

Wild animals of various kinds occur, though not in great number, on the Mesa Verde, and were hunted by the cliff-dwellers. Among them was a species of lynx or wild cat, the bones of which have been found in the ruins. The skin of deer and other large animals was dressed and made into clothes, moccasins, belts, etc. The bones were used in the manufacture of needles, awls, and scrapers.

Among the products of the mineral kingdom the mesa sandstone supplied an excellent and easily worked building material. Volcanic rocks, quartzites, and hard shales were made into stone axes and knives, jasper and flint into arrow and spear heads.

It thus seems that in these regions nature, though not lavish of her gifts, still bestows all that is indispensable to human existence. Our task is now to investigate the manner in which the cliff-dwellers availed themselves of these supplies, the kinds of implements and weapons which they employed, and the articles — woven, plaited, etc. — which they manufactured with these implements.

In the heliotypes which accompany this work, figures are given of all the more important objects found during my researches among the ruins of the Mesa Verde, and to these plates are appended brief descriptions. I therefore refer the reader to these descriptions, and here give only a summary of the different objects represented in the heliotypes.

As I have mentioned in a preceding chapter, the cliff-dwellers were *entirely ignorant of the use of metal*. The thick piñons and cedars of which the beams supporting the roofs between the stories are hewn, were felled with stone axes, beyond doubt a laborious and protracted operation. An idea of the work necessary in felling such a tree may be gained by examining the ends of the beams. They are as it were worn through. The stone axes were probably more efficacious as weapons.

Pl. XXXIV and Pl. XXXV show some of the most common types of *stone axes*. All of them have the groove characteristic of the North American stone axes, and intended for the attachment of the handle, but this groove is perhaps somewhat shallower than in axes from more eastern tracts. The slight elevations which coast this groove in most of the axes made by the Mound Builders, are wanting.

Some of the axes are two-edged, for example those represented in Pl. XXXVI: 4,6. In these instances the handles too are preserved. Some coarse pliant osiers have been bent round the axe in the hollow at its middle, and then attached with cord and thongs of hide to some thick sticks, added to increase the strength of the handle. The simple ornament on the axe fig. 4, consisting of straight lines obliquely crossing each other, is of interest. They have been carved only on the side visible in the figure; on the other side there are merely a few indistinct scratches. It must have cost great labour to execute this simple ornament in the hard stone. This is the only instance in which I observed any ornamental design on a stone implement from the cliff-dwellings. A simpler form of handle for a stone axe is shown in Pl. XLII: 19. — Stone axes and other implements of stone were sharpened on the face of the rock; the marks left by this process may be seen in fig. 12 (p. 28).

Stone hammers (Pl. XXXIV: 8, XXXV: 8 and XXXIX: 2) are similar in form to the axes, and are also furnished with the groove round the middle; but they are blunt at both ends and vary greatly in size. These tools were helved in the same way as the axes. They were probably used for many different purposes, for example in dressing the stones of which the cliff-dwellings were built, in driving chips of stone into the chinks in the walls, and in crushing various objects, such as fragments of pottery to be mixed in the paste of new vessels, colouring matter, etc. Pl. XXXVIII: 2 represents a large stone club of hard conglomerate.

A common type of *scrapers* is figured in Pl. XXXVI: 8, 9 and XXXVII: 2, 3. They are of oblong shape and flat, tapering towards the end held in the hand, and broader at the other end, which was ground to a fairly sharp edge. The material is usually silicious slate, which is often very brittle, and thus hardly adapted to the manipulation of any hard substance. They were probably employed without handle as *skinning-knives* in flaying the carcases of animals or in preparing the hide. The scraper Pl. XXXVI: 10 is a somewhat modified form of the same implement and was used with a handle.

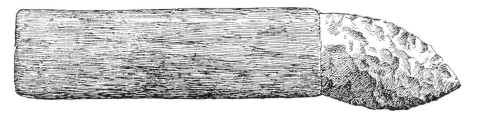

FIG. 59. KNIFE WITH HANDLE. FROM WETHERILL'S COLLECTION. (¹/₂.)

Knives of different types are shown in Pl. XXXVI: 3, 7 and XXXVII: 1, 8, 10. The material is hard quartzite or flint, and the knives were thus quite suitable for carpentry or other work in which durable implements were necessary. My collection contains a knife with a small lump of pitch still adhering to it. The pitch was evidently intended to fasten the stone blade in the cleft end of the wooden handle. The method in which the haft was fitted to the blade may be seen in fig. 59.

Arrow heads of various forms are found in the cliff-dwellings, but are not very common, perhaps because Indians have visited the ruins, and secured all which they could find, for use in the making of their own arrows. Pl. XXXVII: 11, 12 shows two very carefully wrought arrow heads of flint or jasper. Two deep notches are intended to receive the yucca cord with which the head was fastened to the shaft. WETHERILL's collection comprises some perfect arrows tipped with stone; in my collection there is only one well-preserved specimen (Pl. XLII: 1), and this has a wooden point.

The implement shown in Pl. XXXVII: 6 is probably a *spear head*. It is somewhat thicker and stronger than the knives.

Fig. 60 represents a large fragment of flint, pieces of which have probably been made into arrow heads and other small implements of stone. Traces still show in some parts of the fragment that thin flakes have been chipped off at the edges.

Tools for *drilling* holes were also tipped with flint, the handle consisting of a long, thin stick, as represented in Pl. XXXVI: 1. The tip, which in shape resembles a sharp tooth, is attached to the handle with yucca fibre. Pl. XXXVI: 2 and Pl. XXXVII: 7 are probably the points of similar implements.

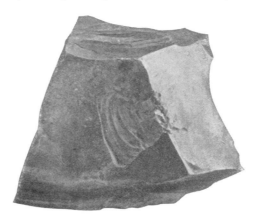

FIG. 60. BLOCK OF FLINT FROM WHICH ARROW HEADS HAVE BEEN CHIPPED. STEP HOUSE. (¹/₂.)

Metate stones [1] were principally used in the crushing of maize. One of these corn-mills is figured in Pl. XXXVIII: 1. They consist of large slabs of hard sandstone or quartzite, deeply concave on one side. Metate stones are fairly common in

FIG. 61. SANDSTONE MORTAR. STEP HOUSE. (¹/₃.)

FIG. 62. SMALL MORTAR OF QUARTZITE. SPRUCETREE HOUSE. (¹/₂.)

most of the cliff-dwellings. They were built in a slightly sloping position between four upright slabs of stone, which prevented the meal from being spilt during the process of grinding. Similar mills, constructed in the same manner, are still employed among the Moki Indians. A smaller stone, oblong in shape and convex on one side, was used to crush the corn.

[1] See p. 42., note.

Other substances were pounded or grounded in rough *mortars* of sandstone. A specimen is figured in Pl. XXXVIII: 3. It is roughly hewn of a large piece of soft sandstone, and could not be used for the crushing of hard substances. Other mortars of similar form (fig. 61 and Pl. XXXVIII: 4), but of various sizes and more or less careful execution, were found during the excavations. Small quantities of colouring matter and the like were ground in mortars of less capacity and made of round pieces of quartzite with concave upper surface. One of these mortars was found in Sprucetree House, and may be seen in fig. 62. The pestle was probably a round pebble.

I have still to mention a number of stone implements the use of which is unknown to me, first some large (15—30 cm.), flat, and rather thick stones of ir-regular shape and much worn at the edges (Pl. XXXIX: 4, 5), second a singular object consisting of a thin slab of black slate, and presenting the appearance shown in Pl. XXXIX: 6. My collection contains only one such implement, but among the objects in WETHERILL's possession I saw several. They are all of exactly the same shape and of almost the same size. I cannot say in what manner this slab of slate was employed. Perhaps it is a last for the plaiting of sandals or the cutting of moccasins. In size it corresponds pretty nearly to the foot of an adult.

Bone implements.

Among this class of implements *awls* (Pl. XL) are the most common. They are found in great numbers in all the cliff-dwellings and also among the fragments of pottery in the barrows on the mesa. They were made of the bones of birds and small mammals, and sharpened on the face of the sandstone cliff. Long grooves crossing each other and probably indicating the places where the awls were ground, I observed on several occasions. These tools may have been applied to miscellaneous purposes, for example to the piercing of holes in hide to receive the thread with which it was sewn, and to the perforation of soft substances in general. To Pl. XL is appended a list of all the awls and other implements of bone which could be determined. Dr. L. JÄGERSKIÖLD has very kindly performed this task wherever the somewhat scanty materials possessed by our museums from this part of North America rendered it possible to determine the bones.

Implements presenting the appearance shown in Pl. XLI: 1, 2, 4, 5 are frequently found. They generally consist of the *humerus* of a deer. The bone has been shaved on one side to an edge, which has then been sharpened to the form of a chisel. These implements were probably used in the preparation of skins, perhaps to remove the fat adhering to the hide.

A bone object very common in the cliff-dwellings is figured in Pl. XL: 13, 17, 22, 24, 26, 28, 29; it is usually made of the middle part of a large bird's *ulna*. These tubular bones were probably threaded on a cord and worn as necklaces or amulets. In a room at Sprucetree House eight similar pieces of bone were found strung on a fine thong of hide, as shown in Pl. XL: 5. The Ute Indians wear amulets of similar form, but made of ivory.

Wooden implements.

From most of the implements of bone and stone we can deduce with fair probability the purposes to which they were applied. It is often much more difficult to ascertain the uses of the many different and often extremely simple tools of wood found in the ruins.

The timber was worked with axes and knives exclusively of stone. It may be objected that metal implements were possibly employed as well, and that no such instruments have been found merely because the excavations have not been sufficiently comprehensive. But a single glance at the ends of the rafters or of the different articles made of wood is enough to show that no sharp edged metal tools have been used in the work.

The most common wooden implement, figured in Pl. XLIII: 10—13, is a rather thick stick 0.7—1.4 m. long, pointed like a sword at one end and often furnished with a round knob at the other. This instrument closely resembles the sticks used by the Moki Indians in planting maize. With these a hole about 50 cm. deep is made in the ground, and a kernel of maize is then dropped into the hole. I assume that the implements now in question were employed in the same manner. They probably served besides as spades for general purposes. A circumstance which apparently bears out my conjecture that these tools answer to the "planting-sticks" of the Moki Indians, is the custom sometimes resorted to by the cliff-dwellers of providing the dead therewith (see for example, p. 40). J. W. Fewkes has informed me that the Mokis commonly lay beside the corpse, which is buried in a sitting posture, one of these planting-sticks, considering that the deceased ought not to enter upon his new existence without this important adjunct to the planting of maize. It seems as if the same idea obtained among the cliff-dwellers.

Fewkes also succeeded, thanks to his knowledge of the Moki Indians, in giving an explanation of another implement in my collection, at the use of which different guesses have been made. In rooms *39* and *40* at Long House we found seven sticks of the appearance represented in Pl. XLII: 2—8. Nearly all of them were broken off short at the end turned downwards in the plate. The other end is carved as shown in the figure. Sticks carved in precisely the same manner are deposited by the Moki Indians on certain occasions in secluded sacrificial shrines. They are tied in pairs, and each pair symbolizes a man and a woman who are consecrated to the gods. From the perfect similarity of form it appears that the votary sticks of the Moki Indians and the above-mentioned objects from Long House were originally used in the same manner. But still it is not certain that among the cliff-dwellers these articles had merely a religious purpose. Among the Moki Indians we often find that an object, originally of great usefulness in daily life, has been entirely restricted to a symbolic purpose on the introduction of an improved implement.

Among weapons of wood *arrows* and *bows* deserve mention. Arrows were made partly of long thin sticks, partly of reeds. The heads consisted either of stone or hard wood. Arrows with stone points were probably used in war and in hunting big game, arrows with wooden points when a smaller animal was the quarry. Wooden arrow heads may be seen in Pl. XLII: 15, 22, 25. The slender part was inserted in the end of the reed. A rim prevented the arrow head from slipping in too far. Pl. XLII: 16, 17 represent the ends of broken reed arrows with the points

FIG. 63.   REEDS FOR THE MANUFACTURE OF ARROWS.   STEP HOUSE.   ($^1/_5$.)

attached. The latter were bound fast with fine sinews. Fig. 63 shows a bundle of reeds tied with a yucca string, probably intended for use in the manufacture of arrows. It was found in the refuse heap at Step House. I never found a perfect bow, but only the broken ends of one (Pl. XLIII: 8). Two bows in WETHERILL's collection are about 1.5 m. long. The bowstring is made of sinews.

The *tinder* of the cliff-dwellers resembles the apparatus formerly used for the same purpose by several Indian tribes, and consists of a drill (Pl. XLII: 24) composed of a singular, brittle wood, and a piece of wood hollowed into conical depressions. The drill was inserted in one of these depressions, and then set in rapid

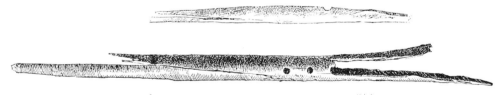

FIG. 64.   FRAGMENTS OF A FLUTE.   SPRING HOUSE.   ($^1/_3$.)

rotation, until a spark was caused, at which a bunch of fine strips of cedar bast (Pl. XLII: 21) or grass (Pl. XLVII: 5) was lit.

Among the wooden objects some fragments of a *flute*, found in Spring House, should also be mentioned. They are represented in fig. 64. The flute was made of a bough, its diameter was 2.5 cm., the longest fragment measured 45 cm. and was pierced with three holes. In a smaller fragment, which could not be fitted together with the rest, was a trace of a fourth hole.

A number of other wooden implements, the use of some of which I cannot conjecture, are figured in the plates.

Wickerwork, woven articles, etc.

In Chapter VI is described and figured an osier mat of the kind in which the dead were shrouded. The osiers have then been placed with the thick ends alternately to the right and left, and fastened together with strong yucca cord passed through fine holes pierced at intervals of about 10 cm. The largest mat of this sort in my collection (Pl. XLVIII: 1) measures 1.78 x 1.08 m., and is in an excellent state of preservation.

Besides these mats baskets were made of willow. A thick round osier was laid in a spiral, and fine osiers were then braided at right angles to it. The braiding was performed with great care and is very close. All that was necessary to render the basket watertight was a coat of pitch or some other suitable substance on the outer surface. One of the baskets in my collection seems, from the fragments adhering to its surface, to have been coated with some substance of the kind. Baskets of this description are figured in Pl. XLIV: 3, 4, 5.

a   b

FIG. 65. DIFFERENT METHODS OF BRAIDING.

In Pl. XLIV: 1, 2 and Pl. XLV: 1, 2 baskets of another type may be seen. They are braided of strips of yucca leaf, which are often arranged in handsome patterns. The pattern is sometimes further elaborated by placing in one direction strips of leaf darker than those at right angles to them. This type of basket is not so strong as the preceding one.

Sandals, which seem to have been the most usual covering for the feet, were also plaited of yucca leaf. Only on one occasion did I find a moccasin (Pl. XLVI: 4), and this was in a bad state of preservation. It was sewn of raw hide. The sandals are of several kinds. The most common type is represented in Pl. XLVI: 5. This sandal is plaited of narrow strips of yucca leaf. Sometimes whole leaves of the same plant were used (Pl. XLVI: 1), in which cases layers of maize leaves were often placed on the upper surface, in order to render the sandal softer to the foot. A third kind of sandal (Pl. XLVI: 2, 3) was plaited of twisted cord. These, which are somewhat rare, were attached to the foot by means of loops through which the toes were passed. In sandals of the other types the sides were usually fringed with loops (Pl. XLVI: 5) to which might be fastened the cords or thongs with which the shoe was laced. Different methods of braiding employed in the making of sandals are shown in fig. 65 *a* and *b*. The first method (*a*) was generally used in braiding whole leaves. The second method (*b*), which is the more common, was chosen for sandals of narrow strips of leaf.

A smaller species of yucca afforded material for hairbrushes, which were prepared simply by binding the slender leaves in a bunch, with the sharp tips turned in the same direction (Pl. XLVII: 8). Similar brushes are used among the modern Indians. A kind of finer brush (Pl. XLVII: 12) was made in the same manner, but of fine grass.

In the manner shown in fig. 65 *b* large rush mats, used in carpeting the floors, were also braided. Pl. XLVIII: 4 represents three fragments of one such mat with a handsome plaited border. The mat was found whole, covering the floor of a room in Sprucetree House. Its size was 1.2 × 1.2 m. In course of transportation it unfortunately fell to pieces. — The yucca plant also afforded, as I have mentioned above, raw material for cordage. The cords were twisted of the fine fibres separated from each other. They are usually composed of only two strands (Pl. XLIX: 4),

FIG. 66. PLAITED ROPE. RUIN II. (¹/₁.)

rarely of three. In workmanship and strength they are not inferior to cordage of the same thickness from our rope-works. The finest string is less than 1 mm. in diameter. Cord of a greater diameter than 5 mm. is rare. Very coarse cord, or rather thin rope, was sometimes plaited of eight fine strands, in a method often employed by sailors (see fig. 66). I also found cords twisted of strands of different colours, red and undyed, or blue and undyed. Finally I may mention among the objects made of yucca the rings mentioned in the chapter on the pottery, and used to support the round-bottomed vessels (Pl. XLVII: 3, 10).

Yucca cord was employed in the manufacture of a textile fabric peculiar to the cliff people, the fabric above denoted by the name of feather cloth. Fig. 67 shows how this feather cloth, or more correctly perhaps, down cloth, was made. Yucca cords were tightly wrapped in down 4—6 cm. long, and then knotted together in the manner shown to the right of the figure, where the down is removed. I found in the pumpkin (Pl. XLV: 4) mentioned on p. 42 and dug up in the refuse heap at Step House, materials intended for the manufacture of feather cloth, including a quantity of down of varying length, pieces of down cut to a suitable

length and tied in bunches (fig. 68), and cords wrapped in down. It is evident
that a weaver engaged in making feather cloth had been compelled for some
reason or other to abandon the work and conceal the materials.

Narrow thongs of hide were probably employed on some occasions instead of
down. I have found loose cords wrapped in strips of hide, as shown in fig. 69.
A mummy found in Step House was shrouded in a net made of similar cords, but
only loosely knotted.

The finest woven fabrics were made of cotton. Fragments of cotton cloth
are fairly common in most of the cliff-dwellings. Figs. 70 and 71 are reproductions
in the natural size of two somewhat different varieties of cotton cloth. The only
difference between them is that in fig. 70 the woof is rather coarser than the warp,

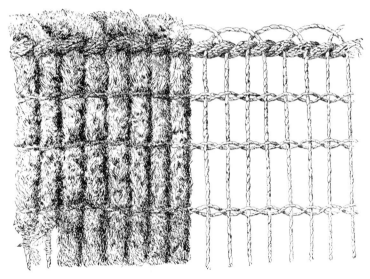

FIG. 67. FEATHER CLOTH. STEP HOUSE. (¹/₂.)

while in fig. 71 the threads in both directions are of the same thickness. I have
found only one textile specimen with woven design (Pl. L). It was discovered in
a room in Mug House. The fragment is of interest, for to the best of my knowledge, cotton cloth with a pattern has never been woven by any Indian tribe of the
United States.

A cloth woven or rather knotted in a singular fashion is represented in fig. 72.
It is somewhat rare, and was generally made of human hair twisted into cord, sometimes of yucca cord. I have found only small fragments of this fabric.[1]

Among the textile fabrics I have still to mention some carefully woven belts of
yucca (Pl. XLIX: 1, 2). They are 7 cm. broad and about 34 cm. long. One of them
is furnished at both ends with short sticks sewn in the cloth. The Moki Indians

---

[1] Fragments of similar cloth have been found in ancient graves on Santa Cruz Island off the
coast of California. U. S. Geogr. Surveys W. 100th Mer., Vol. VII, Wash. 1879, p. 239.

carry heavy loads on their backs by the aid of a broad band passed round the forehead.   These belts were probably used in just the same manner.

Objects sewn of hide are not common.   My collection contains hardly more
than a few belts, a moccasin, and some skin pouches.   One of these pouches (Pl.

FIG. 68.   DOWN FOR THE MAKING OF FEATHER CLOTH.
STEP HOUSE.   (¹/₂.)

FIG. 69.   CORD WRAPPED IN A THONG OF HIDE.
RUIN 9.   (¹/₁.)

XLIX: 3), which was found in the refuse heap at Step House, was full of common salt,
almost pure.   A whole jacket of skin was once found in a grave by J. WETHERILL.

I have now to mention among the finds made in the cliff-dwellings some
objects which have served as personal ornaments or amulets.   To the former class

FIG. 70.   FIG. 71.

COTTON CLOTH.   RUIN 9.   (¹/₁.)

belongs the necklace of shells figured in Pl. LI: 2.   All of the shells were found at
the same spot in a room at Mug House.   They were perforated with fine holes,
and there is thus scarcely any doubt that they once composed a necklace.   The
object shown in Pl. LI: 6 is probably a head-dress; it consists of ten feathers tied
in two rows.   In a painting executed on a fragment of pottery and figured in the

G. Nordenskiöld, Cliff Dwellers.   14 following chapter (p. 108), a man is represented whose head is adorned with something that may perhaps be explained as a similar ornament. Among the articles in my collection which should probably be regarded as amulets, I will mention the bones described on p. 99, a very small, round, white bead (Pl. LI: 4), probably mother-of-pearl, pierced with a fine hole and found in Long House, and an oblong, black bead of jet (Pl. LI: 7). A small polished cylinder of hematite (Pl. LI: 8), found in ruin 16, was perhaps a fetish. Turquoises of the New Mexican variety have been observed by WETHERILL. The simplest ornaments or amulets consist merely of a small fragment of pottery, perforated with a fine hole.

From the short account given in this chapter and the preceding one of the objects found in the cliff-dwellings of the Mesa Verde, a fairly accurate picture may be drawn of the life led by the ancient inhabitants of these ruins. The description

FIG. 72. SINGULAR CLOTH. STEP HOUSE. (¹/₁.)

of the implements, weapons, and household utensils of the cliff-dwellers is certainly not very defective. After investigating a few ruins and one or two graves, the explorer finds that each new room, each new grave examined, contains in the main objects similar to those already discovered. During the latter part of my excavations, it is true, we often found objects of interest, as completing series already elucidated in part; but it was only seldom that anything quite new was brought to light. The extensive collection belonging to WETHERILL indeed comprises some few objects not in my possession. But in all essential respects the picture of the cliff-dwellers' manner of life would be the same, even if I had taken into account the said collection and thus doubled the material employed.

This is a (probable) storage basket found in Step House; it is strictly utilitarian, as it is unornamented. It is a fine example of Cliff Dweller technique. Photo courtesy MVNP.

Nordenskiold found this rough utility basket and it is presently in his collection in Helsinki; the poor construction suggests it may have been for temporary use. Photo courtesy MVNP.

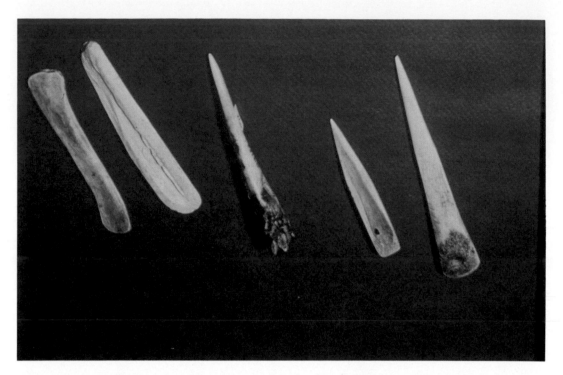

One thing that seems to last forever is bone; above are five representative bone tools in the museum collection at the Park. These are fine examples, probably of awls, punches and needles. Courtesy MVNP.

A ruler suggests the scale size for the bone tools pictured above. These appear to be different from the tools pictured above, but are typical of similar items found frequently. Courtesy MVNP.

CHAPTER XI.

Paintings and Rock Markings from the Mesa Verde.

In this chapter I have brought together the scanty materials which I succeeded in obtaining of the paintings and rock markings probably executed by the cliff-dwellers of the Mesa Verde. As regards the former of these pictorial representations there is hardly any doubt that they are the work of the people who inhabited the cliff-dwellings. The few paintings that came under my observation were all found on the walls of the ruins. With respect to the rock markings here figured, on the other hand, it is difficult to show that they were executed by the cliff people, even if it appears extremely probable that this is the case. In several parts of the Mesa Verde we find figures cut in the sandstone cliff; these figures are of two types, one of them closely resembling the picture writing of modern Indians, which commonly delineates natural objects easy of recognition. But the rock markings of the other type are quite different in appearance. They are characterized by grotesque figures, spiral and zigzag lines, etc., only seldom to be interpreted as reproductions of any object. The markings of the former type show but slight traces of weathering, while the figures of the latter type bear the stamp of great age. They are already partly effaced by the elements, though cut to some depth in the sandstone. These figures of apparently greater antiquity are generally found near the ruins, sometimes within the caves where the cliff-dwellings are situated.[1] It therefore seems highly probable that the rock markings of this type are the work of the cliff-dwellers, while the rest of the figures cut in the cliffs of these regions should apparently be ascribed to modern Indians.

As I have just mentioned, it is only seldom that we find among these petroglyphs figures intended to represent natural objects. Such drawings are equally rare on the richly decorated pottery from the cliff-dwellings. The other objects found among the ruins, as I have already stated, are nearly always unornamented, and when they do possess any ornament, it is always entirely textile in character. Among all the pottery from the Mesa Verde contained in my collection, or of which I have seen figures, there are only four specimens on which natural objects have been depicted. On the potsherd shown in fig. 73 a bird is painted in a somewhat conventional style. The same figure is found on the fragment of a bowl

---

[1] HOLMES (Pottery, p. 312) gives a figure of a vessel belonging to the ancient pottery of Northern Arizona, the bottom of which is inscribed with a drawing of a man and a woman, executed in the same primitive style as we generally meet with in the occasional representations of the human figure to be found among the rock carvings just mentioned.

shown in Pl. XXVIII: 3. On a fragment of pottery belonging to Wetherill's collection, a hunting scene is reproduced, a man shooting an arrow at an animal. Both the archer and his quarry are somewhat stiffly drawn, and the execution betrays the artist's inexperience. In Spring House a piece of earthenware was found, with a painting of the singular creature shown in fig. 75. All these three figures were represented on the outer surface of bowls. Their signification was presumably

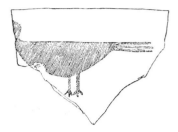

FIG. 73. FRAGMENT OF A BOWL. (¹/₂.)   FIG. 74. FRAGMENT OF A BOWL. WETHERILL'S COLLECTION.
(ABOUT ¹/₄.)

analogous to that of the designs on the outside of the bowls Pl. XXV: 1, 4, 5 and Pl. XXVII: 2, 6.

The paintings which I observed in the rooms of the cliff-dwellings, are executed in dark red or brownish red on the yellow coat of plaster covering the walls. Fig. 76 is a part of the estufa in Ruin 9 described on p. 15. I have already mentioned

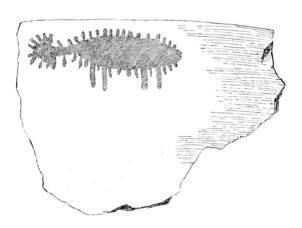

FIG. 75. FRAGMENT OF A BOWL. SPRING HOUSE. (¹/₂.)

in the description of this ruin that the estufa is decorated with a band of dark reddish brown paint lining the lower part of the cylindrical wall, and bordered at the top with triangular points. All round the upper margin and above these points runs a continuous row of red dots. It is difficult to conceive the idea which suggested this singular design. The same figures recur in both of the other paintings here reproduced. The first of them, fig. 77, is executed in a room at Sprucetree House. Here too the lower part of the mural surface is dark red, and triangular points of the same colour project over the yellow plaster; above this lower part of the wall runs a row of red dots, exactly as in the estufa at Ruin 9. To the left two figures are painted, one of them evidently representing a bird, the other a quadruped with large horns, probably a mountain sheep. The painting shown in fig. 78 is similar in style to the two just described. It is to be seen in the south part of the Cliff Palace (see the plan, Pl. XI). In this case too the lower part of the wall is painted red, and the singular figures higher up are executed in the same colour. I do not venture to give even a conjectural explanation of these figures.

In a room situated, like the one just mentioned, at the south end of the Cliff Palace below a large block of stone, which forms one of the walls and a part of the roof, I found the picture reproduced in fig. 79. It is painted in white on the

FIG. 76. ESTUFA IN RUIN 9.
(From a photograph by the author.)

sandstone. The figure to the extreme left is the symbol used by the Moki Indians to denote a cloud. The same figure is painted on a larger scale on a wall in Sprucetree House. It was also observed by GILBERT[1] among the rock markings at Oakley Springs in Eastern Arizona.

Figs. 80, 81 and Pl. XX are representations of rock markings. The pictograph shown in Pl. XX: 1 is carved at the mouth of Moccasin Cañon on a large, loose block of sandstone lying high above the bottom of the cañon, at the foot of the cliffs. The characters shown in fig. 80 are carved in the north-west cliff of Mancos Cañon between Cliff and Navajo Cañons, about $1\frac{1}{2}$ kilom. south-west of a ruin

[1] Fourth Ann. Rep. Bur. Ethn., p. 237. Similar figures, but a different explanation of them, are given by FEWKES, J. W. A Few Tusayan Pictographs. Am. Anthr., Vol. V, p. 9.

figured by HOLMES.[1]   Pl. XX: 3 represents a part of the face of rock at Step House,
quite close to the ruins of the cliff-dwelling.   The original of Pl. XX: 2 is cut in
the sandstone cliff at a ruin in Johnson Cañon.   Fig. 81 was observed near a ruin

FIG. 77.   PAINTING ON A WALL IN SPRUCETREE HOUSE.
(From a photograph by the author.)

in Pool Cañon, high up on a smooth wall of rock, inaccessible without the aid of
a ladder or scaffolding.

On examination of these rock markings we find at once that comparatively few
of the figures can be explained as representations of any definite object.   Fig. 80:

FIG. 78.   PAINTING ON A WALL IN THE CLIFF PALACE.
The figures shown to the left of the wall are reproduced from a photograph, those to the right from a sketch by the author.

1, 3, 4, 6, and 8, and some of the drawings reproduced in Pl. XX: 1 and 3, probably
represent human beings.   This primitive manner of delineating the human figure, as
exemplified by these pictographs, is rather common in the rock markings of these

----

[1] Ruins of S. W. Colorado, Pl. XXXIII: fig. 4.

FIG. 79. PAINTING ON A WALL OF ROCK IN THE CLIFF PALACE.
(From a sketch by the author)

FIG. 80. CHARACTERS CARVED IN THE SANDSTONE CLIFF IN MANCOS CAÑON.
(From sketches by the author.)

regions, for example on the banks of the Rio San Juan [1] in Chaco Cañon. [2] A few zigzag lines, ending in a dot or small circle, are perhaps intended to represent snakes. Pl. XX: 2 shows the outlines of a hand and a foot. The spiral line frequently observed in ancient petroglyphs from these tracts, is stated [3] to be a symbol of the whirlwind among the Moki Indians.

It is well known that the North American Indians have a fairly complete system of picture writing, by means of which the memory of past events is perpetuated in simple, but characteristic symbols, written communications are despatched to distant parts, etc. But Indians of a different tribe from the artist can seldom interpret the meaning of these symbols; much less, of course, a white man. Still it is generally easy to recognize the objects pictured in these drawings. As appears from the figures here given, this is not the case with the rock markings which date from the time of the cliff-dwellers. It is therefore uncertain whether these remains are really pictographs. If they are, the emblems employed to denote the various objects have been so greatly modified that it is no longer possible to trace them to their originals. The inference that these designs are merely creatures of the fancy, is opposed by the fact that, throughout the region once inhabited by the cliff-

FIG. 81. CARVING ON A CLIFF IN POOL CAÑON.
(From a photograph by the author.)

dwellers in Colorado, Utah, Arizona, and New Mexico, all the ancient rock markings are apparently of the same characteristic type, so far as we can judge from the scanty and, in most cases, poor figures which have been published. In rock carvings from parts of this region most remote from each other, we can often recognize the same designs. But for the full elucidation of the extent to which this uniformity prevails within the country formerly inhabited by the cliff-dwellers and their kindred tribes, a much greater number of accurate figures from different localities is necessary than that available at present. These materials will beyond doubt be gradually collected as the regions in question are more thoroughly explored, and with their help it will perhaps be possible to decide whether the petroglyphs are really pictorial symbols, although, even if this problem be solved, it is scarcely probable that any interpretation of them will be discovered.

[1] HOLMES, Ruins of S. W. Colorado, Pl. XLII.
[2] SIMPSON, J. H. Report of an Expedition into the Navajo Country in 1849. Sen. Ex. Doc. No. 64, 31st Congr. 1st Sess., Wash. 1850, Pl. 25.
[3] FEWKES, Pictographs, p. 20.

CHAPTER XII.

Ruins in the South-west of the United States.

In the preceding chapter I have concluded the description of the cliff-dwellings of the Mesa Verde. The account which has been given of the appearance of these remarkable erections, and of the objects discovered there, should enable the reader to form a fairly good idea of the life of the inhabitants, of the difficulties with which they had to contend in order to gain their livelihood, and of the skill with which they overcame these difficulties. The present chapter contains a general survey of the archæological remains akin to the cliff-dwellings of the Mesa Verde, remains which are found in number in the south-west of the United States, and which show the wide extension of the Pueblo tribes. I give the name of Pueblo tribes to all those nations which, judging by the ruins of their habitations, were closely approximated to the cliff-dwellers in their manner of life. The above remains are spread over an extent of country embracing the southern parts of Colorado and Utah, nearly the whole of Arizona, the western half of New Mexico, and the north of Mexico. The limits of their territory in the last country are not yet known. It is not my intention in the present chapter to give an exhaustive description of all the ruins within this area, a task which is indeed impossible with the aid of the somewhat scanty literature on this subject. Only few ruins have been described at length. Most of them are known merely from a cursory notice in some book of travels, the main object of the journey having generally prevented any minute investigation of their details. Hence I can here give only a brief description of the most remarkable and best known monuments in the above region. To this description I shall append a summary of the other less important or more obscure ruins.

If we take into account the geographical situation of the ruins, we find a natural principle of classification in the various river systems. The ruins in Southern Arizona on the Rio Gila, for example, are distinct in type from those in the north of the same state on the Rio San Juan or the Colorado Chiquito. We may conveniently adopt three divisions:

1. *Ruins along the upper course of the Rio Colorado with its tributaries (from the Rio Virgin inclusive);*
2. *Ruins on the Rio Grande del Norte with its tributaries;*
3. *Ruins on the Rio Gila with its tributaries.*

As to the ruins belonging to each of these divisions I shall still adhere to the classification adopted in Chapter II:

    I. *Ruins in the valleys, on the plains, or on the plateaux.*
    II. *Ruins in caves in the walls of the cañons.*

The latter group may be conveniently treated under two heads:

    1. *Cave-dwellings or caves inhabited without the erection of any buildings within them;*
    2. *Cliff-dwellings or buildings erected in caves.*

1. Ruins in the basin of the Rio Colorado (upper course).

Cave-dwellings. On the banks of the Rio San Juan, about 16 kilom. above the mouth of the Rio Mancos, lies a collection of cave-dwellings described by HOLMES.[1] The river bed is bordered by low lines of bluffs, formed of shales, 10—12 m. in height at the place where the cave-dwellings were discovered. The caves, which extend in a long row along the middle of the cliff, have been hollowed by the hand of man. Remnants of mortar indicate that the walls were lined with plaster. The floor is composed of a harder stratum of rock, which projects in many places, forming a platform on which one may pass from one cave to another. The entrances of some of the caves are half concealed by fallen stones. Here, as is generally the case with the cave-dwellings, some stone buildings were found close by. At the very brink of the cliff in which the caves are hollowed, stand the ruins of a round tower, 3.6 m. in diameter, and enclosed by an outer wall, also cylindrical, but open towards the cliff, 6.6 m. in diameter. It seems not improbable that this tower served the inhabitants of the cave as a look-out and at the same time as a defence against attack from the plateau. The ruins of a similar tower with double walls, but of considerably greater dimensions, and the remains of a rectangular building, were found, the former south-west, the latter north-east of the tower first mentioned, situated like it close to the edge of the cliff. Caves similar to those just described were also discovered in the cliffs towards the mouth of the Rio Mancos.[2] In this case the mouths of the caves had been partly walled up, only a quadrangular opening being left. The construction of the caves on the Rio San Juan had perhaps been the same, though the walls had collapsed. Above the cave-dwellings on the Rio Mancos too a cylindrical tower, which had probably been employed as a point of observation, stood at the top of the cliff. Towers of the same description[3] are very numerous along the Rio Mancos, especially in the lower part of its course. From these towers the inhabitants of the different villages, when menaced by any

---

[1] HOLMES, Ruins of S. W. Colorado, p. 388.
[2] Ibid., p. 390.
[3] See also above p. 71.

danger, could communicate with each other at considerable distances by means of signs. I cannot refrain from once more reminding the reader that the population of these regions must have been in constant peril, and that for this reason they always thought first of defence in the construction of their dwellings.

Near the San Francisco Mountains, south-west of the Colorado Chiquito, cave-dwellings have also been found.[1] In form the caves resemble ovens with the opening turned towards the bed of the cañon. They are plastered inside. Some of the largest among them are partitioned by walls into several rooms. The maximum dimensions are a diameter of 3 m. and a height of about 2 m. Within these larger caves smaller ones were found, still more like ovens. Fragments of pottery, some ornamented in black and white, others with corrugations, were found in the neighbourhood.[2]

Cliff-dwellings. The smallest cliff-dwellings really differ but slightly from the cave-dwellings. The partition-walls which sometimes divide the latter into separate rooms, have been joined by cross walls so as to form small, rectangular apartments. Even in the cliff-dwellings the innermost wall of a room often consists simply of the rock at the back of the cave.

Nearly all the Mesa Verde ruins described above belong to this group, which is very numerously represented in several parts of the basin of the Colorado. This basin actually contains almost all the cliff-dwellings known in the United States. It is the home of the cliff-dwellers. All these ruins are similar in so many respects to those already described in this work that there is not the slightest doubt that they are the work of the same people. As I have above described a considerable number of cliff-dwellings, I shall hereafter confine myself to a short list of the most important of these ruins.

Along the banks of the Rio San Juan, the river into which the Rio Mancos flows, numerous cliff-dwellings may be seen in the rocky walls on both sides of the stream,[3] some of them quite small, others so large that there was plenty of room within them for several families. McElmo Cañon, Montezuma Cañon, and Epsom Creek, all of which open upon the north bank of the Rio San Juan below the Rio Mancos, as well as their numerous subdivisions, contain many cliff-dwellings,[4] most of them, however, of insignificant size. Further west, in the now almost uninhabited

---

[1] WHIPPLE, A. W. Itinerary Report of Explorations for a Railway Route near the 35th Parallel. Sen. Ex. Doc. No. 78, 33d Congr. 2nd Sess., Vol. III: Pt. I, Wash. 1856, p. 81.

MÖLLHAUSEN, B. Tagebuch einer Reise vom Mississippi nach den Küsten der Südsee. Leipzig 1858, p. 320.

The Fifth Ann. Rep. Bur. Ethn. (p. XXIII) contains a mention of cave-dwellings near the San Francisco Mountains. During the excavations were found fragments of ornamented pottery resembling those from other ruins in Arizona, metate stones, stone axes, corn cobs, and various seeds.

[2] Cave-dwellings in Utah are mentioned in: PALMER, E. Cave-dwellings in Utah. Eleventh Rep. of the Trustees of the Peabody Mus., Vol. II, 1878, p. 268. I have not had access to this publication.

[3] JACKSON, W. H. Report on the Ancient Ruins examined in 1875 and 1877. Rep. U. S. Geol. and Geogr. Survey of the Terr. 1876, p. 415.

[4] Ibid., pp. 413, 425, 427.

tracts of S. E. Utah, between the Rio San Juan and the Rio Colorado, there are also numbers of cliff-dwellings,[1] though no description of any of them has yet been published. The regions west of the Rio Colorado have been little explored, but there too ruins are apparently common. Not even the immediate neighbourhood of the Grand Cañon, that gigantic gorge between whose precipitous walls the Rio Colorado flows 2,000 m. below their summits, was too gloomy, too desolate to afford the cliff-dwellers a home. On the contrary, it seems as if they had often resorted by preference to the wildest cliffs, the highest precipices as a site for their dwellings. The ruins of these tracts are also undescribed. My statements are based merely on the accounts of travellers who had visited these regions.

South of the Rio San Juan the cliff-dwellings seem to be rarer, with the exception of a small tract of country which in the number and size of its ruins almost rivals the Mesa Verde. I shall return hereafter to the ruins of this tract. About ten kilometres below Bluff City, a Mormon village situated on the Rio San Juan, is a good ford. Not far below this point the river is joined from the south by the Rio de Chelley. During the warm season this stream, like most of the other affluents of the Rio San Juan, is apparently quite dry. The water is entirely absorbed by the sandy bed of the river. Towards the end of its course the Rio de Chelley traverses a cañon with precipitous walls of red sandstone. About ten kilometres from the mouth of the stream JACKSON discovered in a vaulted cave a ruin of considerable size and in a fair state of preservation.[2] The entire length of the buildings was 172 m., and the ground plan shows about 75 rooms. At about the centre lay a cylindrical chamber, probably an estufa. The thickness of the walls varied as a rule between 15 and 30 cm. They were built of long, thin slabs of sandstone, roughly trimmed down to the required size. Judging from JACKSON's description, the building exactly resembles one of the cliff-dwellings of the Mesa Verde. Amongst a heap of refuse at one end of the ruin a jar was found. It has the same ornament as one of the vessels in my collection from the Mesa Verde. In the same cañon, further from its mouth, another ruin, not so well preserved, was found.[3]

Gradually the cañon widens into a broad valley extending southwards through the entire length of the Navajo Indian reservation. Along the middle of the valley winds the wide, but very shallow bed of the river, like a broad road strewn with the finest white sand. I have visited these regions in person. The surroundings are of a desolate character, the ground produces only a scanty vegetation, and the landscape almost bears the stamp of a desert. To the east the valley is bounded by the Sierra Tunecha, a mountain range running north and south. A tributary of the Rio de Chelley rises in these mountains. Its bed is worn deep in the

---

[1] According to the verbal statements of persons who had visited these localities.
[2] JACKSON, l. c., p. 421.
[3] JACKSON, l. c., p. 424.

subjacent strata of sandstone, and forms a cañon with precipitous walls 200—300 m. in height. This cañon is named after the Rio de Chelley, by which it is drained. Its two main forks, the Cañon del Muerto and the Monumental Cañon, seem to have been favourite resorts of the cliff-dwellers. The precipices are hollowed into numerous vaulted caves, such as this strange people preferred for the erection of their dwellings. In these caves stand ruins of considerable size and often in a very good state of preservation. From the rather brief descriptions[1] which have been published of them, it seems that there is here a rich field for future explorations. In most respects, however, the ruins in the Cañon de Chelley seem to differ but little from the cliff-dwellings of the Mesa Verde. It is a remarkable fact that in the former the same singular circumstance has been observed as I have pointed out in the case of some of the latter, namely that all the roof-timber has been removed. Some earthenware which I procured from the Navajo Indians, and which they stated was from the Cañon de Chelley, exactly resembles in form and ornament the pottery which I discovered on the Mesa Verde. The same remark applies to the pottery from the same tract figured by STEVENSON.[2]

West and south-west of the Rio de Chelley the cliff-dwellings are apparently fewer in number; but these regions are as yet imperfectly explored. South-west of the Colorado Chiquito, near the line of watershed which divides the basins of the Colorado and the Rio Gila, cliff-dwellings have been found in Walnut Cañon,[3] 22 kilom. S. E. of Flagstaff. They differ in one respect from the ruins I have hitherto described, the doors beeing so high that a full-grown man can pass through without stooping. The rooms- are large, and the walls 0.6—0.12 m. thick. The fireplace is set in a corner of the room on an elevated rock. Unfortunately nothing more is known of these ruins, which probably contain much that would prove of interest.

Ruins in the valleys and on the plateaux. Throughout the basin of the Colorado ruins of stone buildings are very common. Though we sometimes find those of quite insignificant structures, the villages on the plains were generally of greater dimensions than those situated in the caves; the ample space afforded has enabled small communities to gather in settlements of wider extent. These villages in the open are always in a much further advanced state of decay than the cliff-dwellings; but, as I have already mentioned, this does not prove that the former are older than the latter, being perhaps due exclusively to the more exposed site of the buildings. It is only seldom that entire walls are found. In most cases they are

---

[1] SIMPSON, Report, p. 104.

STEVENSON, JAMES. Ancient Habitations of the Southwest. Bull. Am. Geogr. Soc., 1886, No. 4, p. 329.

BICKFORD, F. T. Prehistoric Cave-dwellings. Cent. Ill. Mag., Oct. 1890, p. 903.

In the Fifth Ann. Rep. Bur. Ethn. (p. XXV) it is stated that a complete survey of the Cañon de Chelley has been made, and a thorough investigation of its ruins carried out. No less than 134 ruins are contained in this cañon and its forks. To the best of my knowledge nothing has been published of this exploration.

[2] Second Ann. Rep. Bur. Ethn., p. 418.

[3] Fifth Ann. Rep. Bur. Ethn., p. XXIV.

so dilapidated that extensive excavations would be necessary to ascertain the arrangement of the rooms.

The same motives as led the inhabitants of the cave villages to build and dwell
in the most inaccessible cliffs, also seem often to have influenced the people of the
plateaux and valleys. On the plateau the site selected was often some isolated rock,
surrounded on all sides by precipices, and well suited for purposes of defence. In
the valleys, where no natural fastness could be found, the village itself was sometimes fortified by enclosing all the buildings within a common outer wall four or
five stories high and not pierced with any doorways. The remarkable villages in
Chaco Cañon are of this structure.

Most of these ruins, as mentioned above, have not been subjected to scientific
investigation, though excavations would certainly bring to light many objects of
great interest, and also give a better idea of the original appearance of the buildings.
I confine myself here to giving a short list of the places where the largest heaps of
ruins have been discovered. Only in the case of some few groups of ruins better
preserved than the rest, shall I give a more detailed description.

In Mancos Valley and throughout the Mesa Verde, on the plateaux and in
the cañons, lie numerous heaps of ruins, some of which have been mentioned above.
East of Mancos there are ruins of considerable size on the Rio La Plata [1] and
Rio de las Animas.[2] Both these valleys were once densely populated. West of
Mancos, at Aztec Spring in Montezuma Valley, a well now dried up, a group of
ruins covering an area of 44,000 sq. m. is situated.[3] I give a plan of these ruins
(fig. 82) after HOLMES, as a specimen of a pueblo belonging to a very common
type. The arrangement of the rooms after the fashion of the cells in an organic
tissue is characteristic. The walls are built with a regularity which does not exist
in the cliff-dwellings. The building seen at the top of the plan is rectangular
(24 × 30 m.). The walls seem to have been double, with a space of 2.1 m. between
them. A number of cross walls at regular intervals indicate that this space has
been divided into apartments as shown in the plan. The walls are 0.6 m. thick
and built of roughly dressed stones. Enclosing this great house is a network of fallen
walls, so completely reduced that none of the stones seem to remain in place. It
is difficult to decide whether this was formerly a cluster of irregular apartments with
low walls, or a large building of adobe.[4] In the southern part of these ruins lie
two rooms with well defined circular outlines (estufas?). The larger is 18 m. in

---

[1] HOLMES, Ruins of S. W. Colorado, p. 387.
[2] ENDLICH, F. M. Geological Report etc. Rep. U. S. Geol. and Geogr. Survey of the Terr.
1875, p. 177.
    BIRNIE, ROGERS. Report on Ruins Visited in New Mexico. Rep. U. S. Geogr. Surveys W.
100th Mer., Vol. VII, p. 347.
    MORGAN, L. On the Ruins of a Stone Pueblo on the Animas River in New Mexico. Twelfth
Rep. Peabody Mus., Vol. II, p. 536.
[3] HOLMES, Ruins of S.W. Colorado, p. 399.
[4] Sun-dried brick.

diameter, and is surrounded by a low stone wall. The spring lay in the centre of
the ruins. West of the rectangular building described first a small open court is
situated, which probably had a gateway opening to the west. The building seen
at the bottom of the plan measures 54×60 m. The north wall is double and contains a row of eight rooms about 2.₁ m. broad and 7.₂ m. long. The other three
walls are single, and probably served simply to enclose the great court, near the
centre of which lies a large walled depression (estufa? reservoir?).

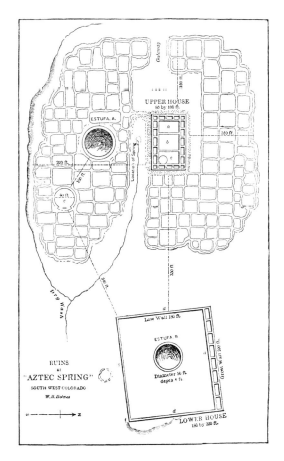

FIG. 82. PLAN OF THE RUINS AT AZTEC SPRING. AFTER HOLMES.

Between the Mesa Verde and the Rio Dolores there are numerous ruins, none
of which has been described. Near a dry wash that enters the McElmo Cañon from
the south, lies a ruin[1] the plan of which shows about the same arrangement of the
rooms as the pueblo at Aztec Spring. A cylindrical tower (fig. 83) with triple walls
had been erected at one end of the building. The space between the two outer
walls is divided in the same singular manner as in the tower on the Rio San Juan

<hr />

[1] HOLMES, Ruins of S. W. Colorado, p. 398.

and in some towers on the Rio Mancos, into cells, fourteen in number and measuring about 1.5 × 1.5 m. The different cells seem to have communicated with
each other by means of openings in the partitions; no openings were found in the
outer wall. It is difficult to determine the object with which these singular towers
were built. Perhaps they were erected for some religious purpose.

On the Rio San Juan,[1] on the Hovenweep, in McElmo Cañon, and in Epsom
Creek,[2] there are according to JACKSON several remarkable Pueblo ruins. In Montezuma Cañon,[3] which joins the Rio San Juan some kilometres west of the mouth
of McElmo Cañon, 16—18 isolated rocky promontories, surrounded by cañons, were
found within 20 kilom. of each other. All these rocks were covered with the remains of massive stone buildings, one of which is especially remarkable, some of the
walls consisting partly of colossal blocks of stone standing upright and in some cases
1.5 m. high and more than half a metre thick. In general, however, the walls are
built of smaller stones in the ordinary style. As at Aztec Spring, the rooms consist
of an agglomeration of small quadrangular cells. The ruins last described are situ-

FIG. 83.   SINGULAR TOWER IN A RUIN NEAR MC ELMO CAÑON.   AFTER HOLMES.

ated in the south-east corner of Utah. Throughout the south of this state similar
ancient remains occur.[4]

North of Montezuma Cañon all traces of a numerous ancient population cease.
Only an hour's ride north from a tract literally thick with ruins, the explorer enters
upon a region where he seeks in vain for a single heap of ruins, a single potsherd.
Nor on the slopes of the Sierra Abajo (Blue Mountain), a group of lofty peaks
with their luxuriant woods and rich pastures forming as it were an oasis in the
desert between Mancos and the Rio Colorado, are there any ruins to be found.

---

[1] JACKSON, Ancient Ruins exam. in 1875 and 1877, p. 415. Ruins on the Rio San Juan are
also mentioned by ENDLICH (Geol. Rep., p. 179).

[2] Ibid., p. 413. The Hovenweep, McElmo Cañon and Epsom Creek lie in Southern Utah,
and join the Rio San Juan.

[3] Ibid., p. 427.

[4] REMY, JULES. A Journey to the Great Salt Lake City. London 1862, Vol. II, p. 305.
Mentions ruins at Cedar City.

THOMPSON, G. Notes on the Pueblos and their Inhabitants. U. S. Geogr. Surveys W. 100th
Mer., Vol. VII, p. 324. Mentions ruins at Pipe Spring and in Escalante and Colorado Cañons.

HOLMES, Pottery, p. 287. Mentions a barrow at S:t George.

What can have induced an agricultural people to prefer desolate cañons and dry sandy plains to fertile mountain slopes, watered by never failing streams? Another of the many riddles which confront the student of the prehistoric inhabitants of these tracts! Perhaps a nomad people, more powerful and more warlike, held these more fortunate regions.

In Northern Arizona, on the wild plateaux around the Grand Cañon and at the bottom of that grand monument of erosive action, lie ruins [1] of the same type as those just described. This is also the case along the whole course of the Colorado Chiquito,[2] a tributary of the Colorado. I have crossed the strip of country between the Colorado Chiquito and the San Juan on horseback, and I then observed that this tract is also rich in archæological remains. In this region are also situated the villages of the Moki Indians, and in their neighbourhood lie numerous ruins,[3] showing that the Mokis were formerly a more important tribe. Some of these ruins have been deserted in historic times.

The western limit of the geographical extension of the Pueblo ruins intersects the northern half of Arizona, roughly speaking through Aztec Pass, in Long. 113° W. From this line west to the Colorado and the Pacific Ocean [4] there is not a single ruin.

In New Mexico, not far from the boundary of Arizona, the Zuñi Indians have their home. Their villages are situated on the Zuñi River, an affluent of the Colorado Chiquito. The neighbourhood contains many deserted pueblos, some of

---

[1] POWELL, J. W. The Cañons of the Colorado. Scribners Monthly, Jan., Feb., March 1875, pp. 402, 407.

HOLMES, Pottery, p. 281: "The remarkable desert-like plateau lying north of the Grand Cañon contains many houses and village sites. At intervals along the very brink of the great chasm we come upon heaps of stones and rased walls of houses about which are countless fragments of this (the coiled) ware."

[2] SITGREAVES, L. Report of an Expedition down the Zuñi and Colorado Rivers. Sen. Ex. Doc., 33d Congr. 1st Sess., Wash. 1854, p. 9 (Pl. 12): "All the prominent points of the plateau (near the Colorado Chiquito) were occupied by the ruins of stone-houses of considerable size and in some instances of three stories in height. They are evidently the remains of a large town, as they occurred at intervals for an extent of eight or nine miles. The ground was thickly strewed with fragments of pottery."

WHIPPLE, Itinerary, p. 76.

MÖLLHAUSEN, Tagebuch, p. 301: "Immer neue Ruinen, auf welche wir stiessen, liessen uns vermuthen, dass die wandernden Völkerstämme im grauen Alterthume ausgedehnte Ansiedelungen in diesem Thale besessen hatten, wo Alles, was zur Existenz der Menschen nöthig ist, geboten wurde."

HOFFMANN, W. J. Ethnographic Observations on Indians Inhabiting Nevada, California, and Arizona. Rep. U. S. Geol. and Geogr. Survey of the Terr. 1876, p. 477.

West of the San Francisco Mts., on Pueblo Creek, ruins are mentioned by:

WHIPPLE, Itinerary, p. 92.

WHIPPLE, A. W. Report upon the Indian Tribes. Pac. R. R. Rep., Vol. III: Pt. III, Wash. 1855, p. 15.

MÖLLHAUSEN, l. c., p. 348.

[3] BOURKE, J. G. The Snake-dance of the Moquis of Arizona. London 1884, pp. 86, 90, 294, 316, 327.

See also: Third Ann. Rep. Bur. Ethn., p. XXI, Fourth Rep., p. XXXVIII, and Fifth Rep., p. XXIV, where a number of ruins are mentioned without further description. Some of the ruins near the Moki villages have recently been subjected to a most searching examination by FEWKES, who is the chief of the Hemenway Expedition. Unfortunately I have not been able to procure more than a few of the papers he has published as the result of his investigations.

[4] WHIPPLE, Report, p. 15.

which have been inhabited in historic times.[1] But others were probably in ruins long before the Spaniards reached these regions at the middle of the sixteenth century. In addition to these Pueblo remains, some of which remind us in their construction of the buildings in Chaco Cañon more fully described below, ruined towers also occur, similar to those so common in Mancos Valley, and isolated cliff-dwellings. In one of these towers FEWKES observed the same structural peculiarity as I have pointed out in my description of some of the cliff-dwellings, notably the Cliff Palace, namely that the upper part of the walls is carefully built of hewn blocks, while the lower part consists of rough stones.

The most remarkable and the largest Pueblo ruins in the basin of the Colorado are situated in the north-west of New Mexico, in Chaco Canon,[2] which is drained by the Rio San Juan. Both sides of the bed of the stream, which is now dry, are skirted by a narrow plain, shut in by steep cliffs. For an extent of 30 kilom. at the foot of these precipices, lie the remains of several large villages, noteworthy for the skill displayed in the erection of the walls, and especially for the systematic and often perfectly symmetrical distribution of the rooms. I here give plans, accompanied by a short description, of the most important ruins, following JACKSON's account of his investigations.

Pueblo Pintado lies on a bench 8—9 m. above the valley. The main building (see the plan fig. 84: 1) forms an **L** enclosing a court bounded on the outer side by a low arched wall. The surface of the ground in the court is very irregular and broken, as if it once contained underground rooms, the roofs of which have fallen in. The two outer walls, still rising in some places to a height of 9 m., indicate an original elevation of at least 12 m., unbroken by any apertures except the smallest kind of windows. The two interior longitudinal lines of walls are two or three stories high, while the inner wall hardly reaches the second story. In the north-west angle of the court lie two circular rooms (estufas). They are each 7.5 m. in diameter. The inside walls are perfectly cylindrical. One of these rooms contains two pillars, the other four, built into the cylindrical wall. Both the round estufas are erected

[1] SIMPSON, Report, p. 117.
    WHIPPLE, Itinerary, p. 69.
    MÖLLHAUSEN, Tagebuch, p. 270.
    FEWKES, W. J. Reconnoissance of Ruins in or near the Zuñi Reservation. Journ. Am. Ethn. and Arch., Vol. I, Camb. 1891, p. 95.
[2] GREGG, J. Karawanenzüge durch die westlichen Prairieen. Dresden und Leipzig 1845, Th. I, p. 183.
    SIMPSON, Report, p. 76.
    JACKSON, Ancient Ruins exam. in 1875 and 1877, p. 431.
    LOEW, O. Report on the Ruins in New Mexico. U. S. Geogr. Surveys W. 100th Mer., Vol. VII, p. 337.
    MORRISON, C. C. Notice of the Pueblo Pintado and of other Ruins in the Chaco Cañon. Ibid., p. 366.
    BICKFORD, Cave-dwellings, p. 896.
    GREGG was the first to mention the ruins in Chaco Cañon. SIMPSON published the first description. JACKSON has given a fuller description, accompanied by accurate plans. BICKFORD, LOEW, and MORRISON have made less important contributions to the study of these ruins.

Examples of Cliff Dweller cradle boards. Very young children were, in effect, strapped onto theses boards while the mother went about her daily chores. Photo courtesy MVNP.

Cradle boards of the Cliff Dwellers were sometimes ornamented, as the picture above indicates. Perhaps these aboriginies were not totally classless, after all. Photo courtesy MVNP.

One ancient tool nearly universal around the world is a "digging stick"; this was used by the Cliff Dwellers to dig a hole into which was planted seeds. Photo courtesy MVNP.

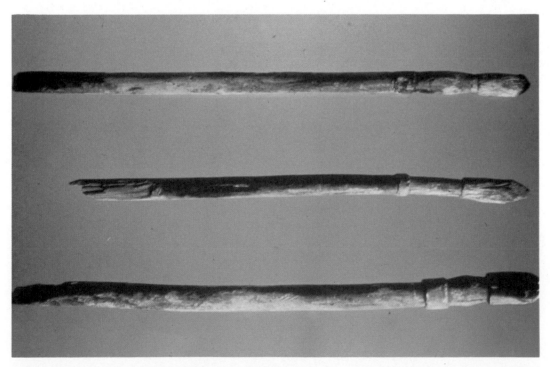

Cliff Dweller "prayer sticks", found by the author and now in the Nordenskiold collection in Helsinki. Each stick represents a particular prayer to a particular deity. Photo courtesy MVNP.

in square rooms, the space between the circle and the adjoining straight walls being filled with solid masonry. No openings are to be found at the sides; the entrance was probably in the roof. Besides these two estufas there is another circular room just outside at the south-west corner of the building. This structure is 15 m. in diameter, and is enclosed within a rectangular wall (17 × 24 m.). JACKSON explains this room too as an estufa. But is it not more probable that circular walls of such dimensions are the remains of open reservoirs? It is hard to believe that the ancient inhabitants of this pueblo, however skilful they may have been in architecture, could

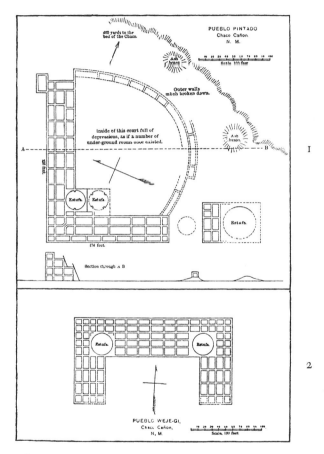

FIG. 84. PLANS OF PUEBLO PINTADO AND WEJE-GI. AFTER JACKSON.

roof a building so wide, especially as cedar and piñon logs, the timber generally used in these buildings, are seldom more than 10—12 m. long. Below the plan (fig. 84: 1) is given a vertical section of the ruin in the line A B, according to JACKSON's ideas of its original appearance. It is probable that the walls descended in terraces towards the court, from which the rooms were reached by ladders, the high outer wall thus forming a protection against hostile attacks, and giving the whole building the appearance of a fortification. The plan is devoted principally to the second story.

The ground floor is divided into a still greater number of rooms. No rafters are left. Each room has one or more entrances in the form of small doorways, the largest of which measured 0.6 × 1 m. The sills of these doors are generally about 0.6 m. above the floor. The walls of the first floor are 70—75 cm. thick, those of each ascending story being a little less. The structure of the walls is not the least remarkable point in these buildings, and forms a striking contrast to the rude method in which the Pueblo Indians of modern times run up their villages. The building material, a grayish-yellow sandstone breaking readily into thin slabs, was quarried in the neighbouring cliffs. The stones are about as large as an ordinary brick, but as the larger pieces were irregular in size, the interstices were filled in with very thin plates of sandstone. And with such skill has this task been accomplished, so exactly do the different pieces fit together, that at a little distance the walls bear every indication of being a plain solid surface. Mortar composed of clay was used plentifully within the body of the wall, but does not appear anywhere upon the surface. Great care was bestowed upon the construction of the doorways, the stones being here more regular, and the corners dressed down to perfect right angles. The lintel consisted usually of small round sticks of cedar laid side by side, sometimes, when the opening was not so large, of a single slab of stone. Though the stones in the walls vary greatly in size, they are still arranged in perfectly horizontal layers, courses of smaller stones alternating with rows of larger ones. Just outside the court are two refuse heaps, full of potsherds and chips of flint.

Nineteen kilometres from Pueblo Pintado lies another remarkable ruin, *Pueblo Weje-gi*. Between these two pueblos numerous smaller ruins are situated. Fig. 84: 2 is a plan of Weje-gi. The perfectly regular arrangement of the rooms is worthy of note. Here, as at Pueblo Pintado, the outer wall rises to the full height of the building, unbroken by any doorways or other openings, save very small windows.

Four kilometres farther down the cañon are the ruins of *Pueblo Una Vida*, a structure similar to Pueblo Pintado. A further descent of $1\frac{1}{2}$ kilom. brings the explorer to *Pueblo Hungo Pavie* (Crooked Nose), which resembles Weje-gi in the perfectly symmetrical arrangement of the rooms. The main building forms three sides of a court. A curved wall joins the two wings, and forms the outer wall of the court. At least four stories have once existed. The single estufa occupies the centre of the building. It is 7 m. in diameter. Six quadrangular pillars are built into the cylindrical wall at equal distances from each other. The height of the rooms is 2.7 m. in the second story, 2.1 m. in the third. Some of the rafters still remain.

The Pueblo Chettro Kettle, 3 kilom. from the preceding ruin, resembles the latter in the plan of the building, but is considerably larger (132 × 75 m.). Much of the floor timber is preserved, and the beams forming the roof of the first floor project 1.2—1.5 m. beyond the outer wall, where they probably served in former times to support a balcony. SIMPSON [1] describes the interior of a room still in a perfect state of preservation. The floor measured 4.2 × 5.2 m., the height 3 m. One large niche (96 × 135 × 120 cm.) and some smaller ones had been built in the walls. The roof was supported by two large beams laid transversally, above these lay small poles in a longitudinal direction, and on the top of the latter, transversally and in close contact, a kind of lathing, probably cedar bast. JACKSON estimates that 30,000,000 stones were employed in the building of the Pueblo Chettro Kettle.

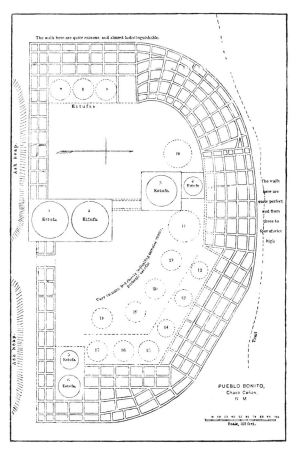

FIG. 85. PLAN OF PUEBLO BONITO. AFTER JACKSON.

Five hundred yards farther down the cañon lie the ruins of *Pueblo Bonito*, the largest of all the pueblos in Chaco Cañon. Its length is 163 m., breadth 94 m. The plan (fig. 85) shows less regularity in the arrangement of the rooms. The whole building has not been erected at the same time, but additions and alterations have been made on several occasions. The court is not closed, as in most of the ruins previously described, by a wall, but by a straight, double row of small rooms. The

[1] Report, p. 79.

walls in different parts of the building are erected in various manners, indicating that they have been constructed at different periods. The court contains about 20 estufas of various sizes. Depressions in the ground suggest that underground rooms once existed.

The next ruin, *Pueblo del Arroyo*, is about 300 yards distant from Pueblo Bonito, and is so called from its close proximity to the *arroyo*, the steep-walled channel cut by the stream in the loose bottom of the cañon. This arroyo has exposed a layer of potsherds, chips of flint, and small bones, firmly embedded in coarse

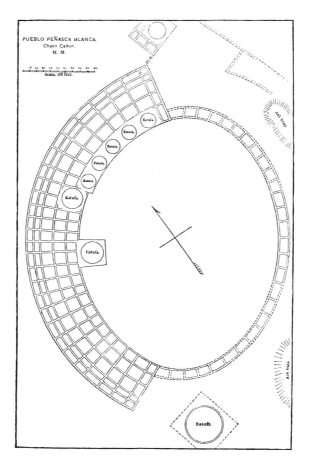

FIG. 86. PLAN OF PUEBLO PEÑASCA BLANCA. AFTER JACKSON.

gravel and lying 4.2 m. below the surface. The said layer determines the ground level at the period when the village was inhabited. Since that time 4 m. of sand and gravel have been deposited, and subsequently the present arroyo has been worn in the stratum thus formed.

Five kilometres from Pueblo del Arroyo the ruins of *Pueblo Peñasca Blanca* are situated. Between these two pueblos are two smaller ruins. Pueblo Peñasca Blanca and one other are the only villages built above the bottom of the cañon.

This pueblo also differs from all the rest in another respect, the outer walls forming an almost perfect ellipse (fig. 86). The western half of this ellipse is occupied by a massive structure containing five rows of rooms; the eastern half by a single row of small chambers, shutting in the court like a wall. The outermost tier of rooms in the main building has probably consisted of four stories. The roofs between the different stories were built of beams in the method described above. A thick layer of willow twigs rested on the beams, and supported a floor of hard clay. The large rooms measure 6 m. from wall to wall. The bottom story seems to have been divided into much smaller rooms. The walls are composed of stones, each of about the same size as an ordinary brick, cemented with mortar. This building method resembles that employed in the cliff-dwellings of the Mesa Verde.

North of Pueblo Bonito, but on the plateau, about half a kilometre from the brink of the cañon, lie the remains of *Pueblo Alto*. From the great height at which the buildings have been erected, a magnificent and extensive view may be gained on all sides. Not far from the ruins JACKSON discovered some "water pockets," or holes in the sandstone where rainwater collects, prevented from evaporation by the overhanging rock. From these reservoirs a stairway hewn in the very wall of the cañon led down to Pueblo Bonito. The labour necessary for the construction of such a stairway seems to show that even the villages at the bottom of the cañon drew their supply of water from these holes on the mesa. In that case there was no running water in the arroyo of Chaco Cañon even when this tract was densely populated, and the intervening period between that time and the present has thus been attended with no essential change of climate.

On comparison of the ruins in Chaco Cañon with the cliff-dwellings of Mancos, we find several points of resemblance. In both localities the villages are fortified against attack, in the tract of Mancos by their site in inaccessible precipices, in Chaco Cañon by a high outer wall in which no doorways were constructed to afford entrance to an enemy. Behind this outer wall the rooms descended in terraces towards the inner court. One side of this court was protected by a lower semicircular wall. In the details of the buildings we can find several features common to both. The roofs between the stories were constructed in the same way. The doorways were built of about the same dimensions. The rafters were often allowed to project beyond the outer wall as a foundation for a sort of balcony (Balcony House, the Pueblo Chettro Kettle). The estufa at Hungo Pavie with its six quadrangular pillars of stone is exactly similar to a Mesa Verde estufa (see p. 16). The pottery strewn in fragments everywhere in Chaco Cañon resembles that found on the Mesa Verde. We are thus not without grounds for assuming that it was the same people, at different stages of its development, that inhabited these two regions.

Several others among the numerous ruins found in the north-west of New Mexico, and the south-west of Colorado, seem to be constructed in a similar manner to those just described; but with the exception perhaps of the ruins on the Animas

River, this territory possesses no archæological remains so well preserved and so magnificent as the pueblos in Chaco Cañon.

2. Ruins in the basin of the Rio Grande.

Cave-dwellings. West of Santa-Fé, at the head of the Rio Grande, numerous cave-dwellings have been found. Some of them, situated north of Cochiti, an Indian village, are described by STEVENSON.[1] A cañon the Indian name of which is Gunuye, is bounded to the north by perpendicular cliffs of soft tuff, which tower to a height of 15—30 m. above the more gradual slope extending to the stream at the bottom of the cañon. In the lower part of these cliffs a number of small caves have been hollowed. One of them proved on closer examination to be of a round, but some-what irregular shape (4.5—3.5 m. in diameter). The roof was arched, 2.5 m. high at the middle, and blackened with smoke. The entrance of the cave consisted of a small opening on a level with the ground, 0.7 m. high and nearly 0.6 m. wide at the bottom, but much narrower at the top, it being just possible for a man of or-dinary stature to gain ingress. Two holes of irregular form, pierced in the outer wall, had perhaps served as windows. Many of the caves examined contained a firm and level floor of fine, red clay. In some places the remains of a coat of plaster, consisting of red and yellow clay, might still be seen on the walls. The lower part of the walls was sometimes plastered in one colour, the upper part and the roof in another, a broad, dark brown stripe being the line of demarcation. Small niches were often constructed in the walls. On several occasions smaller caves were found at the back of the larger ones, communicating with the latter by means of tiny doorways. Here and there the caves were more scattered and situated higher up the cliff, while below their mouths lay rectangular hollows, once the rear walls of rooms. This was shown by the plaster still to be seen on parts of the walls. The front walls must have been built of stone, for immediately at the foot of the cliff a quantity of rough-hewn blocks were found. By this method of construction a lower room was erected, with the front wall and both side walls built of stone, while the rear wall consisted of the cliff. The roof of this room formed a platform in front of the main cave above it. The caves here described extended along the lower part of the north side of the cañon for a distance of about 3 kilom. In some places they were crowded close together in two or three rows, in others more scattered. In some instances the stone walls with which the caves had been fronted were partly preserved. No weapons or implements were found, but fragments of pottery and pieces of obsidian were strewn everywhere on the ground. The slopes below the caves were dotted with ruins of stone buildings.

---

[1] STEVENSON, Ancient Habitations, p. 339.
Illustrated Catalogue of the Collections obtained from the Indians of New Mexico in 1880. Second Ann. Rep. Bur. Ethn., p. 430.

Cliff-dwellings are unknown in the basin of the Rio Grande, or I can at least find no reference to any in the literature to which I have had access.

Ruins in the valleys and on the plateaux. In the north-west of New Mexico[1] these remains are similar to those belonging to the adjoining parts of the Rio Colorado and its affluents.

Along the Rio Grande and several of its tributaries, in regions where there still exist pueblos with a numerous population, a great number of deserted villages occur,[2] more or less entirely destroyed. In many of them, which have been inhabited in historic times,[3] there is of course a Spanish element; and as it is often impossible to determine whether a certain ruin is prehistoric or not, these remains possess less interest for the present work, where it is my chief purpose to give as faithful a picture as the records permit, of the life and extension of the cliff people and their kinsmen the Pueblo tribes, in prehistoric times and before they had been influenced in any manner by the whites. The Indian villages on the Rio Grande differ from the ruined pueblos previously described in being often built of adobe and not of stone. This depends probably on the greater ease with which a supply of the former material might be procured.

3. Ruins in the basin of the Rio Gila.

Cave-dwellings. Some cave-dwellings in the valley of the Rio Verde, an affluent of the Rio Gila, are mentioned by MEARNS[4] without further description.

Cliff-dwellings have been discovered in several parts of the same valley. One of them, known by the name of "Montezuma's Castle," is described at length both by HOFFMAN[5] and MEARNS.[6] In the site and the general arrangement of the building the castle closely resembles the cliff-dwellings of the Mesa Verde. Even small details, the method of building the roofs of beams covered with a layer of withes and finally overlaid with a coat of clay, and the construction of the

---

[1] HOLMES, Ruins of S. W. Colorado, p. 401.

COPE, E. D. Report on the Remains of Population observed in North-western New Mexico. U. S. Geogr. Surveys W. 100th Mer., p. 351. The author describes ruins in the neighbourhood of Gallinas Creek, N. W. of Abiquiu. The ruins are situated at the top of steep cliffs. COPE is of the opinion that these tracts formerly had as numerous a population as the more densely peopled districts in the east of the United States.

YARROW, H. C. Notice of a Ruined Pueblo and an Ancient Burial-place in the Valley of the Rio Chama. Ibid., p. 362. The author mentions a village on a mesa bounded by perpendicular cliffs in the Rio Chama valley near Abiquiu. It is built in the form of an E.

[2] LOEW, Report, p. 337.

BANDELIER, A. F. A Visit to the Aboriginal Ruins in the Valley of the Rio Pecos. Papers of the Archæol. Inst. of Am., Am. Ser. I, Boston 1883, p. 37.

Scattered mentions of ruins in these regions occur in several of the works quoted in this chapter.

[3] Ruins were already to be found, however, when CORONADO first reached the valley of the Rio Grande. See CASTAÑEDA, Relation, pp. 177, 178.

[4] MEARNS, E. A. Ancient Dwellings of the Rio Verde Valley. Pop. Science Monthly, Oct. 1890, p. 749.

[5] HOFFMAN, Ethnographic Observations, p. 477.

[6] MEARNS, l. c., p. 749.

G. Nordenskiöld, Cliff Dwellers.

doorways and of the small holes by means of which the different stories communicated with each other, all are exactly the same, in spite of the great distance between the two localities.

I cannot refrain from mentioning one more cliff-dwelling in the same neighbourhood, where the end which the builders seem always first and foremost to have had in view, namely the fortification of the structure, has been attained by a singular device. Between 10 and 12 kilom. from the ruin just mentioned lies a deep spring, or rather a small lake, named "Montezuma Wells" and entirely surrounded by steep cliffs. It was the general custom in the construction of fortifications to select as a site some eminence difficult of approach; but here the depression surrounded by perpendicular cliffs has been utilised as a fastness. There is only one path down the rocks to the spring, and this path is defended by two cliff-dwellings, one on each side. In small hollows of the cliff some other buildings of quite insignificant size are situated. The spring is drained by a subterranean outlet.

Ruins in the valleys and on the plateaux. The Rio Verde valley also contains numerous ruins belonging to this group.[1] One of them is described by MEARNS.[2] It consists of two buildings, which were probably erected in terraces. The walls, which were of stone at the bottom, but had probably been completed with adobe, were 0.5—1 m. thick. The arrangement of the rooms calls to mind the ruins at Aztec Spring. Settlers in the neighbourhood have partly demolished the walls still remaining, in order to employ the stones in the reparation of a canal (acequia) dating from the time of the Pueblo people. During these operations a number of objects had been unearthed. Excavations were afterwards instituted by MEARNS. He gives figures of some earthenware vessels which are of a type quite different from the pottery of the Mesa Verde. They closely resemble the ware from the Casas Grandes in the Gila valley and from those in Chihuahua (Northern Mexico). The buildings, on the other hand, remind us in certain respects of the ruins in the basin of the Rio Colorado. This is also the case, as I have mentioned above, with the cliff-dwellings, which in MEARNS's opinion are the work of the same people as erected the structures on the plains.

The so called *Casas Grandes* on the Rio Gila differ in several architectural respects from the ruins previously described. EMORY, who followed the course of this river from the east, found the first ruins in Long. 109° W.[3] From this point all the way to the place where the river emerges from the mountains, numerous

[1] BARTLETT, J. R. Personal Narrative of Explorations and Incidents in Texas, New Mexico etc., London 1854, Vol. II, p. 247. The author, citing as his authority a trapper named LEROUX, mentions ruins in the San Francisco (Rio Verde) valley. Both WHIPPLE (Report, p. 14) and MÖLLHAUSEN (Reisen in die Felsengebirge Nordamerikas. Leipzig 1861, Bd. II, p. 140) drew their information from the same source. A list of the ruins in the Rio Verde valley is given by MEARNS, E. A. in the paper just quoted.

[2] L. c., p. 757.

[3] EMORY, W. H. Notes of a Military Reconnoissance, from Fort Leavenworth, in Missouri, to San Diego, in California. Sen. Ex. Doc. No. 7, 30th Congr. 1st Sess., Wash. 1848, p. 64.

ruins were found. Even farther down the plain on both sides of the river architectural remains were discovered. Of the ruins in the Rio Gila the Casa Grande is
the best known and the most thoroughly examined. The first description [1] of this
remarkable building is from the pen of Padre MANGI, who accompanied the Spanish
Jesuit missionary Padre KINO in 1697. In 1775 the ruins were visited by Padre
PEDRO FONT, who has given a description in his diary.[2] Since that time several
travellers have described these remains.[3] BARTLETT quotes MANGI's description, and
remarks that during the intervening 150 years the ruins had not undergone any
great change. The figure given in FEWKES's paper closely resembles the drawing
reproduced in BARTLETT's work. Thus the weathering of the last forty years does
not seem to have greatly affected the structure. It appears that buildings, even those
erected, like the Casa Grande, of so perishable a material as adobe, can long with-
stand the destructive action of the elements in this climate.

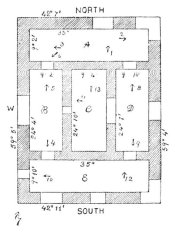

FIG. 87. PLAN OF THE CASA GRANDE. AFTER FEWKES.

The Casa Grande lies 80 kilom. from the mouth of the Rio Gila, as the
crow flies. This name has been restricted to a rectangular edifice (18 × 13 m.),
containing five rooms, and still rising to a height of several stories. The said structure
is surrounded by other ruins in a more advanced stage of decay, which in former
times probably made up a considerable village. Fig. 87 is a plan of the central
building. It is constructed of large blocks (height 0.6 m., breadth 1.2 m.) of gravel
and clay, and the thickness of the walls at the bottom is no less than 1.2—1.5 m.

[1] It is supposed that the ruin mentioned by CORONADO under the name of Chichilticale is
identical with the Casa Grande on the Rio Gila. But it is hardly certain that this opinion is correct.
[2] Extracts from this journal are given in TERNAUX-COMPANS, Relation du Voyage de Cibola, p. 383.
[3] BARTLETT, Personal Narrative, Vol. II, p. 272.
EMORY, Military Reconnoissance, p. 81.
FEWKES, W. J. On the Present Condition of a Ruin in Arizona called Casa Grande. Journ.
Am. Ethnol. and Archæol., Vol. II, p. 179.

The inner walls are perpendicular; but the outer surface of the walls leans sharply inwards, the walls thus being narrower at the top.   The five rooms, the arrangement of which is shown in the plan (fig. 87), communicate with each other by means of doorways 0.6—1 m. broad and 1.5—2 m. high, or of considerably greater dimensions than in most of the cliff-dwellings.   The outer surface of the walls has been roughly plastered.   On the inside the coat of plaster is hard and bright, and looks as smooth as though it had just been applied.   The roofs between the stories were supported by beams 12—15 cm. in diameter.   When BARTLETT visited the ruins, the ends of these beams where still to be seen in the walls.   They seemed to have been burnt down.   At the time of FEWKES's visit (1891) all the timber had fallen or been removed.

Ruins of structures similar in type to the Casa Grande occur in the Gila valley within the limits given above, and also on the Rio Salado,[1] a tributary of the Gila.   Most of these remains are, however, almost entirely razed to the ground. Characteristic of these buildings are the huge central temples, which usually occupy the middle of the village.   The Casa Grande is the ruin of one of these temples.   Numerous remains of canals show that the tract was extensively cultivated in former times.   The ruins in the Salado valley have been subjected by the Hemenway Expedition to careful archæological investigations; but the results have not yet been published.[2]

In the province of Chihuahua in Northern Mexico ruins of the Casa Grande type, also called Casas Grandes, occur.[3]   They are in a better state of preservation than the buildings on the Gila and Salado Rivers; but have not yet been examined with any great care.   The largest and best preserved of these "casas" measures at least 240 m. from north to south, about 75 m. from east to west.   The dimensions of the structure have thus been very considerable.   Although the strict purpose of this chapter is to give a survey of the archæological remains in the South-west States of North America, I have not been able to pass over in silence these Casas Grandes, on account of their close resemblance to the ruins of the Gila and Salado valleys.   There are also other ruins in Mexico which show that the southern limit of the territory inhabited by tribes akin to the cliff-dwellers lies considerably south of the present boundary between this republic and the United States.   Some of these ruins, the only ones where any thorough researches have been carried out, were explored by LUMHOLTZ.   I shall here give a brief description of these ruins, based on the papers quoted below.[4]

---

[1] BARTLETT, Personal Narrative, Vol. II, p. 245.

[2] A short account of this expedition has been published: BAXTER, S.   The Old New World. Salem, Mass. 1888.

[3] BARTLETT, Personal Narrative, Vol. II, p. 345.

[4] LUMHOLTZ, CARL.   Report of Explorations in Northern Mexico.   Bull. Am. Geogr. Soc., 1891, No. 3, p. 386.
    Explorations in the Sierra Madre.   Scribner's Monthly, Oct. 1891, p. 531.

From Nacori, a small village situated on the western slope of the Sierra Madre, 180 kilom. south of the United States frontier, Lumholtz started eastwards. In the wild, rugged, and uninhabited mountain regions through which the expedition advanced, numerous ruins were found, usually built of stone and perched on mountain tops. Occasionally the buildings were surrounded with fortifications. The most remarkable remains, however, were discovered in caves. In these caves lie stone buildings, sometimes three stories high, and furnished with small windows and doors constructed in the shape. of a cross. Here and there among the mountains rose stone terraces, built across narrow glens, and obviously intended for agricultural purposes. Each steep rocky slope was terraced with huge stone blocks 4.5—6 m. high. On the arrival of the explorers at San Diego on the eastern slope of the sierra, an expedition was undertaken down the Piedras Verdes River to Cave Valley, where about 50 cave or cliff dwellings were counted in a stretch of 30 kilom. Some of the caves contained small villages or groups of houses, built with more than ordinary skill. "The rock formation in which these caves occur is porphyry, that in time has disintegrated into a dust, which in some places covers the floor of the cave up to the knee. This dust was made into a pulp and used by this singular people in the construction of their dwellings.... The walls, which are about a foot and a half thick, present a solid surface of as much as eight feet in height, all of one piece and whitewashed." During a visit to a ruin of some considerable size a huge balloon-shaped vessel was found, 3.6 m. in height and of the same diameter, with a mouth 1 m. wide. Lumholtz supposes that this singular jar was used for the storage of grain. Among the objects discovered in these ruins were "bone needles, a complete fire-drill, mats and baskets, mat girdles, threads of fibre or hair sandals; but the most interesting find at this point was the throwing-stick or boomerang used to-day by the Moki Indians for killing rabbits; also some smooth pieces of iron, probably used for ceremonials. We also discovered a bow that had been hidden away on a ledge. The former inhabitants of these dwellings must have been agriculturists, as Mr. Hartman identified beans, corn, and three species of gourds among the remains. As for *datems* — a green, sweet fruit still found in Mexico — we identified it everywhere in the dwellings." Lumholtz further mentions burial caves where several mummies were found, some with hair and eyebrows preserved. The hair was "very slightly wavy, and softer than that of the modern Indian — almost silky in fact. They were of low stature, and bear a marked resemblance to the Moki village Indians, who, as well as the Zuñis, have a tradition that their ancestors came from the south, and who to this day speak of their southern brethren."

Several other bodies were exhumed, which had been buried in the same manner. They wore no ornaments of metal, but only shells. The ankles and wrists were encircled with anklets and bracelets of beautifully plaited straw, which, however, crumbled to dust when handled. Their only clothing consisted of three layers of wrapping round the loins, first a coarse cotton cloth, then a piece of matting, and over that again another strip of cloth. Underneath was a large piece of cotton batting mixed with feathers of the turkey and the large woodpecker.[1] In a few instances the cotton cloth was dyed red or indigo blue. Near the head of the corpse stood a small jar of simple ornament.

LUMHOLTZ' description of the cliff-dwellings of Northern Mexico shows that they closely resemble the corresponding remains in the United States. The structural features are almost exactly similar, and the objects brought to light during the excavations also seem to be about the same as those discovered by me in the ruins of the Mesa Verde, a strong indication that these inhabitants of regions so widely separated had the same habits and customs. But this point cannot be decided with certainty until a more detailed description of LUMHOLTZ' collections has been published. An important question is whether the ornamentation of the pottery illustrates the same simple, characteristic style as that we have seen in vogue among the cliff-dwellers of the Mesa Verde. At present the cliff-dwellings discovered by LUMHOLTZ are the southernmost known to exist. But wide stretches of the rough country around the Sierra Madre are as yet unexplored, and it is not impossible that we may succeed in tracing still farther south this singular people, who were compelled to seek a safe refuge among the most rugged mountains, in the most inhospitable cañons.

CHAPTER XIII.

The Moki Indians.

In New Mexico and Arizona there is a whole group of Indian tribes who have been supposed with greater or less reason to be the descendants of the people that built the ruined structures described above, and of whose geographical extension I have given a brief statement in the preceding chapter. These Indians are most numerous on the Rio Grande del Norte and its tributaries, where they have received the name of Pueblo Indians, a name which properly includes the Zuñis and Mokis as well, but which is often employed in this restricted sense, to designate the Indians of the Rio Grande. The so-called Pueblo Indians inhabit a great number of villages along the course of the Rio Grande, from the southern to the northern frontier of

---

[1] Probably the same feather cloth as that often found in the graves on the Mesa Verde (see above, p. 104).

A street in the Moki-village Oraibe.

From an instantaneous photograph by the author.

New Mexico, and subsist by agriculture. Their houses are built of stone or adobe. They are related to the Zuñis, who live farther west, on a small river of the same name, and to the Mokis, whose seven villages are situated on high mesas in the deserts of North-eastern Arizona. Dwelling in these remote parts, the Mokis have been less exposed to Spanish influences than their kinsmen the Zuñi and Rio Grande Indians, and have actually retained their independence almost without a break. I have therefore chosen for description this people as the representative of the modern agricultural Indians of North America.

After completing the exploration of the Mesa Verde cliff-dwellings, I set out on horseback, together with ALFRED WETHERILL and ETHRIDGE, from Mancos through North-eastern Arizona to the Moki villages, in order to gain an opportunity of studying this singular people. The account of the Moki customs given below is based partly on personal observations made during the said expedition, partly on the descriptions of American writers, above all BOURKE's excellent work.[1]

A ten days' ride through rugged mountain regions inhabited by Navajo Indians brought us to the westernmost of the seven Moki villages. An extensive mesa narrows towards the south, forming a sharp promontory, and at the extreme end of this promontory, on the very brink of the steep cliffs, 150 m. above the plain, lie three small villages, *Te'-wa*, *Si-choam'-a-vi* and *Wol'-pi*. Though the whole supply of water and fuel must be conveyed up to the mesa, only a single Indian family has ventured to infringe ancestral custom and settle on the lowland, near the springs. At the foot of the mesa huge sand-hills have collected, over which winds the trail to the village. The crossing of this drift-sand would have been very arduous, had not the Indians constructed a sort of stairway by laying stones in a row. The ascent is thus rendered much easier, especially for the old squaws, who carry large jars of water from the spring to the village. Higher up the slope grows steeper, but at the same time the ground becomes firmer. Trodden by the feet of many generations, the path winds on among rocks and stones to the top of the mesa. At the steepest places steps have been hewn in the rock. There is also a new waggon road up to the mesa, but it is much longer. The trail leads to Te'-wa, the northernmost village. A few hundred paces from Te'-wa lies Si-choam'-a-vi, and at the very end of the promontory Wol'-pi, the largest of the three villages (fig. 88).

On each side of the village street the houses rise in terraces, the front of the building containing only one story. The next row of rooms is two-storied, the third three-storied (see Pl. XVII). The rooms are generally small and dark (on an average 3 × 4 m. and 2 m. high), the outer ones are living-rooms, the inner chambers on the ground floor are used as storerooms. From the foremost room on the

---

[1] This account does not claim to contain anything new or to be a complete description of the manners and customs of this interesting people. I insert it for readers not conversant with American ethnology, for without a knowledge of the agricultural town-building Indians of the Southwest it would be impossible to understand the development of the Pueblo culture.

ground floor the roof may be gained through a rectangular hole. From the roof
a door opens into the second story, and from this part of the building one generally
ascends through the roof to the next terrace. It is on these terraces, which usually
communicate with each other by means of ladders as well, that the Indians spend
most part of the day, and perform all their domestic duties (Pl. XVII). The doors
of the various rooms are not of the same incommodious dimensions as in the cliff-
dwellings. The smoke is conducted out of the apartments through chimneys, which
are heightened by the addition of bottomless jars, placed one above another and cemented with mortar. The furniture of the rooms shows indications of white influence, and has retained little of its original appearance. Iron stoves and a number

FIG. 88. THE MOKI VILLAGE OF WOL'-PI.
(From a photograph by the author.)

of other household utensils purchased at the neighbouring store may be seen there.
The walls are built of unhewn stone and with far less care and skill than those of
the cliff villages, for example of the Cliff Palace. For the sake of comparison I
give two figures. Fig. 89 *a* is a Moki wall, fig. 89 *b* a wall in the Cliff Palace.
Most of the walls in the Moki villages were probably built after the Spaniards'
arrival and the introduction of iron, for all the beams supporting the floors between
the stories bear traces of metal axes.

　　Here and there in the village streets singular elevations of rectangular shape
meet the eye. At their centre is a square aperture from which two long poles project.
This hole is the entrance of an estufa or, in the Moki tongue, *kib-va*. The kib-va

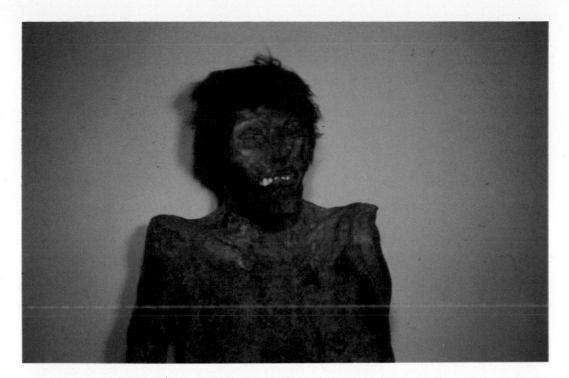

Mummy of a Cliff Dweller, a woman scholars have named "Esther". In the high dry climate of Mesa Verde, the body dessicated instead of decayed. Mummy is not on public display, but may be seen on request. Photo courtesy MVNP.

This is a Cliff Dweller mummy with funerary artifacts; in this case, the body was buried extended. Scholars can deduce a great deal about a past social order by studying burials. Courtesy MVNP.

Bodies of the dead were often placed into a fetal position for interment; scholars call this a flexed burial. Above is a sample flex burial en situ. Photo courtesy MVNP.

The author found this body wrapped in burial mats made of vegetal fibers; it is now in the Nordenskiold collection in Helsinki. Photo courtesy MVNP.

is a large rectangular apartment with sunken foundations, two-thirds of its height lying below the surface of the ground. Its size varies, the length being 7.5—10.5 m., breadth 4.5—7.5 m., height 2—3 m. Along three sides of the room runs a bank of earth and stones, 0.3 m. in breadth and of the same height. In a small rectangular hollow in the floor burns the eternal fire, which is never allowed to burst into flame. The walls of the kib-va are built of stone, in the same manner as the rest of the village. Their inner surface is plastered. Through the above-mentioned hole in the roof, which is constructed of thick beams, a ladder leads down into the room. The two side-props to which the rungs of the ladder are fastened project high above the roof. The rectangular entrance may be covered in case of rain with a mat of straw or yucca. In Wol'-pi there are 5 kib-vas, in Te'-wa 2, and in Si-choam'-a-vi also 2. At Jackson's visit in 1877 the populations of the same villages were respectively 334, 132, and 102. The entire population of the seven Moki villages was then 1,604.

a   b

FIG. 89. *a* WALL IN ONE OF THE MOKI VILLAGES. *b* WALL IN THE CLIFF PALACE.
(From photographs by the author.)

The kib-va of the Moki Indians is a room set apart for quite special purposes. Here, round the eternal fire, are performed the mystic rites connected with the solemn dances which are repeated several times a year, and which possess a profound religious significance, the gods being then supplicated for a good harvest, for bounteous rain, or the like. The kib-va is much frequented in the daytime by the men, who often lie idle on a mat, chatting and smoking, and sometimes busy themselves with weaving or some other of the duties that fall to their lot. Only on exceptional occasions do the women descend into the kib-va; their tasks are performed on the terraces.

Strange to say, the inhabitants of Te'-wa, the northernmost village, do not speak the same language as the rest of the Mokis. Tradition states that the people of Te'-wa fled before the Spaniards from their homes on the Rio Grande, at the end of the seventeenth century. They were invited by the Mokis to settle on the same mesa, and there they live to the present day, speaking a language different from that of their neighbours a few hundred paces to the south.

The Moki Indians are of a small stature, but well-shaped, their limbs being supple rather than robust. The features are often not unpleasing. Among the young girls really handsome faces with regular features may be seen. But at the age of maturity the soft contours of the features disappear; the face becomes angular and repulsive, the skin full of wrinkles. Old men and women are without exception hideous in appearance. The complexion is of a light reddish brown, the hair bluish black. The children's hair sticks out all over the head in the wildest disorder. The men cut it on the forehead into a long straight forelock. This manner of wearing the hair distinguishes them from their neighbours, the Navajo and Ute Indians, and from the Apaches, all of whom simply comb the hair to the sides, and fasten it with a band round the head. The Cohoninos, Hualpais, and Mohaves, on the other hand, dress their hair in the Moki fashion, and the Mokis therefore claim relationship with these tribes.

The dress of the Mokis varies widely. Children of both sexes under eight or nine wander about completely naked. Easy is the life led by these youngsters, who need neither dress nor wash themselves, and have nothing to do from morning to night but play about, nimble and lithe as chamois, in the warm sunshine that bathes the rocks on the mesa. Their elders wear at least a waist-cloth. In cold weather the Mokis wrap themselves in broad thick blankets. Sometimes they are clothed in calico smock and trousers, occasionally in a complete costume of European fashion. The women seem more often to retain their national dress. They wear a sleeveless tunic reaching to the knees and fastened round the waist with a broad belt of variegated colour. Across one shoulder is cast a woollen mantle, the two upper corners being knotted round the other shoulder. The feet are shod with hide moccasins, sewn in such a manner that the foot-covering proper consists of one end of a large piece of hide, which is wound several times round the leg, giving the limb a thick and clumsy shape. The unmarried women comb their hair in a singular fashion (see Pl. XVII, the girl standing highest of all); it is fastened in two large rolls above each ear. The married women comb the hair back and knot it in two queues. Their personal ornaments include necklaces of sea-shell and coral, which according to tradition were formerly fetched by the Mokis themselves from the western ocean, whither they made a pilgrimage, according to BOURKE, once every four or five years. Silver ornaments, such as bracelets, necklaces, earrings, buttons, and the like, are much worn. They are obtained by barter from the Navajo Indians, who manufacture them from silver dollars. Turquoises and a stone of a light green colour are worn as pendants to the necklaces.

Like other Indian tribes of North America, the Mokis are divided into clans, each of which has its own head. These chiefs together elect a common ruler, whose period of office is 1—2 years. Each clan lives in its own quarter of the village, has its own device, from which it is named, and with which its representatives are adorned on solemn occasions. As an example I here quote from BOURKE the clans of Te'-wa, named from their respective emblems: 1 Sun Clan; 2 Corn Clan; 3 Snake Clan; 4 Tobacco Clan; 5 Cottonwood Clan; 6 Pine Clan; 7 Cloud Clan; 8 Bear Clan; 9 Parrot Clan. The Moki has only one wife; polygamy is not allowed. But the husband may divorce one wife and take another at will. The Moki girls are considered eligible for marriage at the age of 10—15; it is said that they are then permitted to choose a husband themselves. All members of the same clan are regarded as brothers and sisters, and marriage between them is forbidden. The children belong to the mother's clan. The Moki women are not conspicuous for their virtue. Illegitimate children receive the same attention as those born in wedlock.

The Moki wives enjoy a better position than the women of most other Indian tribes. They own the houses, the sheep, goats, and other domestic animals, with the exception of the horses and donkeys, which are the property of the husband, and the harvested crops. Indoor occupations in general fall to their lot. The husband has no right to dispose of any household utensil without his wife's consent. It is to her that application must be made in the arranging of all purchase or barter. It is also she who must see that the house is kept in good order. If a wall needs repair, she calls in the aid of the neighbours' wives, and they perform the work together. But the building materials, including timber if any be required, are procured by the husband. Outdoor work in general belongs to the men; they sow and harvest the crops; they own and attend to the horses and donkeys. The plateaux where the villages are situated afford no supply of water with the exception of a few small pools of rainwater, at which no animals but poultry will drink. All the water is therefore fetched by squaws in large jars constructed for the purpose, which are carried on the back from the wells dug in the sand at the foot of the mesa and lined with masonry. Burdens of all kinds are carried on the back with the aid of a band passed round the forehead. Wood is conveyed to the villages from distant places on the backs of donkeys. The immediate neighbourhood of the villages has been stripped quite bare of timber.

Maize is the most important food of the Moki Indians. On the bleak, extensive plains surrounding the cliffs on which the villages are perched, there grows hardly anything but a few stunted bushes. And yet it is from this soil that the Mokis year after year reap good crops of maize. But their agriculture costs them no little trouble, and countless are the difficulties with which they must contend. They must dig deep below the surface of the ground to find a trace of moisture, and the sower therefore bores with a stick a hole 40—50 cm. deep, into which a maize kernel is dropped. Among the greatest dangers that threaten the standing corn, are the inundations following on the frequent and extremely heavy showers of rain. To prevent the crop from being swept away by the torrent which then scours the country, five or six plants are invariably set at the same spot, a greater resistance being thus offered to the current. As a protection from the violent winds that often rage, driving across the plain whirling clouds of sand, small banks of earth and stones are sometimes built. When the ears at length begin to swell and ripen, flocks of crows gather from all quarters to feast upon the corn. Now it is the Moki boys' turn to be on the alert and scare away the greedy pests. At this season whole families sometimes take up their quarters on the plain to guard the precious crop. At last the harvest-time arrives; the maize is reaped and carried up to the village, where the ears are first plucked and then piled in heaps on the floor or threaded on cords and hung to the roof. If the rain-god Oma'-a has been gracious, accepting in good part the dances instituted in his honour, and has neither been too prodigal nor too niggardly of the gifts he so often dispenses with capricious hand, the granaries are full, and the Mokis live a life of unruffled ease until the struggle against drought, against storm and rain, begins afresh with the next sowing.

When the kernels have been removed from the ear, they are ground into fine flour. They are bruised between two stones, one of which, a large, flat, and somewhat concave slab, lies on the ground, surrounded by four upright slabs, which form a kind of pan, and prevent the meal from being scattered about. Kneeling on the floor at this mill, the young girls work with all their might to bray the corn finer and finer. From the flour the skilful housewife prepares multifarious dishes. A singular sort of bread is baked in the following manner. Flour and water are mixed to a thin batter, which is spread by a few pats of the hand on a flat stone shelf, heated from below, which is constructed especially for this purpose in a corner of the room. The batter stiffens at once, forming a thin cake, which is carefully rolled up. The rolls are of a bluish black colour, the maize often belonging to a singular blue variety. I can state from my own experience that the flavour of this bread is not disagreeable, though perhaps a little insipid for lack of spices.

Maize is not the only vegetable cultivated by the Mokis. In the dry sand heaped by the storms of centuries at the foot of the mesa, grow whole orchards of peach-trees, annually yielding rich crops of fruit, which is partly boiled and eaten fresh, partly dried for winter consumption. During my visit to the villages I had my fill of dried peaches. Other vegetables cultivated are wheat, beans, tomatoes, melons, Spanish pepper, and pumpkins. Many wild plants too are laid under contribution by the Mokis. The fruit of the yucca and the Indian fig is eaten, partly raw and partly baked.

The domestic animals of the Mokis consist of horses and donkeys, used as draught cattle, sheep and goats, the flesh of which is the most important animal food, pigs, chickens, and turkeys. A Navajo Indian told me that the Mokis also eat other animals. "No like Mokis," he said, "heap dirt, eat dogs and donkeys." The Navajos, a prouder and more warlike tribe, entertain a certain contempt for their more peaceful neighbours the Mokis.

The street of a Moki village presents a diversified and lively picture. Domestic animals of miscellaneous kinds, two-legged and four-legged, run about grubbing in the refuse before the doors, and in the midst of this hubbub small naked boys are at play. On the roofs men and women, dressed in a motley of colours, sit in groups, gossiping or busied with their household duties. Eatables of all possible kinds, maize, pumpkins, pieces of dried meat, etc., lie strewn about everywhere. Dogs stroll up and down the ladders with the coolest imperturbability, and small naked children make the same experiment with less success, frantically clinging to the rungs until rescued by a mother's helping hand. Plate XVII, a photograph taken in an unguarded moment, for the Indians will not face the camera of their own free will, is a fairly accurate representation of the life in a Moki street.

Among the productions of Moki industry we first remark the textile fabrics. Both of wool and cotton they weave mantles, blankets, and rugs of artistic designs. Leggings too are knitted of wool. Cotton they formerly cultivated at home, but now they find it more convenient to buy the cloth ready-made at the store. Yucca is used in braiding mats and baskets, of which several different sorts are manufactured. Some baskets are made of thin dyed osiers, plaited in ornamental designs often representing some animal regarded as sacred. White cotton cloth is embroidered with variegated patterns; at the dances mantles of white cotton with gay-coloured borders are worn.

A kind of quilt is made of hare-skin, sewn together in long narrow strips. These quilts are laid under the bed, to render it warm and snug. They are sometimes used in winter as door-curtains to keep out the cold.

Pottery of Moki manufacture is still in extensive use, though American china has already begun to supersede the home-made ware. The potter's art is practised exclusively by the squaws. The body of the vessels consists of clay, which is first freed from all foreign substances, then kneaded with water to a paste, in which pulverised fragments of old pottery are mixed. From the plastic mass thus prepared the vessel is shaped by hand, without the aid of a potter's wheel. No implement is used other than a small bit of a gourd shell, with which the surface is constantly moistened and smoothed. When the vessel has assumed the shape desired, it is dried in the sun and afterwards polished, generally with a small flat stone. With small brushes made of the fur of the hare or yucca fibre, the ornament is applied in different colours, red and yellow (ferruginous ochre), white (kaoline), and black (charcoal?). Finally the vessel is carefully set on some small stones and covered with fuel, consisting of sheep-dung dried and compressed. The fuel is kindled, and in an hour's time the vessel is ready baked and sufficiently cool for removal from the improvised kiln.

The modern Moki ware is in every respect far inferior to the Mesa Verde pottery and to the ancient ware of these regions in general. The body is less firm, more porous, and the vessels are more fragile. The surface is dull and may be scratched with the nail, while even steel leaves no traces on the surface of some earthenware from the cliff-dwellings. The colours are different; instead of sharply prominent black patterns on a white ground, brown and reddish ornaments are painted on a ground of yellow. The tasteful, though simple ornament characteristic of the cliff-dwellers on the Mesa Verde is not seen among the Mokis. Here we find intricate, tasteless patterns of oblique and crooked lines, combined in every possible manner, and carelessly executed. Representations from the animal and vegetable worlds, so extremely rare on the ancient pottery, are much in vogue among the Mokis. Not only the ornament, but also the shape is entirely different. In this respect too simplicity and grace have given way to more complicated and tasteless

FIG. 90.   FIG. 91.

MOKI POTTERY.

designs. Instead of the simple rounded bowl we find bowls with the upper part curved outwards (fig. 93), bowls approaching to a rectangular shape, or bowls with serrated rim and furnished with a handle like a basket. The larger spherical vessels do not show the same handsome, regular, rounding as the ancient pottery. They often have a flattened form (fig. 92). Fig. 90 represents a water canteen of a type not found in the cliff-dwellings. No mugs of the singular cylindrical or conical type (Pl. XXIV: 1, 3, 4, 6) occur among the Mokis. Nor do we meet with any coiled and indented ware, answering to Group I among the pottery of the cliff-dwellers.

The ceramic art of the other inhabited pueblos in Arizona and New Mexico differs somewhat in ornamental respects from that of the Mokis, but the vessels show far greater resemblance to Moki ware than to the ancient pottery.

The original weapons of the Moki Indians were the bow and arrow. At present, however, almost all of them are armed with Winchester rifles. In hunting the rabbit a singular missile is used, a flat crooked stick, not unlike a boomerang, though it does not recoil when thrown. At the time of BOURKE's visit to the Moki villages (1881), stone axes were often employed, but at the present day they have been entirely abandoned for metal implements. Stone mills for the grinding of maize, similar to those found in the cliff-dwellings, are still in general use.

Barter is extensively carried on with the neighbouring tribes, even those at so great a distance as the Rio Grande Indians. For purposes of trade the Mokis

FIG. 92.

FIG. 93.

FIG. 94.

MOKI POTTERY.

undertake long journeys. In former times, it is said, they even made expeditions to the Pacific Ocean, in order to fetch coral and sea-shell, being absent for several years. But in general they are very reluctant to leave their homes. I once tried to persuade an old Indian to act as our guide on an excursion from the villages of some days' duration. He replied that he could not be away from his wife so long: "May be me homesick," was his apprehension.

In the treatment of diseases the Mokis have recourse to sweating baths of the same description as among other Indian tribes. The bathroom is a small and very low, conical hut, built of poles covered with earth or sand in order to keep in the steam, which is produced by pouring water over heated stones. Emetics too are often administered. In serious cases the medicine-man is consulted.

The dead are buried, according to BOURKE, at the foot of the mesa. They are wrapped in blankets, and their heads are turned to the east. GILBERT [1] states that one of the Moki chiefs informed him that the tribe interred their dead in cysts built of wood or slabs of stone. The body was laid in a sitting posture, with the hands placed close to the knees and grasping a stick, one end of which projected above the ground. By the aid of this stick the deceased was to climb out of the grave. FEWKES has observed the same method of burial. Several objects, consisting for the most part of pottery, were deposited in the grave together with the corpse.

The religion of the Moki Indians and the ceremonies, dances, etc. connected therewith, have but recently been chosen as the subject of systematic study. The Hemenway Expedition in particular, with FEWKES at its head, has made important contributions to our knowledge of this phase of Moki life. But it would lead me too far to enter into this question, and in the present work the point is of little weight, for we know next to nothing of the cliff-dwellers' religious ideas, and are thus debarred from instituting any comparisons.

CHAPTER XIV.

The Pueblo Tribes in the Sixteenth Century.

In order to form a correct judgment of the relations between the Pueblo tribes and the cliff-dwellers, it is of importance not only to study the life of these tribes in modern times, but also to investigate their customs as well as their geographical extension, at a period so far removed from the present as our historical records will admit.

Only a few decades after the discovery of America the Spaniards, spurred by insatiate lust of new conquests, of gold and riches, had penetrated to the tracts which now compose the northern portion of the Mexican Republic. From this time dates our first information [2] of the Pueblo Indians, which is based, however,

---

[1] YARROW, H. C. A Further Contribution to the Study of the Mortuary Customs of the North American Indians. First Ann. Rep. Bur. Ethn., p. 114.

[2] Before CABEZA DE VACA's travels the Spaniards had heard vague rumours of great towns to the north, by which were possibly meant the Pueblo villages. NUÑO DE GUZMAN had been told by an Indian in his service that the Indian's father had made long journeys to the north for purposes of barter, exchanging variegated feathers for gold and silver, which metals were common in those regions.

merely on statements made by other Indians to CABEZA DE VACA during his memorable journey across the North American continent. I here give a brief account of his experiences.

Most of the expeditions despatched, after the discovery of Florida by PONCE DE LEON, to explore the coasts of the new country, disastrously failed. PANFILO DE NARVAEZ' squadron of five ships and 600 men, equipped for the subjugation of Florida to the Spanish crown, shared in the general fate.

After numerous adventures the coast of Florida was reached on the 11th of April, 1528. Here NARVAEZ parted from his fleet, which he never succeeded in regaining. With 300 men he advanced, first by land and afterwards in boats along the coast of the Gulf of Mexico, probably beyond the mouth of the Mississippi. At this juncture all the boats were wrecked; their crews, already thinned by want and hardships, perished with the exception of a few men, four of whom succeeded after a long captivity among different Indian tribes, in joining each other and making their escape. These four were CABEZA DE VACA, who had been *alguazil mayor* under NARVAEZ, ANDRES DORANTES, CASTILLO MALDONADO, and a negro named ESTEVANICO. They forced their way from one Indian tribe to another, and thanks to their success in achieving a reputation as great medicine-men, they were everywhere received with awe and reverence. In this manner they gradually approached the Spanish settlements on the Pacific coast, where they arrived in 1536, their travels having thus lasted eight years from beginning to end. From the accounts of the journey which have survived to the present day, it is impossible to ascertain the exact route followed. The Rio Grande was probably crossed far south of the Pueblo villages. We are indeed told [1] that the travellers met with Indians who had permanent domiciles (*maisons fixes*), and who wore cotton garments. But their houses were built of earth or rushes. These Indians could, however, give particulars of lofty mountains to the north, from which they procured emeralds and turquoises, and which were densely populated, the people sometimes living in very large houses. These tales refer, beyond doubt, to the Pueblo Indians. The Indians with fixed habitations who were visited belonged to other tribes, and like the modern Pimas and Maricopas, cultivated maize and had permanent dwellings, similar in appearance, however, to ordinary Indian huts.

CABEZA DE VACA and his companions reported to the Mexican Viceroy ANTONIO DE MENDOZA, the information they had received from the Indians of great and

---

On one or two of these expeditions he had accompanied his father, and had then seen towns so large that they might be compared to Mexico, the suburbs included. It was this tale that induced NUÑO DE GUZMAN, at the head of a powerful army, to march northwards and explore the country, an undertaking attended with no results worthy of mention, except the foundation of San Miguel de Culiacan (CASTAÑEDA, Relation, p. 1). This is probably the origin of the tales regarding the *Septem Civitates*, a fiction which was so often repeated in subsequent times, and which played an important part in the history of discovery.

[1] Relation et Naufrages d'ALVAR NUÑEZ CABEÇA DE VACA. TERNAUX-COMPANS, Sér. 1: Tom. VII, p. 243.

powerful towns north of their route.[1] The Viceroy communicated the intelligence
to the governor of Nueva Galicia, FRANCISCO VASQUEZ DE CORONADO, who at once
repaired to Culiacan, and despatched MARCOS DE NIZA, a Franciscan friar, in quest
of the famous towns. NIZA was accompanied by another friar ONORATO and the
negro ESTEVANICO who had attended CABEZA DE VACA on his travels.[2] On the 7th
of March, 1539 they started from San Miguel de Culiacan, a Spanish colony on
the Gulf of California.

At Petatlan ONORATO fell ill, and had to be left behind. NIZA continued the
journey with his negro companion. They met with a good reception everywhere.
The 25—30 leagues[3] between Petatlan and the desert were covered without any
noteworthy adventures. They came across Indians from a supposed island in the
Gulf of California which had been visited by CORTEZ in 1533. Their route then
lay for four days across a desert. At the end of the desert they came to Indians
who had never seen or heard of the Spaniards, and who therefore regarded them
with astonishment. Still their reception was friendly. The Indians were questioned
as to their knowledge of the great towns to the north. They stated that in the
interior, four or five days' march from the point where the mountain ranges began
to slope ("at the foot of the mountains" according to HAKLUYT), there lay on a
very extensive plain a considerable number of large towns, the inhabitants of which
were dressed in cotton cloth. NIZA also showed the Indians some articles made of
various metals. They took the gold and remarked that the inhabitants of the said
towns had vessels of this substance, that they wore in their nose and ears round
objects of gold, and that they had small scrapers of the same metal, with which
they cleansed their skin of sweat. But it was said that this densely populated plain
lay far from the sea, and NIZA was unwilling to leave the coast; he therefore determined to visit the locality on his way back.

For three days they advanced through a country inhabited by the same
hospitable Indians. They arrived at a town named Vacapa. Here NIZA halted for
a time, and despatched Indians by three different routes to the coast, which was
said to be only 40 leagues distant. ESTEVAN the negro was sent on ahead to the
north. NIZA and he had agreed that if the latter ascertained beyond doubt that
there really lay rich, inhabited tracts in this quarter, he should not proceed alone,
but should either return or send Indian messengers with a cross. If the country
were of moderate size, the cross should be white and a palm long. If it were of
considerable extent, the cross should be two palms long, and if it were greater than
New Spain, the sign should be a large cross. Four days after ESTEVAN's departure

---

[1] CASTAÑEDA, Relation, p. 9.
[2] The account of NIZA's expedition is taken from: Relation de Frère MARCOS DE NIZA. TERNAUX-
COMPANS. Sér. 1: T. IX, p. 256. I have also looked through HAKLUYT's English version (A relation
of the reuerend father Frier *Marco de Niça* etc. HAKLUYT, RICHARD. Voyages, Navigations etc.,
Vol. III, London, 1600, p. 366) of the same narrative; this relation differs only in a few details
from the former.
[3] A Spanish league (*legua*) = 5 1/2 kilometres (SIMPSON).

from Vacapa the messengers arrived with a cross as large as a man. They brought word from ESTEVAN, urging NIZA to follow with all speed in his line of march, and stating that he had found people who had told him of a country, the largest in the world. The Indian sent by ESTEVAN had also much to relate of Cibola. From ESTEVAN's present position to the first town was thirty days' journey.

NIZA considered himself, however, in duty bound to await the natives whom he had despatched to the coast. They returned soon afterwards, accompanied by some of the coast Indians. At the same time NIZA was visited by three Indians belonging to a tribe called Pintados, and tattooed on the face, breast, and arms. They lived farther east, some of them in the neighbourhood of the Seven Cities, of which they gave in the main the same information as NIZA had received through ESTE-VAN. In company with these Indians NIZA left Vacapa. New messengers from ESTEVAN met him, bringing another cross as large as the first, and exhorting him to follow with promptitude. The land to which they were bound was the most wonderful ever heard of. After three days' march NIZA reached the Indians who had told ESTEVAN of the seven towns which they had visited. They repeated that it was thirty days' march to Cibola, adding that besides the Seven Cities there were three other kingdoms called Marata, Acus, and Totonteac. To the question why they had wandered so far from their homes, they answered that they had been to Cibola to fetch turquoises and other objects which the Cibolans possessed in abundance. They had been set to till the ground and perform other labour, for which they were paid in buffalo hide[1] and turquoises. Handsome turquoises were worn as personal ornaments in the nose and ears, and the principal gates of Cibola were adorned with these stones. The inhabitants were dressed in a long shirt of cotton cloth, reaching down to the feet, and buttoned round the throat; at the waist it was fastened with a belt of turquoises. Over the robe a mantle of buffalo hide was often worn.

After another day's journey NIZA arrived at a village where he was very hospitably received. Here ESTEVAN had left a third cross, in token that the news of Cibola had gained in definiteness. For five days NIZA continued his march, everywhere received with friendship and with new and still more marvellous descriptions of Cibola. The natives stated that the route now lay for four days across a desert. Before reaching the desert, however, a visit was paid to another village, where important information of Cibola was obtained. NIZA was dressed in a suit of gray cloth, which attracted the attention of the natives. They asserted that there was plenty of similar stuff in Totonteac, and that the inhabitants used it in making articles of clothing. When NIZA questioned the truth of this, he was answered: "Do you suppose that we are ignorant that this cloth is different from our own? You will find that at Cibola all the houses are full of the same cloth as we wear; but in Totonteac there are small animals which afford material for the manufacture

---

[1] "Cuirs de vaches."

of this fabric." Of these animals they further related that they were as large as either of the two greyhounds which ESTEVAN had with him. They were plentiful in Totonteac.

In the course of the next four days the desert was crossed, and the travellers now reached a densely populated valley. The inhabitants wore ornaments of turquoise and mantles of buffalo hide. They were well acquainted with Cibola, and supplied NIZA with a number of details as to the appearance of the buildings etc. When he told them it was impossible that the houses were such as they described them, in order to convince him they took ashes and earth, which they moistened, and then showed how the walls were erected by laying stone on stone with mortar between.

For five days[1] the march was continued along the same valley, which had a numerous population. The villages were situated at a distance of a quarter of a league or half a league from each other. Everywhere intelligence was obtained of Cibola. The travellers even met with a native of that town who said that he had fled from the person whom the chief of the Seven Cities had appointed to supersede him at Cibola. This chief resided at Ahacus. To the other towns he sent deputies, who governed in his name. The man from Cibola was handsome in appearance and much more intelligent than the inhabitants of the valley and the surrounding country. Of Cibola he gave NIZA further information: "It was a large town with a very numerous population; of streets and open places there were plenty; in some quarters there were very large houses, with as many as ten stories, where the chiefs held meetings at appointed times. The houses were of stone and mortar, as the first Indians had stated; the entrances and facades of turquoise. The other seven (six?) towns were built in the same manner; some of them were still larger; the most important was Ahacus."

He went on to relate that to the south-east there was a kingdom, Marata, which was densely peopled. The inhabitants had been and still were at war with the ruler of the Seven Cities. This war had much weakened the resources of Marata, but the kingdom was still powerful and could hold its own. To the west, he added, lay the kingdom of Totonteac, which was one of the mightiest states in the world, thickly populated and very wealthy. The people were dressed in cloth like that worn by NIZA; nay, there was even still more handsome stuff. The material was obtained from animals such as those previously described to him. The inhabitants were highly civilised and quite different from the natives he had already seen. According to this Indian there was another very extensive kingdom, named Acus

---

[1] NIZA tells us in his narrative of the journey, before giving an account of the continuation of the march up the valley, that he learnt of the Indians that the coast-line ran due north, and that he personally investigated the truth of this assertion: "Comme il était très-important de côtoyer dans cette direction, je voulus m'en assurer par mes yeux. Je partis donc pour la rechercher, et je vis clairement qu'à la hauteur de trente-cinq degrés elle tourne à l'ouest." This statement must depend on some mistake.

(not Ahacus, which was the name of the capital of the Seven Cities). Of the Cibolans he further stated that they slept in beds raised above the ground and made of cloth; these beds were covered with canopies.

For three days NIZA advanced along the same valley. The natives continued to give him a friendly reception and confirmed what he had previously been told of Cibola and the other great kingdoms. At one place in the same tract NIZA was shown "a skin half as large again as a buffalo hide; it was said to belong to an animal which had only one horn on the forehead. The horn was bent down to the breast and then turned up in a sharp point, which gives the animal such strength that it can break to pieces any object whatsoever." These animals were stated to be very common farther north. The colour was like that of goatskin, and the hair was of a finger's length.

NIZA now received from ESTEVAN, who was still hastening on in advance, further intelligence to the effect that he was on his way through the last desert, that he was highly satisfied, and believed that the goal of the journey was a very great country. As yet he had never detected the Indians in falsehood, but had always found the country to be such as they had described it. NIZA concurred in this opinion, and therefore concluded that the case must be the same with Cibola.

NIZA was now only four leagues (four days according to HAKLUYT) away from the desert which still separated him from Cibola. From the beginning of the desert to Cibola was fully 15 days' journey. ESTEVAN had already set out, accompanied by a troop of more than 300 Indians, who acted as an escort and conveyed provisions. The Indians also offered their services to NIZA, and after three days' preparations a start was made. During these three days NIZA had gathered additional information of Cibola from a number of different Indians, whose versions invariably coincided with what he had previously learnt.

On the 9th of May NIZA began his march through the desert. In several places he found the remains of huts and the traces of camp fires, showing that the Indians often employed this route to Cibola. The journey had lasted twelve days, when he met an Indian of ESTEVAN's escort. His appearance was pitiable, and he was bathed in sweat. His whole bearing indicated great mental distress. He made the following statement: "The day before his arrival at Cibola ESTEVAN according to his usual custom, sent messengers with his gourd, to announce his approach. To this gourd were attached a string of bells and two feathers, one white, the other red. When the messengers were brought into the presence of the chief who acted as the king's representative at Cibola, they gave him the gourd. He took it, but on seeing the bells flew into a passion of rage, cast it on the ground, and dismissed the messengers, saying that he knew these strangers, that they had better warn them not to enter the town. If they did so, he would put them all to death. The messengers returned, and gave an account of their reception to ESTEVAN. He replied that this meant nothing, and that the people who showed displeasure at his approach always received him better than others did. He continued his march to Cibola. On the point of entering the town, he was met by Indians who opposed his passage. They conducted him to a large building situated outside the walls, and at once plundered him of all his effects, including articles for barter, turquoises and many other presents which he had received on the route. He passed the night in this building, neither he nor his followers being supplied with any food or drink. Next morning the relater felt thirsty, and left the building to drink at a neighbouring brook. Shortly afterwards he saw ESTEVAN in flight, pursued by the inhabitants of the town, who were killing his native companions. As soon as he noticed this, the Indian followed the course of the brook, concealing himself from sight, and retraced his steps across the desert."

These particulars caused great dismay among NIZA's Indian followers. He endeavoured to console them, he distributed among the chiefs part of the cloth and other commodities which he had brought with him. The whole company then proceeded, and at length were only a day's journey from Cibola. Here they met two other Indians who had been with ESTEVAN. They were bleeding and covered with wounds. When they had somewhat recovered from their panic, they told their tale, which agreed in the main with the first Indian's version. ESTEVAN had been conveyed to a large house outside the town. On the morning after his arrival he went out, accompanied by some of the chiefs in his train, when a great crowd of Cibolans at once appeared. On seeing them ESTEVAN and his Indians immediately took to flight. But a shower of arrows hurtled about their ears, the Cibolans raised a battle-cry and rushed in pursuit. The narrators had barely effected their escape. They had heard loud cries from the town, and seen a multitude of people standing on the terraces. They saw no more of ESTEVAN, but supposed that he had been killed by an arrow, like all his companions except the two bearers of the news.

NIZA was utterly crushed by this intelligence. Some one gave him a hint that his followers, laying the blame of their countrymen's death on his shoulders, intended to kill him. In order to reconcile them, he distributed among them all the remaining merchandise. Before commencing the return journey, however, he advanced, escorted by a few Indians, until he could see Cibola. The town was situated on the slope of a rounded knoll, and was handsome indeed; it was the largest NIZA had seen in these regions, and in size even surpassed Mexico. The houses, as the Indians had said, were built in several stories, rising in terraces one above another. "In my opinion," says NIZA, "this is the greatest and the best country hitherto discovered."

On the spot from which NIZA had viewed Cibola, he piled a high cairn, erected a cross on the top, and solemnly took possession of the Seven Cities and the kingdoms of Totonteac, Acus, and Marata, under the name of "Nuevo Regno de San Francisco."

The retreat was made with headlong haste, and "with more panic than provisions." NIZA soon reached San Miguel, and then went on to Compostela, where he reported his adventures to CORONADO, the governor of Nueva Galicia.

The above sketch of NIZA's journey is taken from his own account thereof. The description of Cibola is based on hearsay and the statements of natives and of neighbours to Cibola, not on personal observation; and it contains numerous exaggerations. But apart from these it affords a fairly correct idea of the most characteristic features of the pueblos and their inhabitants, as described by later writers. That the city visited by ESTEVAN was really the famous Cibola afterwards taken by CORONADO, seems probable from the mere fact that NIZA accompanied CORONADO, without any doubt being expressed on this head either by the leader of the expedition or anyone else. The version given by CASTAÑEDA, the historian of CORONADO's expedition, of the negro's arrival at Cibola,[1] differs in some points from NIZA's account, and contains some details which the latter purposely omits. He relates that ESTEVAN the negro came to Cibola, bringing with him a great quantity of turquoises and some beautiful women, presents which he had received on the route. He had besides a numerous train of Indians, who believed that in his company they could march the whole world through. But the Cibolans were suspicious, and imprisoned ESTEVAN in a house outside the village. Here he was interrogated by the elders and chiefs as to the object which had brought him to their country. After an inquiry lasting three days, they assembled to decide his fate. As the negro had told the Indians that he was the forerunner of two white men, the emissaries of a mighty prince, they thought him to be the guide or spy of some nation who had designs of subjugating them. Above all they considered it improbable that he, a black, should be the messenger of white men. ESTEVAN had coveted their wealth and their women, but it seemed hard to acquiesce in this. They accordingly determined to put him to death, and did so, without harming his followers in any way. The latter returned to NIZA, who was then 60 leagues from Cibola. He was so terrified by the news of ESTEVAN's death that, mistrusting the Indians, he at once distributed among them all his effects. Then the retreat was commenced by forced marches, without NIZA's seeing a glimpse of the wonderful town. NIZA's assertion that he saw the city with his own eyes, is probably a mere invention, as well as his statement that, after passing the first desert on his way to Cibola, he went in person to the coast, in order to investigate the truth of the information given him on this head by the natives.

When CORONADO returned to Culiacan from his expedition in search of Topiza, a kingdom situated, according to the Indians, north of the Spanish colony, he met NIZA, who described his march in such lively colours, relating the negro's discoveries and telling of the great riches which the Indians had said might be procured from

---

[1] CASTAÑEDA, Relation, p. 12.

the Southern Sea, that CORONADO immediately made up his mind to go to Mexico, taking NIZA with him, so that the latter might give the Viceroy a personal account of all he had seen. By disclosing the discovery to his most intimate friends alone and only under a promise of secrecy, he led people to over-estimate its importance. At Mexico he had an audience of the Viceroy. He proclaimed everywhere that he had discovered the Seven Cities sought for in vain by NUÑO DE GUZMAN, and that he was mustering troops for their conquest. Father MARCOS was elected provincial by the members of his order; he should serve as a guide. Noblemen of the best families hastened to join CORONADO's army. In a few days he had collected 300 Spaniards and 800 Indians. FRANCISCO VASQUEZ DE CORONADO himself was appointed commander-in-chief by the Viceroy. The army assembled at Compostela, the capital of Nueva Galicia, in the spring of 1540, and marched first to Chiametla and then to Culiacan.[1]

Before commencing the description of CORONADO's march from Culiacan to Cibola, I will say a few words of an expedition which, though it did not penetrate to the renowned Seven Cities, added several particulars to the knowledge of their inhabitants. Simultaneously with the departure of CORONADO and NIZA from Culiacan in order to report to the Viceroy, the latter had commanded Captains MELCHIOR DIAZ and JUAN DE SALDIVAR to set out and explore the country visited by Father MARCOS.[2] They started on the 17th of November, 1539, accompanied by fifteen men, and penetrated to Chichilticale, "situated at the beginning of the desert and at a distance of 200 leagues from Culiacan." Without making any noteworthy discovery, they returned and at Chiametla met CORONADO's army, which was just about to leave. Though they could not recount any personal observations of Cibola, they had obtained from the natives on their line of march certain information, which the Viceroy, having received a letter from DIAZ, communicated to CHARLES V. The main purport of DIAZ' statements is as follows:

"On crossing the great desert the traveller finds seven towns within about a day's journey of each other; they are collectively called Civola. The houses are roughly constructed of stone and mortar. They consist of a long wall fringed on each side with rooms twenty feet square and partitioned by cross walls. The roof is supported by beams. An entrance into these houses is gained by ladders from the street; the buildings are three or four stories high. The stories are more than nine feet high, except the ground floor, the height of which is hardly more than

---

[1] The account of CORONADO's expedition is chiefly taken from CASTAÑEDA's relation (quoted on p. 95), which supplies us from all accessible sources with most of the details touching the inhabitants of the newly discovered countries etc., and which gives the impression of great veracity. I have further consulted the following authorities:

JUAN JARAMILLO. Relation du Voyage fait à la Nouvelle-Terre. TERNAUX-COMPANS, Sér. 1: T. IX, p. 364.

The relation of *Francis Vazquez de Coronado.* HAKLUYT, Voyages, Vol. III, p. 373.

[2] Lettres de Don ANTONIO DE MENDOZA à l'empereur CHARLES V. TERNAUX-COMPANS, Sér. 1: T. IX, p. 292.

Another flex burial en situ. The position of buried bodies is of particular interest to anthropologists; gravesites often reveal important information. Photo courtesy MVNP.

A semi-extended burial; only the knees of this body were flexed. This skeleton en situ reveals a lack of consistency in funerary and interment ceremonies. Photo courtesy MVNP.

A Cliff Dweller "dog" jar, intact, highly decorated and quite rare. Some aborigine had a good imagination and an artistic bent to create such an item. Photo courtesy MVNP.

Another interesting and rare type of pot — a square vessell with a square opening, and beautifully ornamented. This may have been a ceremonial pot. Photo courtesy MVNP.

a fathom. From ten to twenty houses have one ladder in common; the lower stories are used for various domestic purposes, the living rooms being situated on the upper floors. The walls of the ground floor are obliquely pierced with loopholes, as in Spanish forts. The Indians say that, when they attack the inhabitants of Civola, the latter shut themselves up in their houses, and then defend themselves. When the Civolans go on the war-path, they carry round shields and wear a dress of dyed cowhide (buffalo hide). They fight with arrows, small stone clubs, and wooden weapons of which I could procure no explanation.[1] They are cannibals, and use their prisoners as slaves. They have much poultry of a kind peculiar to the country,[2] great quantities of beans and maize, and melons. They breed in their houses furry animals as large as Spanish dogs. They shear these creatures, and make the hair into dyed head-dresses and also into cloth. The men are small, the women white. Their demeanour is graceful. Their dress consists of a shirt reaching to the feet. They part their hair, combing it to the sides so as to leave the ears free.[3] In their hair, round their necks, and on their arms, they fasten numbers of turquoises. The men are dressed in mantles, and over these they wear buffalo hides like those used by CABEZA DE VACA and DORANTES. Their heads are covered with a kind of cap. In summer they wear leather shoes adorned with painted designs or dyed. In winter they are shod with high boots (*brodequins*) of the same material.

"I have not succeeded in tracing the use of any metal, nor do they speak of any metal implements. They have turquoises in plenty, though not in such abundance as the Father Provincial stated. They possess small crystal stones like those which I sent to Your Highness. They till the ground as in New Spain; they carry burdens on the head, as in Mexico. The men weave cloth and spin cotton. They season their food with salt, which they procure from a lake two days' journey from Civola. The Indians accompany their songs and dances with flutes, marks on the instrument indicating the places where the fingers should be set.[4] They are very fond of music.

"The soil is good for maize, beans, and other kinds of corn. They know nothing of saltwater fish. They have no cows, but are aware that such animals exist.[5] Farther in the interior of the country there are a great number of wild goats, which in colour resemble light gray horses. The Indians say that the Seven Cities include three very large communities and four of smaller size. As far as I could understand from their gestures each of these towns is three bowshots square.

"Totonteac lies about seven days' easy journey from Civola. The country, the houses, and the people are of the same appearance as in Civola. Cotton was said to grow there as well, but I doubt this, for the climate is cold. Totonteac was stated to contain twelve towns, each one of them greater than the largest in Civola.

---

[1] Perhaps the throwing-stick still employed by the Mokis.
[2] Tame turkeys were kept by the cliff-dwellers, and are still bred by the Mokis (see p. 95).
[3] Probably with a reference to the singular coiffure still to be seen among the young Moki girls.
[4] Possibly of the same sort as the flute from Spring House (fig. 64).
[5] Buffaloes are meant.

"A day's journey from the last province is a town the inhabitants of which are at war with each other. Both the houses and their inhabitants resemble those of Totonteac. This town, they assured me, was the largest of all."

In conclusion a few words are added of the negro ESTEVAN, to the effect that he had been killed as stated by NIZA. The inhabitants of Civola had sent the following message to the neighbouring tribes: "If the Christians come, you shall not receive them, but shall put them to death; we know that the Christians are mortal, we have in our possession the bones of the man who came to us; if you dare not do so, you need only send for us, we will come at once and kill them."

Of the natives met with on the way, DIAZ says that they had no fixed habitations, except in a valley situated 150 leagues from Culiacan and densely populated. Here there were houses built of earth, and many natives were seen, "from whom no profit, however, can be gained, save to make them Christians."

NIZA's and DIAZ' accounts of the great towns in the north are based, as mentioned above, merely on the statements of Indians. Not before CORONADO's expedition did the Spaniards obtain authentic descriptions of the Pueblo Indians' remarkable villages. NIZA's tale proved to have been not a little exaggerated.

I now return to CORONADO's march, following the narrative of CASTAÑEDA. As I have mentioned, the army advanced from Chiametla to Culiacan, where a halt of some duration was made.[1] With a small troop CORONADO pushed on ahead to Chichilticale on the outskirts of the desert.[2] Chichilticale turned out to be a ruined house without roof. From this place he marched in a fortnight to a point eight leagues from Cibola. The following night Cibola was only two leagues away, and the next morning they caught sight of the first Indian town. But what a disappointment! Instead of a great and wealthy city they beheld a wretched village. The soldiers burst into open threats against NIZA. "The village was so insignificant that in New Spain there were farmhouses of greater size." It was estimated to contain 200 warriors, and was built on a cliff. The houses had three or four stories, but were small and incommodious, without separate courtyards. A single courtyard was allotted to a whole quarter. Cibola belonged to a province consisting of seven towns; some of them were more important and better fortified than Cibola.[3]

---

[1] Almost at the same time as CORONADO started, HERNANDO ALARCON sailed on a coasting voyage of discovery to the north; it was his intention to follow CORONADO's army by sea. ALARCON penetrated to the head of the Gulf of California, and even sailed up the Rio Colorado, probably to the neighbourhood of the mouth of the Rio Gila. From the natives he procured information of Cibola. But his relation is of little interest for the studies to which the present work is devoted. (Relation de la Navigation .... faite par FERNANDO ALARCON. TERNAUX-COMPANS, Sér. 1: T. IX, p. 335.)

[2] Several attempts have been made to ascertain from the existing accounts of CORONADO's march the route which he followed. Most of the details on this head are to be found in JARAMILLO's narrative (see the note on p. 152). It is too lengthy an undertaking for the scope of the present work to enter in detail into this question, which has already been discussed in an able manner by SIMPSON. I shall therefore refer the reader to his work (SIMPSON, J. H. CORONADO's March in Search of the "Seven Cities of Cibola" .... Smith. Rep. 1869, Wash. 1871, p. 309).

[3] Cibola is identical with the modern Zuñi.

As the inhabitants of Cibola, who had collected at some distance from the village, paid no attention to the Spaniards' friendly overtures, the signal was given for attack, and the Indians were quickly put to flight. It still remained, however, to take Cibola, a difficult task, for the approach was narrow and tortuous. But in less than an hour the village was stormed. Provisions were found there in plenty, a very welcome booty to Coronado's men.

The main army had meanwhile advanced from Culiacan to Sonora, where it awaited Coronado's orders. He sent word from Cibola that the army should march to join him. The junction was accomplished, the journey to Cibola being performed without adventure.

While Coronado was waiting for the main army, he endeavoured to gain information from the natives with respect to the neighbouring countries. They said that there was a province with seven towns like their own. Its name was Tusayan, and it was 25 leagues distant from Cibola.[1] Coronado despatched Don Pedro de Tobar in search of these towns. He was accompanied by seventeen cavalry, three or four foot-soldiers, and a Franciscan friar. They reached Tusayan at night and were not observed by the Indians until morning, when the natives marched against them, armed with arrows, clubs, and shields. The Spaniards called upon them through interpreters to surrender, but they drew a line on the ground and forbade the Spaniards to cross the line. The latter, however, charged upon the Indians, killing a great number of them. The survivors dispersed and fled towards the village, but soon returned, begging for mercy and bringing presents. Hostilities were abandoned, and the villages were handed over to the Spaniards. The Indians now told them of a great river, adding that if they followed the river in its downward course for some days, they would find a people of a very great stature.

On the accomplishment of his commission, however, Don Pedro de Tobar returned to Cibola, and reported what he had seen to Coronado. The general at once sent Don Garcia Lopez de Cardenas with twelve followers to explore the river spoken of by the Indians. Cardenas was well received in Tusayan. He then proceeded westwards, and after twenty days' march came to a river the banks of which were so high that the Spaniards supposed themselves to be three or four leagues up in the air.[2] For several days they tried in vain to discover a path down to the river, and even made a fruitless attempt to descend the cliffs. After three or four days' march their Indian guides declared that it was impossible to advance further, for they would find no water for four days. When the Indians made this journey, they were accompanied by their wives, carrying gourds full of water. Some of these gourds were buried on the route, for use on the return journey. On their way back the Spaniards came to a waterfall rushing down a precipice. The guides said that the white crystals hanging from the rocks hard by were composed of salt.

---

[1] Tusayan is identical with the Moki villages.
[2] The Grand Cañon is undoubtedly meant.

While these explorations were being made, there arrived at Cibola some Indians from a village situated 70 leagues to the east, in a province named Cicuye. They brought presents for the Spaniards, and said that they desired the preservation of peace. They further described the cows[1] to be found in their country. "It was evident," says CASTAÑEDA, "that they were cows, for one of the Indians had a painting on his body, representing one of these animals. None could have conjectured this from seeing the hides, which were covered with woolly and curly hair like sheep's wool."

HERNANDO DE ALVARADO received orders to accompany the Indians with twenty men to the country of the buffaloes and to return within eighty days. After five days' march he reached a village named Acuco and built on a cliff.[2] The inhabitants, who could muster about two hundred warriors, are dreaded throughout the province for their plundering propensities. This village was very well fortified by nature, for there was only one way of approach. It was built on the crest of a precipice so high that a musket ball could scarcely reach the top. The only path to the village was carved by human agency in the rock. Towards the summit this path or stairway was so steep that the climber must cling fast with both hands. At the very brink of the cliff lay a heap of large stones, which might easily be precipitated on the head of a venturous enemy, so that not even the strongest army could have taken this fastness. The plateau afforded sufficient space for the sowing of a considerable quantity of maize and for the construction of cisterns to collect water and snow. The Indians received at first the Spaniards with hostile manifestations, but when they saw them advancing to the assault, they sued for mercy.

After three days more ALVARADO came to a province called Tiguex. Here the Indians were peaceably disposed, and ALVARADO sent messengers to the general, inviting him to come and winter in this country. At a distance of five days' march lay Cicuye, a well fortified village of four-storied houses.[3] The inhabitants received the Spaniards with lavish demonstrations of rejoicing, conducting them up to the village to the music of drums and flutes. Presents of cloth and turquoises cemented the friendship. Here the Spaniards rested for some days, during which time an Indian, to whom they gave the name of the Turk (*el Turco*), regaled them with highly exaggerated tales of great towns, of gold and riches, possessed by his countrymen. This induced ALVARADO, after marching far enough to see some of the famous buffaloes, the discovery of which was the object of his mission, to return and bring the good news to CORONADO. He halted, however, in Tiguex and awaited CORONADO's coming. Here the natives spoke of numerous villages to the north.

---

[1] Buffaloes.

[2] Identical with Acoma.

[3] Cicuye was probably situated on the Rio Pecos, east of the Rio Grande. Tiguex and most of the towns mentioned below are represented at the present day by pueblos or pueblo ruins on the latter river or its tributaries, though it is often impossible to identify the several villages.

Meanwhile the main army had reached Cibola. Immediately on its arrival CORONADO, who had been told of a province containing eight villages, equipped a troop of thirty men and marched to explore this province. The army was to rest for twenty days and then proceed straight to Tiguex. After eight days' march he reached Tutahaco, the goal of his expedition. The Indians informed him here of several other villages farther down the river[1] on which their own town lay. But CORONADO marched instead up the river to Tiguex, where he met ALVARADO. The latter communicated to him the inspiriting tale of the Turk, who repeated his exaggerated descriptions of his country's fabulous wealth.

In the meantime the main army, in obedience to CORONADO's orders, had commenced their march to Tiguex. The first night they encamped in a village, the most handsome, the best, and the largest in the whole province. There were houses with seven stories, the only instance hereof; these buildings served as fortresses and resembled towers. During the army's stay here snow began to fall, and the soldiers took shelter under the village roofs (*alaves*), which jutted out like balconies, resting on wooden pillars. Ladders were used to reach these roofs, and the rooms were entered from the latter, there being no doorways in the wall of the ground floor. — After ten days' march the army entered Tiguex. The entire province was in an uproar, for the Spaniards had just burnt a whole village to the ground. The first cause of discontent was that CORONADO, on some pretext or other, had arrested BIGOTES, a chief in the province of Cicuye. Shameless extortions and other acts of injustice contributed to provoke the natives, who rose in revolt and retired to their fortified villages. After many fierce battles, in which the Indians often fought with great valour, the Spaniards at last succeeded in reducing to submission the province of Tiguex. One village held out for fifty days, and even then surrendered only because most of the Indians had been forced for lack of water to quit their posts. These events took place at the end of 1540.

During the war in Tiguex CORONADO had paid a visit to Cicuye, and had pacified the natives by a conditional engagement to restore to them their chieftain BIGOTES. On the conclusion of the war he sent one of his officers to Chia, which had promised submission. This place was a populous village, situated four leagues west of the river. Six other Spaniards were despatched to Quirix, a province containing seven villages. In this manner the whole country was gradually appeased, the inhabitants of Tiguex alone still cherishing a distrust of the Spaniards. CORONADO awaited only the breaking up of the ice on the river to pursue his march to Quivira, the country where, according to the Turk, gold and silver were to be found, though not in such abundance as in some other places named by this person. On the 5th of May, 1541 the army left Tiguex and marched to Cicuye, a distance of 25 leagues. BIGOTES, who had been set at liberty, accompanied the army. Four

---

[1] The Rio Grande.

days' journey beyond Cicuye they reached a large and very deep river which flowed past Cicuye as well, and to which they therefore gave the name of the Rio de Cicuye. They were forced to halt and build a bridge. Ten days after crossing the river they sighted some Indian huts. The inhabitants of this country were called Querechos and lived like Arabs, dwelling in tents of buffalo hide and hunting the buffalo.

The Spaniards had thus quitted the country of the Pueblo Indians. The last village to the east was Cicuye, which is probably represented in modern maps by Pecos, a village deserted by its inhabitants at the middle of the present century. The eastward extension of the Pueblo tribes was consequently about the same as in our times.

Touching the situation of the other villages I have given in the notes the modern pueblos most probably answering to some of them. Here I have followed BANDELIER,[1] to whose erudite work I may refer the reader especially interested in this question. For the studies to which the present work is devoted, most attention must be paid to the descriptions which treat of the Pueblo Indians' customs, or from which conclusions may be drawn as to the geographical extension of these tribes in the earliest historic times. With this object in view it is less important to endeavour with certainty to identify each single village. For the same reason I also omit CASTAÑEDA's account of the journey to Quivira, which lay far beyond the boundaries of the Pueblo country.

Scarcity of provisions had induced CORONADO on the way to Quivira to send back most of his followers and to continue the march with a few men. Immediately on arriving at Tiguex, Don TRISTAN DE ARELLANO, the leader of the retreat, despatched FRANCISCO DE BARRIO-NUEVO with a few soldiers along the river[2] to the north. Two provinces were visited, one, Hemes, consisting of seven villages, the other named Yunque-Yunque. The Indians in Hemes submitted; but the inhabitants of Yunque-Yunque fled to the mountains, abandoning two fine villages situated on the banks of the river, and taking refuge in four others, which were fortified and extremely difficult of access.[3] These villages could not be approached on horseback. In the two deserted villages they found plenty of provisions and very handsome pottery, well glazed and richly ornamented. They saw too large jars full of a bright metal, which was used in glazing this *faience*.

Twenty leagues farther up the river lay a large and powerful village named Braba; the Spaniards called it Valladolid. It was built on both sides of the river, which was crossed on bridges constructed of pine beams very well dressed. In this village they saw estufas larger and more remarkable than anywhere else in the whole country. The estufas were supported by twelve pillars, each two fathoms (*brasses*)

---

[1] BANDELIER, A. F. Historical Introduction to Studies among the Sedentary Indians of New Mexico. Papers Arch. Inst. of Am., Am. Ser. I, Boston 1883, p. 3.

[2] The Rio Grande.

[3] Possibly a reference to the cliff-dwellings, where the population sought refuge at the approach of danger.

in circumference and two fathoms (*toises*) high. ALVARADO had already visited this village on his march in quest of Cicuye. From this place BARRIO-NUEVO returned to camp.

Another officer followed the river downwards, in order to explore some other watercourses situated in that quarter. He marched 80 leagues, discovered four large villages, which submitted, and reached a place where the river sinks into the ground. He did not advance to the place where, according to the Indians, the river again emerges, larger than at its disappearance. On the return of this officer to Tiguex, Don TRISTAN marched east in search of CORONADO, as the latter had not come back from Quivira at the time agreed upon. In Cicuye he was attacked by the inhabitants and thus detained for four days, during which period he learnt that CORONADO was on his way back and therefore abandoned the march. CORONADO shortly arrived, after an unsuccessful search for the gold and riches of which he had heard so much. From Cicuye he marched at once to Tiguex, where he decided to winter, intending to renew his explorations of the interior in the spring.

Here ends the first part of CASTAÑEDA's narrative. He breaks off his account of the course of events to give in the second part a description of the countries and peoples visited during the above expeditions. This description is of such interest that I here append a literal translation of those parts thereof which relate to the Pueblo Indians. After describing Culiacan, the northernmost town in Nueva Galicia, and the countries lying between this place and Chichilticale, a name by which is meant, it is supposed, the ruin situated on the Rio Gila and now known as the Casa Grande (see above, p. 131), CASTAÑEDA proceeds:

Chapter III.

Of Chichilticale and the Desert of Cibola. — Of the manners and customs of the inhabitants.

"The name of Chichilticale was given in former times to this place because the friars found in the neighbourhood a house which had long been inhabited by a people who came from Cibola. The soil of this country is red; the house was large, it seemed to have served as a fortress. It appears to have been destroyed in olden times by the natives, who are the most barbarous nation yet found in these regions. These Indians live in isolated huts, and support themselves merely by hunting; all the rest of the country is waste and covered with pine forests. There is abundance of the fruit of this tree, which has no branches at a less height than two or three fathoms above the ground. They have a kind of oak that yields acorns similar to sugar-plums and with a kernel sweet as sugar; one finds cress in certain springs, rosebushes, penny-royal (*pulegium*) and marjoram (*origanum*).

"In the desert watercourses there are barbel and *picones* like those in Spain. On entering the uninhabited country one observes a kind of fawn-coloured lion.

Up to Cibola, which lies eighty leagues to the north, the country rises continually. From Culiacan the march had been made with the north always a little to the left.

"The province of Cibola contains seven villages; the largest is called Muzaque; the houses of the country ordinarily have three or four stories; but at Muzaque there are some which have as many as seven. The Indians of this country are very intelligent. They cover the middle of their bodies with pieces of cloth like napkins, furnished with tassels and embroidered at the corners; they fasten them round the loins. These natives also have a kind of fur-coat made of feathers[1] or hareskin, and cotton cloth. The women wear on their shoulders a sort of mantle which they knot round the throat, passing the mantle under the right arm; they also make themselves clothes of hide, which are very well prepared, and they fasten their hair behind the ears in the shape of a wheel, resembling the handles of a tankard.

"It is a very narrow valley between steep mountains. Maize does not grow to any great height; nearly all the ears project from the bottom of the stalk, and each ear contains seven or eight hundred kernels, a thing which had not yet been seen in the Indies (America). There are in this province bears in great number, lions, wild-cats, lynxes, and otters with very fine fur; very large turquoises are found there, but not in such numbers as had been stated. The inhabitants collect and preserve piñon nuts for their wants.

"A man never marries more than one wife. They (the Cibola Indians) can build estufas (*étuves*), which may be seen in the courtyards and in the places where they assemble in council. There are no appointed chiefs as in New Spain, nor any councils of the old men. They have priests who preach; these are advanced in years; they ascend the most elevated terrace in the village and deliver a sermon the moment the sun rises. The people sit round about and observe a profound silence; these old men give them advice as to their manner of life; I believe even that they have commandments which they are bound to obey, for among them there is neither intemperance nor unnatural crime; they do not eat human flesh; they are no thieves, but very industrious. Estufas are rare in this country. They consider it sacrilege for women to enter a place two at a time. The cross is to them a symbol of peace. They burn the dead and with them the implements which they have used in the exercise of their craft.

"Twenty leagues to the north-west is another province containing seven villages;[2] the inhabitants wear the same dress, have the same manners and the same religion as the people of Cibola. It is estimated that three or four thousand men are distributed among the fourteen villages of these two provinces. Tiguex lies to the north, at a distance (from Cibola) of about forty leagues. Between these two provinces is the rock of Acuco, of which I have spoken in the first part.

---

[1] Probably feather cloth of the kind found in the cliff-dwellings (p. 104).
[2] The Moki villages.

Chapter IV.

Manners and customs of the inhabitants of the province of Tiguex and the neighbouring country.

"The province of Tiguex contains twelve villages situated on the banks of a great river; it is a valley about two leagues broad. It is bounded to the west by very high mountains, covered with snow. Four villages are built at the foot of these mountains, and three others on the heights.

"Farther north lies the province of Quirix, which contains seven villages; seven leagues to the north-east the province of Hemes, which contains the same number; forty leagues in the same direction lies Acha; four leagues to the south-east is situated the province of Tutahaco, which contains eight villages. All these provinces have the same manners and the same customs; but each of them has some peculiar to itself.

"They are governed by a council of old men. The houses are built in common; it is the women that mix the mortar and erect the walls. The men bring the timber and do the joinery. They have no lime, but they make a mixture of ashes, earth, and charcoal which replaces it very well; for, though they build their houses to a height of four stories, the walls (*parois*) are no more than half-a-fathom thick. They collect great heaps of thyme and rushes, and set them on fire; when this mass is reduced to ashes and charcoal, they cast a great quantity of earth and water upon it and mix the whole together. They knead this stuff into round lumps, which they leave to dry and use instead of stone. They coat the whole with the same mixture. Thus the work bears no little resemblance to a structure of masonry.

"Young people who are not yet married work for the public in general. It is they who must find wood for fuel and store it in the courtyards, where it is fetched for household use by the women. They live in the estufas, which lie under ground in the courtyards of the village. Some of these estufas are square, some round. The roof is supported by pillars made of pine trunks. I have seen estufas with twelve pillars, each two fathoms in circumference, but usually there are only four. They are paved with large polished stones, like baths in Europe. In the centre is a hearth, on which a fire burns; a handful of thyme is now and then thrown on the fire; this is enough to keep up the warmth so that one feels as if in a bath. The roof is on a level with the ground. There are some which are as large as a fives court (*un jeu de paume*).

"When a young man marries, it is by order of the old men who govern. He must spin and weave a mantle; he is then led to the young girl, whose shoulders he covers with the mantle, and she is now his wife.

"The houses belong to the women, the estufas to the men. The women are forbidden to lie down in the latter, or even to enter them, except to bring food to their husbands or sons. It is the men who spin and weave; the women attend to the children and prepare food. The soil is so fertile that it is unnecessary to till it for sowing; after this the snow falls, covering the seed, and the maize grows underneath. Their harvest in one year would be enough for seven. The country contains numbers of cranes, ducks, crows, and partridges, which live on the houses. When they begin sowing, the fields are still covered with maize which they have not been able to harvest.

"In this province there were a great number of indigenous fowls and *gallos de papada;*[1] they could be kept for sixty days without being plucked or drawn and without emitting any bad smell. It was the same with human bodies, especially in winter. Their villages are very clean; they void their excrement at a distance, and collect the urine in large vessels, which are emptied outside the village. The houses are well arranged and very tidy. One room is appointed for culinary purposes, another for the grinding of corn; the latter is isolated and contains an oven and three stones cemented firmly together. Three women sit before these stones; the first crushes the corn, the second grinds it, and the third reduces it quite to a powder. Before entering they take off their shoes, tie up their hair, cover their heads, and shake their clothes. While they are at work, a man sits at the door and plays on a pipe (*musette*), so that they may work in time; they sing to this accompaniment in three voices. They prepare a great quantity of flour each time; to make bread they mix the flour with hot water and mould it into a wafer-like cake (cf. p. 140). They collect a great quantity of herbs, and when these are quite dry, they use them all the year round in their cookery. In this country no other fruit occurs but pine-cones.

"They have preachers; they commit no unnatural offences; they are not cruel, offer no human sacrifices, and are not cannibals. When the army entered Tiguex, it was forty days since the natives had murdered Francisco Hernando; yet he was found among the dead, unharmed save for the wound that had caused his death. He was as white as snow and emitted no evil smell.

"I have gained a little information as to their customs from an Indian of ours who had been a prisoner among them for a year. When I asked him why the young girls went quite naked in spite of the great cold, he answered that they were not allowed to wear clothes until after marriage. The men wear a kind of shirt made of tanned leather and outside this a fur-coat. Throughout this province are found glazed pottery and vessels truly remarkable both in shape and execution.

---

[1] "Literally, *coq à gosier.*"

Chapter V.

Of Cicuye and of the villages in its neighbourhood. — How a strange nation came to conquer this country.

"I have said what I know of Tiguex; it is needless to give a detailed description of the other towns in the province, seeing that they belong to the same nation and observe the same customs. I shall therefore speak now of Cicuye and of some deserted villages in the neighbourhood, some of them on the route followed by the army on their march thither, others beyond the mountains and distant from the river.

"The village of Cicuye can muster about five hundred warriors, dreaded by all their neighbours. It is built on the top of a rock, and forms a great square, the centre of which is occupied by an open space containing the estufas. The houses have four stories with terraced roofs all of the same height, on which one can make a circuit of the whole village without finding a street to bar one's progress. On the first two stories there are corridors like balconies, on which you may walk round the village, and under which you may find shelter. The houses have no doors in the basement; the balconies, which are on the inside of the village, are reached by ladders, which may be drawn up. It is on these balconies, which take the place of streets, that all the doors open by which entrance is gained to the houses. The houses that front on the plain stand back to back with the others, which look upon the court. The latter are the higher, a circumstance of great service in time of war. The village is further surrounded by a rather low wall. There is a spring, which might, however, be turned off from the village. This nation asserts that no other has ever succeeded in subduing it, and that it has vanquished all its assailants. These Indians belong to the same race as those of whom I have previously spoken. Among these too the maidens are quite naked, for they say that in this way, if the girls are unchaste, the consequences will be seen, and that they have no reason to be ashamed, for they were born so.

"Between Cicuye and the province of Quirix there lies a small village, very well fortified, to which the Spaniards have given the name of Ximera, and another which seems to have been very large; it is almost entirely deserted, one single quarter being still inhabited. The remainder appears to have been violently destroyed. This place was called Silos, because a number of pits (*silos*) for the storage of maize were found there.

"Farther off was another large village entirely in ruins, where we found in the courtyards a great number of stone balls of the size of a leather bag containing 1 *arroba* (11.5 kilo.). They seemed to have been cast with the aid of machines and to have been employed in the destruction of the village. All that we could learn was that five or six years ago there had come to this province a very numerous nation, called Teyas, who had taken and destroyed all the villages. The strangers had also laid siege to Cicuye, but without succeeding in its capture. Before they left the country, they had made an alliance with the inhabitants. It seems that they were powerful and had battering engines. The Indians did not know where this people came from; they only supposed that they had come from the north. They call this nation Teyas, which means valiant, just as the Mexicans called themselves Chichimecas or brave. The Teyas, whom we met with on a subsequent occasion, were well known to the inhabitants of Cicuye. They even come to winter beneath the walls of these villages; but the inhabitants do not venture to admit them, for they are people whom one cannot trust. They receive them with friendship, and trade with them, but without suffering them to pass the night in the villages. They even post a guard of trumpeters; the sentries challenge each other as in Spain.

"There are seven more villages between the (army's) route and the Sierra Nevada; one of them, half destroyed by the nation of whom I have just spoken, is subject to Cicuye. Cicuye is built in a narrow valley among mountains covered with pines. It is traversed by a little stream in which excellent trout are caught. Very large otters, bears, and fine hawks are found there.

Chapter VI,

wherein are enumerated all the villages seen on the route.

"Before speaking of the plain where buffaloes are found, I consider it necessary to enumerate all the villages which are scattered about the country, and where the houses have several stories. Cibola is the first province, it contains seven villages; Tusayan, seven; the rock of Acuco, one; Tiguex, twelve; Tutahaco, eight (these villages are reached by descending the river); Quirix, seven; among the snowy mountains, seven; Ximena, three; Cicuye, one; Hemes, seven; Aquas-Calientes, three; Yunque-Yunque on the mountain, six; Valladolid or Braba, one; Chia, one.

"This makes seventy in all.[1] Tiguex is the central point, and Valladolid the last village up the river, to the north-east. The four villages situated on the river, below Tiguex, lie to the south-east; for the river makes a bend to the east; about a hundred and thirty leagues are reckoned from the point reached in the ascent of the river to the point attained in its descent. This belt of country is entirely populated; it is here that the seventy villages of which I have just spoken are situated; they may contain about twenty thousand men, to judge by their appearance. The rest of the country is entirely desolate; not the tiniest hut can be seen there. This circumstance, the customs of these nations and their form of government, which are entirely different from all those observed before, show that they have come

---

[1] "The author enumerates seventy-one."

from the quarter of *la Grande-Inde*, whose coasts abut on those of this country to the west. They came perhaps by following the course of the river after crossing the mountains, and settled in the places that seemed advantageous to them. As they have multiplied, they have erected other villages down to the point where the river failed them by sinking into the ground. On its reappearance it flows towards Florida. There are other villages, it is said, on the banks of this river, but they were not visited; it was preferred, on the advice of the Turk, to cross the mountains where the river rises. I believe that great wealth might be found in the country from which those Indians set out. To judge by the route which they followed, they must have come from the end of Eastern India, and from a part very little known and situated, as the configuration of the coasts suggests, far in the interior of the country, between China and Norway. It must in fact be an immense distance from one sea to the other, judging by the run of the coastline as ascertained by Captain VILLALOBOS, who sailed in this direction to find China. The case is the same when one follows the coast of Florida; it approaches Norway continually till one comes to the country of the Bacallaos.

"To return to our subject, I will say that, in an extent of country thirty leagues in breadth and a hundred and thirty leagues in length along the course of the river, there are no more inhabitants than those whom I have mentioned. A great number of governments in New Spain possess a much more considerable population. In many villages were found bits of silver ore used by the natives in glazing and painting earthenware."

In the last chapter of the second part CASTAÑEDA undertakes a description of the prairies to the east and of Quivira, regions situated without the limits of the Pueblo tribes' extension. Then follows in the third part of his narrative an account of the subsequent adventures of the Spaniards in the new-discovered countries and of their return to Culiacan. This part contains little with reference to the Pueblo Indians, and I shall therefore confine myself to giving a very brief abridgment of his account.

CORONADO, as mentioned above, had gone into winter-quarters in Tiguex, intending in the spring to march east with all his forces to the rich countries which still engaged his fancies. Don PEDRO DE TOBAR had arrived with reinforcements, and at the end of winter preparations were commenced for a speedy departure. But a steadily increasing disaffection might already be traced among the soldiers. Furthermore an accident occurred which, for the time at least, rendered the purposed expedition impossible. At a joust CORONADO was thrown from his horse and trampled so severely that for a time his life was in great danger. During CORO-

NADO's illness CARDENAS, who had designed to return to New Spain, came back with the disquieting news that the inhabitants of Suya, a village on his route, had revolted and killed the Spaniards as well as their horses and cattle. This intelligence aggravated CORONADO's illness and depressed his spirits. He was also informed of the soldiers' discontent. Himself seized with a desire to return to New Spain, he persuaded some of his officers to instigate the soldiers to sign a petition expressing their longing for a return, an undertaking which met with no difficulty whatever. He besides induced his officers to sign a declaration to the effect that they considered it best to return, as no rich country had been found. CORONADO gave orders for the march in the beginning of April, 1542. A Franciscan friar. JUAN DE PADILLA, and a lay-brother named LUIS, expressed their wish to remain. The former proceeded to Quivira, where he was shortly put to death; the latter stayed at Cicuye, and was not heard of afterwards. From Tiguex the army marched to Cibola and then into the desert, following the same route as on their way out. Chichilticale was reached without any noteworthy incident. There they met JUAN GALLEGOS with reinforcements and supplies from New Spain. He had expected to come up with the army in the rich country of which the Turk had spoken, and was therefore greatly disappointed to find them on the return march. New disputes arose. A proposal that they should await orders from the Viceroy, fell through owing to the opposition of the home-sick soldiers. The retreat was continued amid repeated skirmishes with the Indians, and Culiacan was soon reached. From this place the army set out for Mexico, but on the route the discipline, already lax, grew still worse. So many deserted that, when CORONADO arrived at the last-mentioned town, he had at most a hundred men. This retreat, for which CASTAÑEDA blames CORONADO alone, cost the latter his reputation and, shortly afterwards, his appointment as governor of Nueva Galicia.

About forty years elapsed after CORONADO's expedition, before any new explorations of the Pueblo country were undertaken, and not until the end of the century were the Pueblo villages conquered and annexed to the Spanish dominions. It does not enter, however, into the plan of this work to describe these later discoveries and conquests; my object is merely to give a picture of the life led by the Pueblo Indians at the period when they first came in contact with Europeans. For this purpose the history of MARCOS DE NIZA's and, above all, of CORONADO's adventures is most rich in information.

CHAPTER XV.

Summary of our Present Knowledge of the Pueblo Tribes.

In the preceding chapters I have brought together the various records from which we can derive any information as to the Pueblo tribes. I have described the antiquities of the Mesa Verde which afford us a glimpse of the daily life of the cliff-dwellers; I have further described similar remains probably to be ascribed to kindred nations; and I have finally given a brief sketch of the modern Indians whose habits remind us most strongly of the cliff-dwellers, adding to this sketch some details of the life led by the same Indians in the middle of the sixteenth century, as depicted by the Spanish invaders in their narratives. It is now my task, with the aid of the materials here collected, to investigate some points in the history of the cliff-dwellers. This undertaking is no easy one, for the materials are few and fragmentary. Future researches within the wide and hitherto but partially explored field offered by the ruins of the South-western States, will set before us new facts, perhaps of a kind to shed a new light on the circumstances. I therefore do not pretend to give here any version, based on positive evidence, of the cliff-dwellers' or the Pueblo tribes' history. But we already know enough to be able to trace the probable origin and the evolution of the singular culture of these tribes.

We will first examine the former question, that touching the origin of the Pueblo tribes. The primitive Pueblo culture, as we find it in its typical development among the cliff-dwellers of the Mesa Verde, may be traced almost everywhere within a sharply defined region, the extent of which we have considered above. In the south of this region we can trace foreign influences, the antiquities seem here to be of a more diversified character. To the north, on the other hand, within the basin of the Rio Colorado, the prehistoric remains belong to a single characteristic type, in several respects quite peculiar to the tract. There is no conformity of style, there are no steps of transition, that might entitle us to compare the culture of the Pueblo tribes, as it appears in their architecture and their pottery, with that of any other people. In these respects this culture bears the stamp of perfect originality. But if we study the other domestic appliances of the Pueblo tribes, their weapons and implements, we find scarcely any essential differences from the nomadic Indians in general. It is evident that the cliff-dwellers do not compose a race distinct from these Indians, but are related to them. Several other circumstances favour this opinion. The crania found in the graves of the cliff-dwellers differ, according to Professor RETZIUS, in no essential respect from those of the neighbouring nomadic tribes. The round shape of the estufa is most easily explained on the hypothesis that it is a reminiscence of the cliff-dwellers' nomadic period. There must be some very cogent reason for the employment of this shape, for the construction of a cylindrical chamber within a block of rectangular rooms involves no small amount of labour. We know how obstinately primitive nations cling to everything connected with their religious ideas. Then what is more natural than the retention, for the room where religious ceremonies were performed, of the round shape characteristic of the original dwelling-place, the nomadic hut? This assumption is further corroborated by the situation of the hearth and the structure of the roof of the estufa (see p. 15, 57), where we find points of analogy to the method employed by certain nomadic Indians in the erection of their huts.

While we must undoubtedly regard the Pueblo tribes as the descendants of nomadic Indians, the culture of the said tribes, as I have just mentioned, shows some very essential distinctions. In certain respects they unquestionably stood higher than their ancestors, the nomadic tribes. But the characteristics of the Pueblo culture find their explanation in the circumstances under which the said culture was developed. If a nomadic people, living mainly by the chase, have been driven by more powerful neighbours from tracts with abundance of game to desert regions such as the Southwestern States, where game is scarce, this nation must have recourse to some new means of support. Maize has long been cultivated by several roving tribes. It is thus possible that this cereal was known to the ancestors of the Pueblo tribes even during their nomadic period. In spite of the dry climate the tableland afforded excellent ground for the planting of maize, though artificial irrigation was sometimes a necessity. It is therefore easy to explain how the cultivation of maize gradually became the immigrants' most important livelihood. But the raising of corn, the tilling of the soil, no longer permitted a wandering life. The nomadic people became an agricultural nation with stationary dwellings. Then what was the primitive form of these habitations? Do we still find remains of the original type? It seems most probable to me that the immigrants, constantly menaced by their enemies, first took refuge in caves and recesses fortified by the hand of nature and offering a safe retreat. In these caves they learnt to abandon building materials of timber for stone, which, especially in the thinly wooded regions, was much more easily procurable. The cave-dwellings described in a preceding chapter perhaps represent in part this first grade of the Pueblo tribes' development, though many of these caves, as appears from the ornamented fragments of pottery found there, were certainly inhabited in more recent times as well. In many instances the more spacious caves, where extensive cliff-dwellings were subsequently erected, probably contained at first these primitive habitations. I may here adduce the find of two

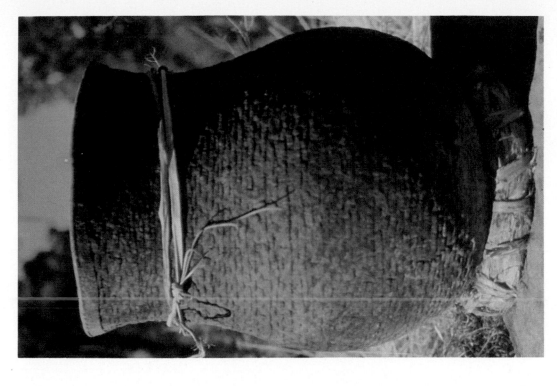

A corrugated plain pot with a carrying handle. Note that it is setting on a pot ring. The flare at the top keeps the carrying cord from slipping. Photo courtesy MVNP.

This is a corrugated pot (pictured upside down) the author found at Step House; several pieces are missing. This is a cataloged item in the Nordenskiold collection in Helsinki. Photo courtesy MVNP.

Funerary pottery of beautiful design and execution. These items are in the Wetherill Collection. Photo courtesy MVNP.

A highly ornamented and useful kitchen ladle, perhaps used in ceremonies. Photo courtesy MVNP.

earthen vessels, clumsily shaped, badly fired, and deviating somewhat from the normal type, in the Step House cave, 0.6 m. below the surface of the ground. It is possible that these rude vessels were manufactured by the first inhabitants of the cave.

The further evolution of the cave-dwellings may be traced without difficulty in their transition to cliff-dwellings, the caves being divided by walls into several rooms. Architecture gradually advanced in these caves. The mason learnt roughly to dress the stones and to lay them in regular courses. In the cliff-dwellings we find different stages of architectural evolution represented. In the interior of the Cliff Palace we see rooms (fig. 38) constructed in the most primitive fashion of large, unhewn slabs of stone. Other walls, in the upper part of Spring House for example (Pl. VIII), are also built of unhewn stone, but more carefully put together. In Long House, in certain parts of the Cliff Palace, and in most of the cliff-dwellings, we find walls of rough-hewn stone, piled without attempt at arrangement. Lastly, in the uppermost, best built parts of the Cliff Palace and also in Balcony House, we find walls of carefully dressed blocks, laid in regular courses (fig. 89 b, Pl. XIII, XV). In one and the same cliff-dwelling we often observe walls built with greater rudeness and greater proficiency, and in most cases several circumstances, for instance the distribution of the apartments, indicate that the cliff-dwellings were gradually enlarged by the addition of new rooms. A time must eventually come, when all the space in the caves suitable for building purposes had been filled. The builders were now compelled to have recourse to the valleys and plateaux. The villages built in these sites seem generally to be constructed in the same fashion as the best parts of the cliff-dwellings. That these ruins are actually remains of the same culture as we find among the cliff-dwellers, is rendered highly probable both by this similarity of architecture and by the resemblance between the fragments of pottery on the mesa and the earthen vessels discovered in the cliff-dwellings. The manner in which the villages are built, the numerous small rooms huddled together in one large structure and the several stories rising in terraces one above another, can be explained only on the assumption that this architecture was developed during the construction of houses in the caves, where the crowded grouping of the apartments and the erection of several stories were necessitated by the confined space. This circumstance has already been pointed out by CUSHING[1] with respect to the Zuñi villages. A pueblo on the mesa is thus in fact nothing but a cliff-dwelling built in the open instead of in the cave.

It is very probable that some of the cliff-dwellings were inhabited contemporaneously with the villages in the open, and perhaps even later than they. This

---

[1] CUSHING, F. H. A Study of Pueblo Pottery as Illustrative of Zuñi Culture-growth. Fourth Ann. Rep. Bur. Ethn., p. 480. In the same paper CUSHING gives an account, founded on his studies of the Zuñi language, of the probable course of this tribe's development. His conclusions, though based on grounds entirely different and somewhat, as it seems to me, rather weak, agree in several points with my conception of the cliff-dwellers' evolution.

is suggested by the excellent state of preservation shown by some of the former, for instance Balcony House. We are forced to conclude that they were abandoned later than the villages on the mesa. Some features, for example the super-position of walls constructed with the greatest proficiency on others built in a more primitive fashion (see Pl. XIII), indicate that the cliff-dwellings have been inhabited at two different periods. They were first abandoned, and had partly fallen into ruins; but were subsequently repeopled, new walls being now erected on the ruins of the old. The best explanation hereof seems to be the following. On the pla-teaux and in the valleys the Pueblo tribes attained their widest distribution and their highest development. The numerous villages at no great distance from each other were strong enough to defy their hostile neighbours. But afterwards, from causes difficult of elucidation, a period of decay set in, the number and population of the villages gradually decreased, and the inhabitants were again compelled to take refuge in the remote fastnesses. Here the people of the Mesa Verde finally succumbed to their enemies. The memory of their last struggles is preserved by the numerous human bones found in many places, strewn among the ruined cliff-dwellings. These human remains occur in situations where it is impossible to assume that they have been interred.

The above remarks as to the cliff-dwellings having been inhabited at two different periods, are based merely on observations made in some of the ruins of the Mesa Verde. Whether they also apply to other cliff-dwellings, is a point on which I will offer no opinion.

I have just mentioned that the ruins on the mesa and in the valleys mark the culmination in the territorial sway of the Pueblo tribes. The cliff-dwellings were mainly confined to the basin of the Rio Colorado. Gradually more and more villages were founded within this area in the open country, and hence the Pueblo tribes spread eastwards and southwards to the basin of the Rio Grande, to the Rio Gila and its tributaries. The causes of the gradual depopulation of these regions and of the destruction of the Pueblo tribes are, as I have just mentioned, difficult to trace. Probably the assaults of strange nomadic tribes skilled in war conduced to these results. CASTAÑEDA relates, as has been stated in the preceding chapter, that in some places the Spaniards found pueblos deserted by their inhabitants and partly in ruins. They had been attacked and destroyed by an Indian tribe called Teyas.

We are not in possession of any facts that might entitle us to draw any con-clusions respecting the date of the Pueblo tribes' ascendancy. It was probably several centuries earlier than the first visit of the Spaniards to their country. To judge by the present condition of most of the ruins, no very long periods can have elapsed since their erection. It is, however, certain that, even at the time of CORONADO's expedition, many tracts were deserted which had supported a numerous agricultural population. As appears from CASTAÑEDA's narrative, both the pueblos of the Gila

Valley and, probably, those of the Rio Verde, were already abandoned at this date, and it is hardly probable that north of the Moki villages, i. e. in the basin of the Rio San Juan, where so many ruins are found, there was any considerable population of agricultural habits. The Spaniards, who first penetrated to these villages under PEDRO DE TOBAR in 1540, heard nothing of any "towns" to the north, though they eagerly listened to every rumour that might possibly convey any intelligence grateful to their insatiate lust of conquest. From CASTAÑEDA's relation it appears that the Rio Grande region was the only one of the said three tracts which still possessed a numerous population. Outside this area there were only the Zuñi and Moki villages, in the situations which they occupy to the present day.

That the modern Pueblo Indians (I include under this appellation the Zuñis and Mokis) are descendants of the Pueblo tribes, that is to say, of the nations who built the cliff-dwellings and villages now in ruins, has been maintained by several writers. This is indicated by the similarity of their architectural productions and of their habits in general, as shown by the descriptions given above of the cliff-dwellers and of the Moki Indians. On studying the ancient Spanish accounts of the Pueblo Indians, we find the resemblance to the cliff-dwellers in some respects even greater, for certain objects (e. g. the feather cloth, p. 103) evidently existed among the said Indians in former ages, though their manufacture has now been abandoned. But the Pueblo Indians of modern times have degenerated in more than one respect. Architecture and the ceramic industry, as I have already mentioned, have fallen into complete decay. The ornament of the pottery has deviated from the ancient types, and betrays a foreign influence, a circumstance to which I shall return below.

From the sixteenth century to the present day the Pueblo Indians have constantly decreased in number. CASTAÑEDA enumerates 71 villages with a population of about 20,000 fighting men. At the middle of the present century, according to WHIPPLE,[1] there were about 30 villages with a total population of 22,000. The number of warriors probably fell short of 4,000. There is little doubt that at no very distant date from the present this last remnant of the agricultural Indians of the South-western States will disappear, or be absorbed in the stream of white settlers which is spreading more and more over the country formerly tilled by the Pueblo tribes, again transforming the parched and barren valleys and plateaux to fertile cornland.

In my attempt to trace the development of the Pueblo tribes I have confined myself to the ruins of their dwellings, these being the only memorials of the said nations whereof we possess any extensive information. I mentioned above that in another respect too the Pueblo culture differed essentially from that of the nomadic Indians, namely in the comparatively high development of the potter's art. As I have already pointed out, we should probably seek the causes of this development,

---

[1] Report, p. 12.

here as in the case of architecture, in the environments of the Pueblo tribes. The dry climate, the lack of springs, often made it necessary to transport water for considerable distances, and to store a considerable supply thereof in the houses. For this purpose suitable vessels were required. Originally, it is probable, gourds were used, or baskets coated with pitch. We find, indeed, that the shapes of the most primitive earthen vessels were copied from gourds. The idea of coiling a vessel by winding a strip of clay in a spiral was probably suggested at first by the spirally plaited baskets. As earthenware came more and more into vogue, gourds and baskets were laid aside. To distinguish between any different stages in the evolution of the ceramic industry, is impossible in the present state of our knowledge of the Pueblo tribes. Yet with regard to the pottery from the Mesa Verde, we may assume with fair certainty, for reasons already given, that it represents an older type than the ware from more southern tracts. If we confine our attention to the Mesa Verde, we feel inclined, judging by a comparison between the fragments on the mesa and the vessels from the cliff-dwellings, to the opinion that the latter represent an earlier stage of development. It seems as if the art of ornamenting coiled ware with corrugations and indented patterns had not made great progress until the mesa was peopled. Fragments of such vessels with greatly diversified ornaments are common on the mesa, but rare in the cliff-dwellings. The red ware too appears to be more common on the mesa. These circumstances agree very well with the results to which we are guided by a study of the ruins, namely that the villages on the mesa represent a later period of the Pueblo tribes' development than the cliff-dwellings.

The further we advance from the Mesa Verde to the south within the Pueblo country, the more numerous and more diversified are the types of pottery. This remark, as has been pointed out, applies in some degree to the ruins as well. Besides the types which I have described in the present work, and which seem to be predominant throughout the basin of the Rio Colorado and are also found in parts of the country drained by the Rio Gila and the Rio Grande, besides these we find in the south of the first-mentioned region, in the basin of the Rio Gila, and probably too in the Rio Grande basin, several other types of entirely different appearance and certainly of later origin. Some of these types are approximated to the modern Pueblo ware. American archæologists distinguish between *ancient ware*, *transitional ware*, and *modern ware*, denoting by the first name vessels of the same type as the Mesa Verde pottery. The term *transitional ware*, however, by which are meant certain types of pottery found in ancient Pueblo ruins and considered to form a transition to the modern ware, is in a manner inappropriate, for there are probably no actual intermediate forms between this ware and the ancient pottery of the Mesa Verde type. The ornamentation of the modern ware is entirely independent, its *motif* consisting of symbolical figures, often very complicated and less attractive from an æsthetic point of view, of which figures we do not find a trace on ware of the ancient type. Similar figures also appear on the so-called *transitional ware*, and they should probably be ascribed to some foreign influence. The fact that the last-mentioned ware does not seem to occur over such a wide extent of country as the ancient ware, suggests that this influence asserted itself when the geographical extension of the Pueblo tribes had suffered considerable reduction. Only in exceptional cases do we find the ancient meanders on the "transitional ware," and in most of these instances they are badly executed, giving us the impression that the potter has copied them from other vessels without comprehending the true signification of the design. No less pronounced than the distinction in ornament is the difference in shape and colour. The pure black and white pigments, which, in addition to red, are the only ones found on pottery of the Mesa Verde type, do not appear on the "transitional" or modern ware. This difference cannot depend merely on the colouring substances and the other materials procurable in the neighbourhood, for the ancient black and white pottery occurs partly in the same tracts as the "transitional" yellow ware with dark brown ornament; the reason is probably that the introduction of new ornaments was accompanied by the adoption of new methods in the manufacture of the pottery.

The ware from the Casas Grandes on the Rio Gila and in Northern Mexico belongs to a distinct type. In its ornamentation it reminds us somewhat of the so-called transitional type, and this may possibly be an indication that the influence which modified the decorative art of the Pueblo tribes came from these southern regions. I am doubtful whether the inhabitants of the Casas Grandes should be included among the Pueblo tribes. Of all the archæological remains of the South-western States these ruins deviate most from the general type.

CUSHING [1] seems to think that the ancient inhabitants of the Gila Valley were related to the Zuñi Indians. I do not know what are his grounds for this assumption. It appears to me that the similarity which crops up in certain respects between the customs of these two peoples, strikes us in those very points where the difference between the Zuñi Indians and the prehistoric Pueblo tribes is most marked, and that this similarity is probably a result of a strong influence exercised by the inhabitants of the Casas Grandes on the ancestors of the Zuñi Indians. The Casa Grande culture seems to be in certain respects more approximated to the comparatively high civilisation which meets us among the tribes of ancient Mexico. It has also been proposed to couple this latter civilisation with the Pueblo culture, and to regard the cliff-dwellings and the Pueblo ruins as the work of the said tribes. During their migration to the south, we are told, they sojourned for some time in the regions where these ruins are now found. But this opinion is quite groundless. There is no resemblance between the cliff-dwellings or the Pueblo ruins and the magnificent architectural remains so numerous in certain parts of Mexico. Nor does the pottery from the cliff-dwellings bear any likeness to the ancient Mexican ware.

---

[1] BAXTER, The Old New World.

I shall conclude with a brief summary of the results at which I have arrived respecting the origin and development of the Pueblo tribes. They were nomadic Indians whose culture had been considerably modified and in certain respects elevated by altered conditions of life. The evolution of this culture had nothing in common with that of the ancient Mexican civilisation; but during its decadence it was perhaps influenced in some respects by the latter.

It is reserved for future research to carry out a careful investigation of the numerous archæological remains of the South-western States, and thus to extend our knowledge of the origin and culture of the Pueblo tribes. The present chapter is merely an attempt to trace, in its main features, the course of evolution pursued by this singular culture, and is based chiefly upon the results of explorations among the ruins of the Mesa Verde.

Plate XVIII.

Scale: $^1/_2$.

1, a and **b** (643). Strongly flattened cranium of an adult.
Found in a small ruin opposite Ruin 14.

2, a and **b** (644). Strongly flattened cranium of a child.
Found in a room in Sprucetree House.

———————————

Note to Plates XVIII—LI. The scale of each plate is either given in the description (below the number of the plate) or indicated by a metrical measuring-tape photographed with the objects.

To the description of each object is appended within parentheses its number in my original catalogue (the same as that of the original label).

Every article is photographed directly and reproduced without retouching. The only exceptions are the bowl Pl. XXXIII, which is lithographed, and the following articles, Pl. XXIII: 1, 2; Pl. XXV: 3, 4; Pl. XXVII: 1, 2; Pl. XXVIII: 5, which have been reproduced from paintings.

———————————

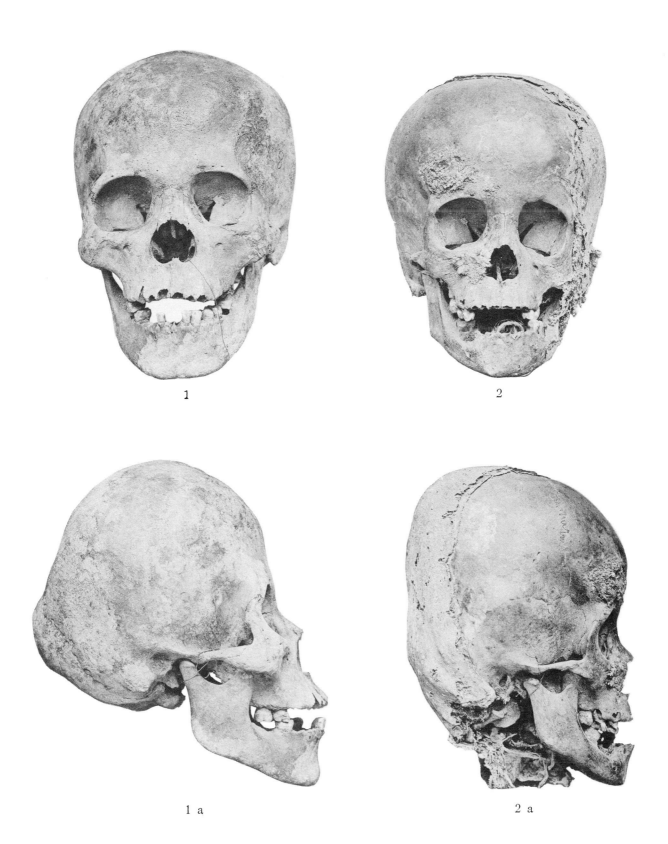

1

2

1 a

2 a

Plate XIX.

Scale: $^1/_6$.

1 (568). Skeleton, probably female. One side decayed, the other mummified. Hands preserved, nails partly left. Shroud of feather cloth remaining, but partly decomposed; shown in the plate below the skeleton.

   Found in Step House.

2 (570). Mummy, shrouded in a network of cords wrapped in thongs of hide, on which the hair is partly present. On the head a skin cap. Hair black, coarse, and well-preserved. Feet clad in moccasins of hide. On the rest of the body remnants of hide clothing. Completely mummified.

   Found in Step House.

3 (607). Mummy of a child. Hands and feet well-preserved. A large piece of feather cloth has been wrapped round the corpse.

   Found in Step House.

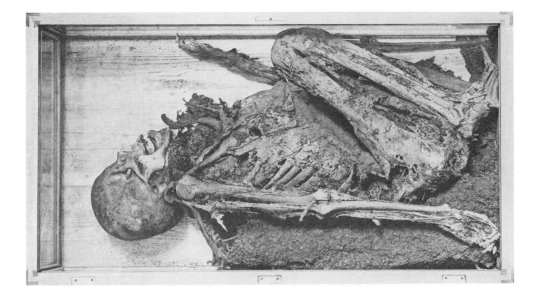

1

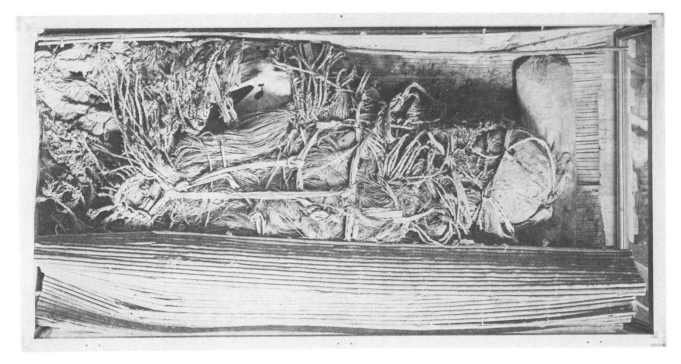

2

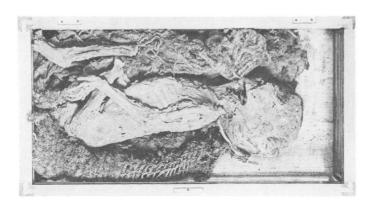

3

Plate XX.

1. Petroglyph at the mouth of Moccasin Cañon.

2. Petroglyph in a cliff-dwelling in Johnson Cañon.

3. Petroglyph in Step House.

1

2   3

Plate XXI.

Scale: ¹/₃.

1 (581). Large vase of the coiled and indented variety. A simple ornamentation has been produced by alternating eight or nine indented coils with four smooth ones. Ware thin (4 or 5 mm.) but of uniform thickness. The baking performed with care, the surface hard, and the execution as a whole excellent. Cubical contents not quite 25 litres.

Found in the refuse heap at Step House, where it seemed to have been purposely concealed.

2 (618). Similar in form to the preceding one, but with the whole surface, except the margin, indented. The bottom smooth, presumably because the jar rested on some object during the process of manufacture. The jar is contained in a net of yucca. A ring, also of yucca leaves, is attached to this net and gives a steady support to the round bottomed jar. The surface covered, especially in the depressions, with a thick layer of soot. Cubical contents 25 litres. Thickness of the ware 4 mm.

Found in the refuse heap at Step House near the preceding jar.

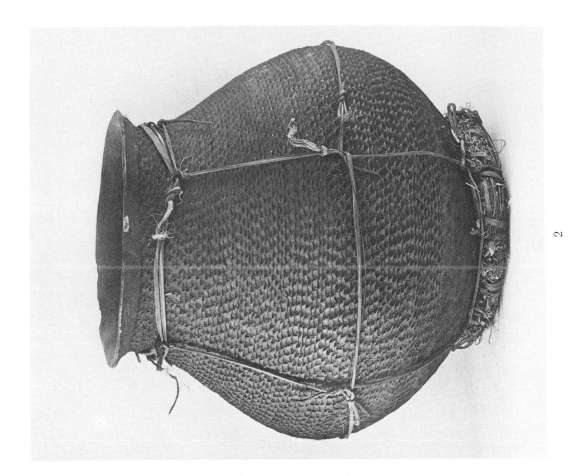

2

1

Plate XXII.

Scale: $\frac{1}{3}$.

1 (370). Jar of the coiled variety. All the coils except three in the middle are indented. The surface of the vessel very hard.

> Found in a small ruin in the cliffs on the west side of Spring House Cañon.

2 (586). Large jar with a tasteful indented pattern, produced by arranging the indentations in triangles, as shown in the heliotype.

> Found at Step House in the refuse heap, not far from the place marked *j* in the plan.

1

2

Plate XXIII.

Scale: $^1/_3$.

1, a and **b** (614). Large, shallow bowl (diam. 50 cm.) of very rough execution. This bowl differs both in form and design from the other vessels found in the cliff-houses. Ware thick (10 mm.), material coarse and rather loose. Surface of gray colour, uneven, and soft. Ornamented with a singular design, composed of small indentations close to each other and forming straight lines.

Found at Step House in the refuse heap at the spot marked *k* in the plan and at a depth of 6 dm.

2 (298). Vessel of singular form, probably a lamp. The WETHERILLS have found similar vessels in which the cotton wicks were still left. The two loops probably served to hold the cord by which the lamp was suspended. Ware very thick; moulding and baking of the vessel carefully executed. Form apparently singular, but possibly derived from another variety of lamp, figured by HOLMES (Pottery, p. 355—357). I once discovered some fragments of a similar lamp that have unfortunately been lost.

Found in Ruin 11 on the west side of Wetherill's Mesa.

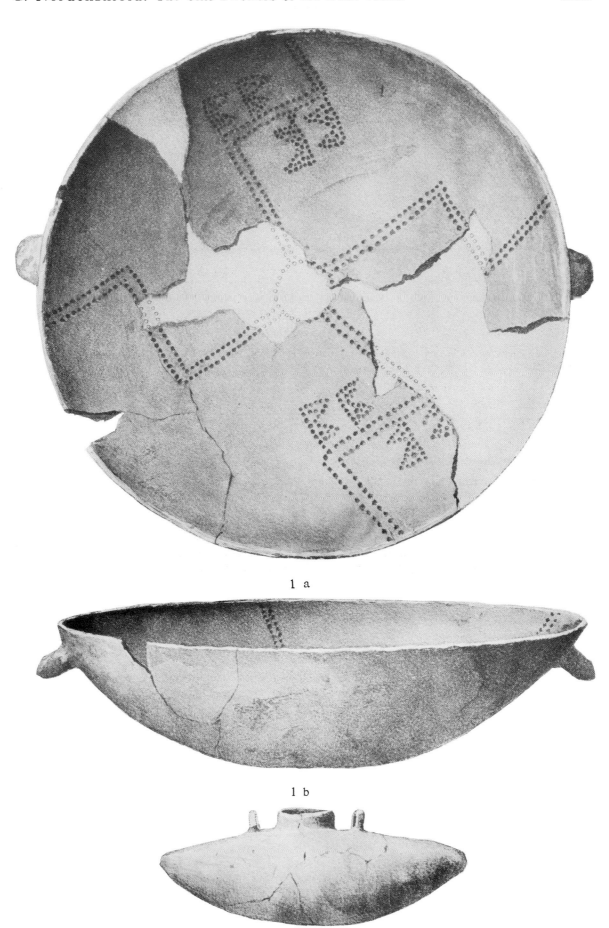

1 a

1 b

2

Plate XXIV.

Scale: $^1/_3$.

1 (331). Jar with two handles. Form unusual. Surface soft, grayish, and fairly even.
Ruin 14 on the east side of Wetherill's Mesa.

2 (613). Large ladle of very rough execution.
Found at the same spot as the large bowl (Pl. XXIII: 1), which it also resembles in the loose texture of the material and the careless execution.

3 (140). Ladle with broken handle, much damaged, and of rough execution.
Mug House.

4 (691). Small vase of incised design, which is, however, indistinct in the heliotype. The design consists of parallel straight lines, arranged in triangular fields. The lines are carelessly and irregularly drawn and rather indistinct.
This vessel was procured of a Ute Indian, who stated that it was from a ruin on the Mesa Verde.

5 (692). Small bowl. On each side of the mouth two fine holes are pierced, perhaps to hold the cord by which a lid was attached. The execution is careful, but the baking has not been thorough, for the surface is soft.
Obtained in the same way as the preceding article.

6, 7 and **8** (94, 93, 83). Small ladles of a singular, dark-brown variety, with extremely hard surface and of excellent material. Perhaps censers.
Found in estufa *1*, Ruin 9 in Cliff Cañon.

9 (128). This is probably the result of a child's experiment in the art of pottery. A portion of the jar is wanting, and the remainder is broken in two across the middle, in a manner possibly indicating that a narrow-necked vessel was made in two pieces, which were subsequently fitted together.
Found in estufa *1*, Ruin 9.

10 (594). Spherical vessel of rough execution. Colour yellow or reddish brown. A few cracks have formed during the process of baking, which has been fairly thorough.
Found in the refuse heap at Step House (*i* in the plan Pl. VII).

11 (129). Ladle of a type very common in the cliff-houses. The form of these ladles is undoubtedly derived, as is further shown by Plate XXX, from a gourd split in two. It is singular to observe how the clay imitation accurately reproduces a point so unessential to the vessel as the curved end of the peduncle. See too the ladle represented in 6.
Found in estufa *1*, Ruin 9.

1   2

3   4   5

6   7   8   9

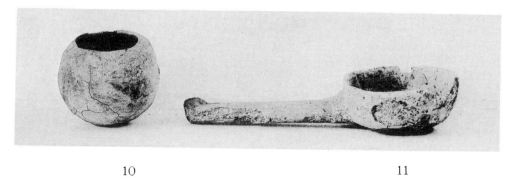

10   11

Plate XXV.

Scale: $^1/_3$.

1 (375). Bowl. Colours bright black and white. The outer margin of the bowl encircled by a black line, from which ten black streaks, single and in pairs, run obliquely downwards for about a third of the circumference.

Found in an estufa in Spring House.

Several of the bowls have marks painted like this figure on the outside. These marks generally consist of crosses or simple designs formed by a few streaks; sometimes they represent birds or other animals. Examples of this are afforded by the bowls Pl. XXV: 4, 5; Pl. XXVII: 2, 6, and by the potsherds figured in the chapter on rock carvings and paintings. The marks may possibly be intended to designate the owners. MALLERY [1] gives examples of similar property marks used by the Arikara and Serrano Indians. In the same grave, however, I found bowls with different marks, though they probably belonged to the same person.

2 (376). Bowl similar to the preceding one. On the outside of the bowl near the margin, at four spots at equal distances from each other, three short, oblique streaks.

Found in Spring House in the same estufa as the preceding bowl.

3 (377). Large bowl with rather flat bottom.

Found in the same place as the two preceding ones.

4 (601). Large, deep bowl. On the outside two markings, only one of which is visible in the heliotype.

Found in a grave (*g*) in Step House.

5 (577). Remarkably handsome bowl. Pattern of sharply marked black on a white ground. Surface extremely hard and glossy. Has a metallic ring when struck. On the outside of the bowl a cross.

Found hidden in the refuse heap at Step House (at *l* in the plan).

6 (651). Bowl. Ornamented with grayish brown on a gray ground. Surface very hard.

Found together with two other bowls in a grave in Pool Cañon (see p. 49).

---

[1] MALLERY, GARRICK. On the Pictographs of the North American Indians. Fourth. Ann. Rep. Bur. Ethn., p. 182.

1   2

3   4

5   6

Plate XXVI.

Scale: $^1/_3$.

1 (650). Bowl of the same type as Pl. XXV: 6. Ornamented too in the same style. On both these bowls the pattern is divided into 10 triangular compartments.

    Found in a grave in Pool Cañon (p. 49).

2 (605). Bowl. The pattern has been black on a white ground, but by the influence of some corrosive agents in the soil this has been altered to a dull reddish brown, the figures being thus almost obliterated. The inner surface of the bowl has been divided into four compartments, which have been filled alternately with straight lines and stair-shaped figures.

    Found in Step House together with an entirely decomposed skeleton (grave *f*).

3 (574). Large bowl with remarkably handsome design of coal-black on a yellowish brown ground. Baking thorough, the inner surface being lustrous and hard. The meander and the parallel lines within which it is enclosed, executed with great skill. Still the potter has not succeeded in calculating the pattern exactly, but has been forced to make the last compartment somewhat longer than the others. On account of the brown colour of the surface a good photograph of the bowl could not be taken. The heliotype is made from a drawing.

    Found in a grave (*c*) at Step House, turned over a basket of cornflour.

4 (612). Large bowl. The surface being much corroded and the pattern half erased, no direct photograph could be taken. Reproduced in the same way as the preceding article.

    Found in a grave (*b*) at Step House.

5 (611). Bowl. Ornament especially handsome and executed in black on a gray ground. The bowl has probably lost its regular form during the process of drying.

    Found in a grave (*b*) at Step House.

6 (302). Bowl. Pattern executed with no great care, in black on a white ground. Half of the bowl much corroded.

    Found in a grave below Kodak House.

————————

1   2

3   4

5   6

Plate XXVII.

Scale: $^1/_3$.

1 (127). Small bowl reconstructed from a fragment. The singular and handsome ornament consists of white zigzags on a black ground and is well executed.

Ruin 9 in Cliff Cañon.

2 (562). Small bowl restored from a fragment somewhat more than half of the full size. Ornament of the simplest description, consisting merely of parallel lines and a row of dots. A singular mark on the outside.

Found in a grave (*h*) at Step House.

3 (610). Small bowl. Pattern a dentated line round the inner margin.

Found in a grave (*b*) at Step House.

4 (260). Small bowl of thick ware.

Found in a much dilapidated cliff-dwelling, 150 metres south of Long House.

5 (579). Small bowl of yellowish brown colour and with simple design of black.

Found in Step House hidden together with two other bowls (at *l* in the plan).

6 (599). Bowl, with *svastika* on the outside.

Found in a grave (*g*) at Step House.

7 (560). Bowl. Not quite so well executed as the preceding ones. Surface soft except where coated with the black colour. It seems as though this pigment had caused a slight vitrification of the surface.

Found in a grave (*h*) at Step House.

1   2

3   4   5

6   7

Plate XXVIII.

Scale: $^{1}/_{3}$.

1, a and **b** (143). Fragment of a large bowl. Design handsome and uncommon, the *svastika* of especial interest. Original diameter 27.5 cm. In the hardness of the surface and the brightness of the colours this bowl ranks among the most perfect specimens of the pottery of the cliff-dwellers. An exceptional point in this bowl is its possession of a design on the outside. I have observed very few instances of this among the bowls from the Mesa Verde.

Found in Mug House.

2 (681). Small bowl.

Found in Square-tower House.

3 (141?). Fragment of a bowl, ornamented with the representation of a bird.

Found in Mug House.

4 (578). Bowl.

Found hidden beside Step House (at *l* in the plan).

5 (126). Large bowl restored from a small fragment. Ornament black on a white ground and consisting of a handsome meander.

Found in Ruin 9 in Cliff Cañon.

6, a and **b** (414). Lid of the jar Pl. XXIX: 7. Both sides of the lid ornamented as shown in the plate.

1 a   1 b

2   3   4

5

6 a   6 b

Plate XXIX.

Scale: ⅓.

1 (609). Mug. Ornamented with black on a grayish brown ground. Surface very hard. Mouth narrow (diam. internally 4.5 cm.).

Found in a grave (*b*) at Step House.

2 (606). Small pitcher of rather rude execution. Handle broken. Ornamented with but little care.

Found in a grave (*f*) at Step House.

3 (273). Cylindrical mug of excellent execution. The broad handle is pierced with a hole (see the appended figure), probably used in hanging up the mug. Contents 250 cc.

Thickness of the ware 0.5 cm. Very elaborately ornamented with glossy black on a clear white ground.

Found together with two small stone axes hidden in a large black jar in Mug House.

The form of these mugs is probably derived from vessels of bark. Fragments of such vessels, found in Ruin 9, show that they were used by the cliff-dwellers.

4 (138). Mug of the form most common among the earthenware of the cliff-dwellers, a truncate cone. Pattern of dull black and white.

Found in Mug House, in a chamber buried by the fall of a large block of stone from the roof of the cave.

5 (139). Jar of especially tasteful form and very handsome execution. Ornamented with great care. The pattern consists of a zone surrounded by concentric circles and divided into three equal compartments. Within these, two white lines, independent of each other, form a singular and complicated design which is best illustrated by the figure. The mouth is surrounded by a raised brim pierced with four pairs of small holes at equal distances from each other. Surface of the jar hard and glossy, colours bright. Material white and fine, ware rather thick.

Found in Mug House in the same chamber as the preceding object.

6 (600). Mug of the same form as 4. Cubical contents 400 cc. The ornament one of the most typical of the cliff-dwellers' pottery. It recurs in 8 and, in a somewhat modified form, in 7.

Found in a grave (*g*) at Step House.

7 (414). Jar similar in form to 5 and of the same excellent execution. Surface hard and of a fairly powerful lustre. Ornament not quite so dull as in the heliotype, black on a white ground as usual. Mouth furnished with a raised brim and closed by a lid, represented in Pl. XXVIII: 6.

Found in the lower portion of Ruin 13.

8 (339). Pitcher with handle and of singular form. Black, when found, with soot that could be partly removed.

Found in Mug House in an estufa filled to the height of the roof with stones and rubbish.

1   2   3

4   5   6

7   8

Plate XXX.

Scale: 1/3. 15

1 (695). Dipper with round, hollow handle, pierced with 5 small holes. Ornamented with two black, spiral lines, each occupying half of the inside of the vessel. The mending is done by a Ute squaw.

   Obtained from the Ute Indians, who had found it in a cliff-dwelling.

   I here append the figure of some fragments of a piece of pottery found in Ruin 9 and showing how earthenware was mended by the cliff-dwellers.

2 (696). Ladle of excellent execution. Form singular, being an accurate copy of a gourd split longitudinally. The pattern consists of rectangular fields divided by parallel lines in two directions at right angles to each other. This arrangement of the lines suggests that the ornamentation is derived from some plaited object.

   Found in the Cañon de Chelley according to the statement of the Navajo Indians.

3 (575). Ladle also of excellent execution. Form developed from that of the preceding vessel, by the addition merely of a partition between the bowl and the handle.

   Found in a grave (*c*) at Step House.

4 (694). Spoon of a form unusual among the pottery from the cliff-houses. Ornamented with a pattern of reddish brown on the grayish surface.

   From the Mesa Verde according to the statement of a Ute Indian.

5 (301). Small ladle.

   Found in a grave below Kodak House.

6 (569). Ladle. Ornament the same as in 5. though the objects were found in different localities.

   Found in a grave (*c*) at Step House.

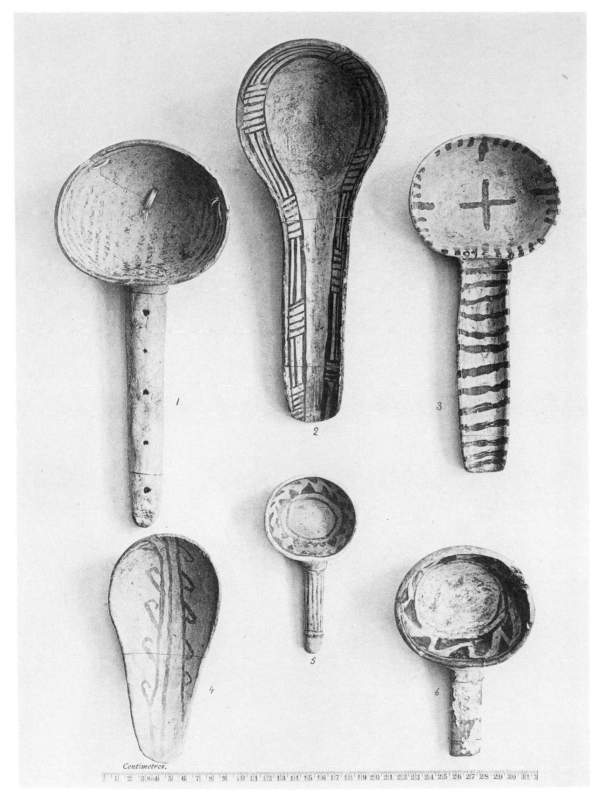

Centimetres.

Plate XXXI.

Scale: $^1/_3$.

1, a and **b** (580). Large spherical jar of masterly execution. Depth 35.5 cm. Thickness of the ware, in spite of the size of the jar, no more than 3 or 4 mm., and the weight no more than 3.6 kgm. Diameter of the neck 8.5 cm. In form this jar is one of the most admirable works of the prehistoric potters. The baking, on the other hand, has not been thorough, for the surface is rather soft. The ornament too is not executed with any special care. At some spots the black colour is so thick that is has been possible to scrape off a quantity thereof. The colour proved on chemical analysis to contain iron, and probably consists of $Fe_3 O_4$.

Found buried beside the ruins of Step House (at *j* in the plan).

1 a

1 b

Plate XXXII.

Scale: $^1/_3$.

1, 2, 3 and **5** (697, 698, 693, 699). Earthenware vessels of different shapes from the Cañon de Chelley in North Arizona (according to the statement of the Navajo Indians). All these vessels are of the fine variety ornamented in black and white.

4 (700). Earthenware vessel ornamented in black and white like the preceding ones. Found in a ruin on the north bank of the Rio San Juan.

———————

1   2

3

4   5

Plate XXXIII.

Scale: $^1/_2$.

1, a and **b** (385). Red bowl. Among all the pottery found by the author in the cliff-dwellings this bowl is the most perfect both in form and design. The unit of the design is shown in 1, *b*, and is repeated three times round the inside of the bowl. Its fine details are executed with great care. The spiral lines of dull white on the outside of the bowl are painted by a practised hand and with a sure eye. This ornament, like figures composed of curved lines in general, is very rare in the pottery from the cliff-dwellings. The colours are almost exactly reproduced in the plate. See in addition the text on p. 84.

Found in Spring House. Restored from fragments forming about half of the bowl.

1 a

1 b

Plate XXXIV.

In the list of the stone axes figured in the plates I give the rock of which they are composed. Whenever it has been possible, I have split a thin piece of the axe and made a microscopical section. When this is the case, it is indicated by an asterisk (*).

1 (374). Stone axe of basalt.*
            Spring House.

2 (521). Double edged stone axe of sandstone.*
            Ruin 11.

3 (567). Stone axe of quartzite.*
            Step House.

4 (685). Stone axe of porphyrite.
            Sprucetree House.

5 (308). Stone axe of porphyrite.*
            Kodak House.

6 (280). Stone axe of petrosilex.*
            Mug House.

7 (133). Stone axe of rhyolite.*
            Mug House.

8 (297). Stone hammer of sandstone.*
            Ruin 11.

9 (387). Stone axe of rhyolite.
            Spring House.

Plate XXXV.

1 (275).   Stone axe of petrosilex.
        Mug House.

2 (665).   Rough-hewn stone axe of quartzite.
        Sprucetree House.

3 (276).   Stone axe of petrosilex(?)*
        Mug House.

4 (338).   Stone axe of porphyrite.*
        Mug House.

5 (337).   Stone axe of sandstone* (same as Pl. XXXIV: 2).
        Mug House.

6 (316).   Stone axe probably of hornblendeschist.
        A little south of Kodak House.

7 (369).   Stone axe probably of gneiss.
        Burial mound on Wetherill's Mesa.

8 (520).   Stone hammer of a kind of green rock not unlike nephrite.
        Ruin 11.

9 (317).   Stone axe of hornblendeschist* (same as 6).
        Kodak House.

Plate XXXVI.

1 (75). Drill. Small point of flint attached by strips of yucca to a stick.
Found in Ruin 9.

2 (224). Drill point of jasper, with the yucca strips for fastening it to the shaft still adhering to it.
From Long House.

3 (682). Knife of quartzite.
Found near Ruin 18.

4 (278). Shafted axe of hard amygdaloidal rock.* Shaft composed of twigs bent round the axe and bound with strips of yucca and hide. Adorned on one side with parallel lines in two directions.
Found in an estufa in Mug House.

5 (208). Scraper of flint, with a cotton string bound round it.
Found in Long House.

6 (271). Shafted stone axe (sandstone?).*
Found in Ruin 11.

7 (701). Knife of quartzite. A shaft, presumably of wood, has probably been fastened to the knife with asphalte or pitch, traces of which still remain.
Found in Long House(?). Label lost.

8 (677). Skinning-knife of hornstone.
Found in Square-tower House.

9 (336). Skinning-knife of the same material.
Found in an estufa in Mug House.

10 (163). Skinning-knife of handsome form. Same material. The handle was found still attached to the knife, but was entirely decayed.
Found in an estufa in Long House.

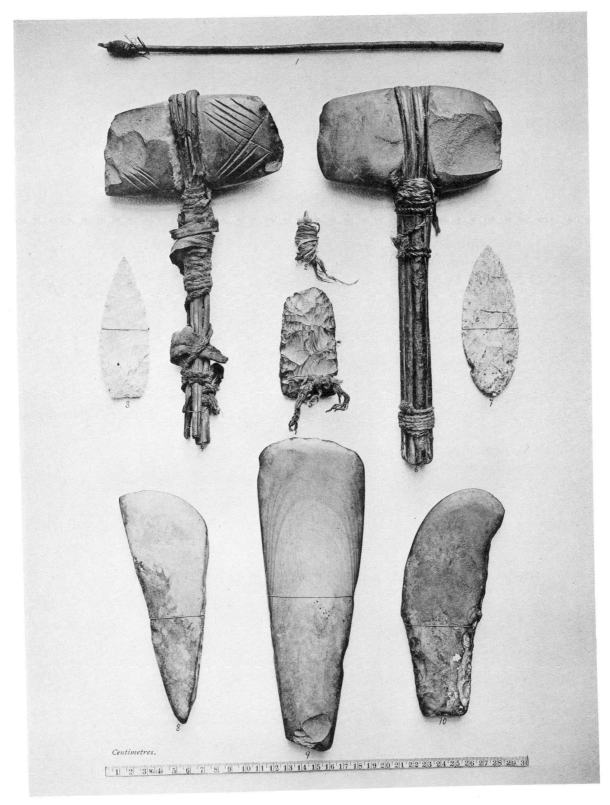

Plate XXXVII.

1 (149). Flint knife.

> Found below a cliff-house in one of the branches of Navajo Cañon (the second branch east of Wetherill's Mesa).

2 (230). Skinning-knife of brittle black slate.

> Found in Long House.

3 (313). Skinning-knife of brittle, variegated black slate.

> Found in Kodak House.

4 (549). Arrow-head of flint.

> Found on the mesa near the Cliff Palace.

5 (474). Piece of silicified wood; probably employed in smoothing the surface of pottery dried but not yet baked.

> Found in Ruin 12.

6 (132). Spear-head of flint.

> Found in Mug House.

7 (550). Drill point of flint.

> Found at the same spot as 4.

8 (314). Spear-head or knife(?) of silicified wood.

> Found in Kodak House.

9 (411). Round quartz stone. Surface highly polished, suggesting that the stone was used in rubbing and polishing some object.

> Found together with another similar stone in Ruin 13.

10 (341). Knife of flint (?).

> Found in Mug House.

11 (564). Arrow-head of flint.

> Step House.

12 (404). Arrow-head of flint.

> Ruin 13.

13 (227). Rude implement consisting of a sharp edged piece of flint wrapped in maize leave. Probably a scraper.

> Found in Long House.

Plate XXXVIII.

1 (591). Metate stone of hard brown sandstone. Greatest length 55 cm.
Found in Step House.

2 (142). Large stone hammer of hard conglomerate. Length 27.5 cm.
Mug House.

3 (378). Large, rough-hewn mortar of light sandstone. Greatest breadth 33 cm.
Spring House.

4 (244). Circular, carefully wrought mortar of sandstone. Diameter 19 cm.
Long House.

1

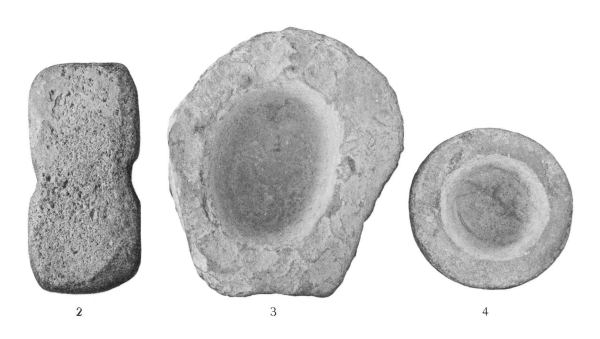

2   3   4

Plate XXXIX.

Scale: $^1/_3$.

1 (191), **3** (193). Rounded stones probably used for grinding some object. Much worn, almost polished on the two large planes.
      Found in Long House.

2 (312). Large stone hammer.
      Found in Kodak House.

3 see 1.

4 (50), **5** (45). Large, rather flat stones of irregular shape, very much worn. Use unknown.
      Found in Ruin 9.

6 (671). Implement of black slate. Form peculiar (see the text).
      Found in Sprucetree House.

1   2   3

4   5

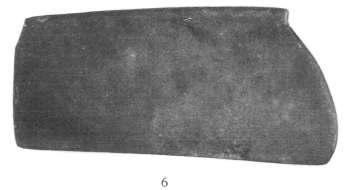

6

Plate XL.

With the description of this plate I here give a brief summary of all the bone implements found during my excavations. Dr. L. Jägerskiöld has kindly undertaken the examination of these bones, and determined when this has been possible, to what animal they have belonged and what part of the skeleton they have formed.

1 (291), **3** (21), **6** (268), **7** (144), **9** (154), **25** (396), and **Pl. XLI: 8** (679). Pieces of so-called "long" mammalian bones, wrought into awls.

Found: 1 and 6 in Ruin 11; 3 in Ruin 9; 7 in Mug House; 9 in Long House; 25 in Spring House; Pl. XLI: 8 in Square-tower House.

Three more bones of this kind were found.

2 (469), **15** (212), **23** (394), **27** (405), and **Pl. XLI: 6** (136), **10** (393). The *tibia* of a species of turkey (probably *Gallopavo sylvestris*). The bones wrought into awls.

Found: 2 in Ruin 12; 15 in Long House; 23 in Spring House; 27 in Ruin 13; Pl. XLI: 6 in Mug House; 10 in Spring House.

15 bones of this kind wrought into awls were found. When any joint is left it is always the lower one.

3 see 1.

4 (306), **13** (525), **17** (523), **24** (473), **26** (221). The *ulna* of a large bird; 4 sharpened to an awl; 13, 17 made into beads; some of the bones probably of the turkey.

Found: 4 in Kodak House; 13, 17 in Ruin 16; 24 in Ruin 12; 26 in Long House.

6 other bones of this kind and 4 or 5 *ulnæ* of smaller birds found, most of them used as beads.

5 (652). Several *ulnæ* and *radii* of birds (turkeys) tied on a buckskin string and probably used as an amulet.

Found in Sprucetree House.

6 see 1. **7** see 1.

8 (287). The *ulna* of a species of *Felis*, wrought into an awl.

Found in Mug House.

An *ulna* of the same species found in Spring House.

9 see 1.

10 (468), **11** (531), **12** (290), **18** (303), **19** (270). The *radius* of a large bird (turkey?). The bones are sharpened to awls.

Found: 10 in Ruin 12; 11 in Ruin 16; 12, 19 in Ruin 11; 18 in Kodak House.

4 awls probably made of the same bone were found.

13 see 4.

14 (678). Lower part of the *femur* of a *Felis*, probably of the same species as 8.

Found in Square-tower House.

In the same locality was found a *humerus* and in Mug House a *rachus* probably both of the same species as 14.

15 see 2.

16 (217), **21** (259), **20** (219). Awls made of the *tarsometatarsus* of the turkey (16, 21 the lower end, 20 the upper end of the bone).

Found: 16, 20 in Long House; 21 in a ruin near Long House.

My collection comprises 15 awls made of the lower, 3 made of the upper end of this bone, and one entire bone. A *tarsometatarsus* and foot of a turkey, dried with the skin was found in Ruin 9.

17 see 4. **18** see 10. **19** see 10. **20** see 16. **21** see 16.

22 (389), **29** (392). Beads made of the *humerus* of a large bird (probably the turkey).

Found in Spring House.

My collection contains one more bone of this kind.

23 see 2. **24** see 4. **25** see 1. **26** see 4. **27** see 2.

28 (282). Awl made of the bone of a bird. Too much worn to be determined.

Found in Mug House.

29 see 22.

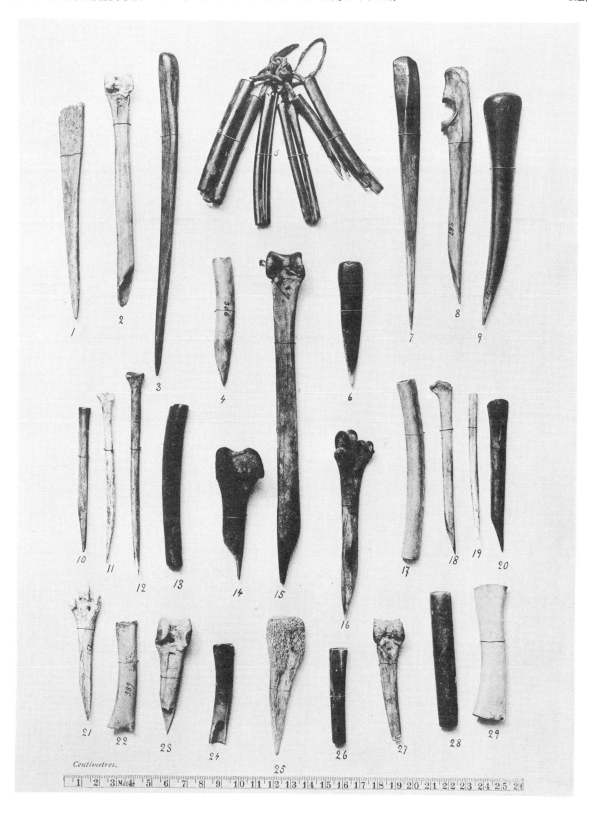

Plate XLI.

1 (416), **2** (335), **4** (107), **5** (251). Scrapers made of the *humerus* of a species of *Cervidæ*.
Found: 1 in Ruin 13; 2 in Mug House; 4 in Ruin 9; 5 in Long House.
One more scraper of this kind was found in Ruin 13.

3 (254). Large scraper made of the *tibia* of a species of *Cervidæ*.
Found in a ruin near Long House.

4 see 1.

5 see 1.

6 see Pl. XL: 2.

7 (360). Implement (scraper?) made of the *cannon bone* of a species of *Cervidæ*.
Found in Ruin 14.

8 see Pl. XL: 1.

9 (150). Horn probably of the mountain-sheep, straightened out.
Found in Long House.

10 see Pl. XL: 2.

In addition to the bones mentioned above Dr. JÄGERSKIÖLD has identified among the bones and bone implements in my collection the *humerus* and *femur* of a species of rabbit and a number of different bones of a large bird, perhaps the turkey.

$(^1/_1)$

The above figure shows a bone implement omitted in the plate. It is a bone pierced with a little hole and perhaps used as a whistle.

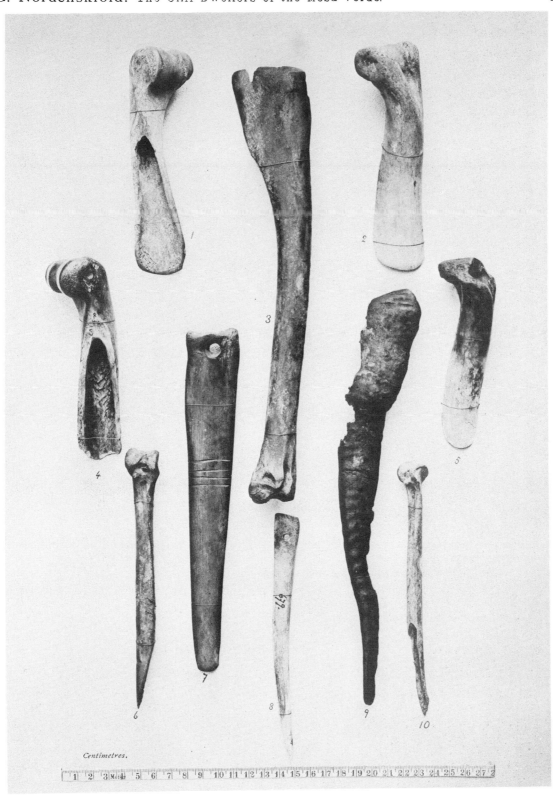

Centimetres.

Plate XLII.

1 (49)   Arrow of wood. Feathers attached with sinews. Length 62.8 cm. The arrow is pointed at the end and does not seem to have had any separate head.
　　　Found in Ruin 9.

2—8 (202—6, 246—7). Implements of wood. (See p. 100).
　　　Found in Rooms *13* and *14* in Long House.

9 (676). Implement of dark brown wood, pointed at one end and adorned with a simple, carved design.
　　　Found in Square-tower House.

10 (627). Implement of oak, rounded on the upper surface, flat underneath, and notched at the ends.
　　　Found in Step House.

11 (633), **20** (475), **26** (632), and **27** (222). Wooden awls.
　　　Found: 11 and 26 in Step House, 20 in Ruin 12, 27 in Long House.

12 (111). Loop of flexible wood. Loops of this description were inserted in the walls on each side of the door-openings, and a stick passed through them to serve as a bolt (see p. 53).
　　　Found in Ruin 9.

13 (641) and **14** (641, *b*). Pegs with a knob at one end.
　　　Dug up in Step House (in grave *b*).

15 (73), **22** (61) and **25** (18). Arrow-heads of hard wood.
　　　Found in Ruin 9.

16 (213), **17** (22). The broken points of arrows. A piece of a fine reed, with a point of hard wood inserted therein.
　　　Found: 16 in Long House, 17 in Ruin 9.

19 (702). Simple handle of a stone axe. A piece of a flexible bough bent and tied with a yucca leaf.
　　　Found in Mug House (?)

20. See 11.

21 (638). A bunch of cedar bast for kindling a fire, tied with yucca leaves.
　　　Found in Step House.

22. See 15.

23 (232). Broken point of a reed arrow; wooden head wanting.
　　　Found in Long House.

24 (48). Fire drill.
　　　Found in Ruin 9.

25. See 15.

26 and **27**. See 11.

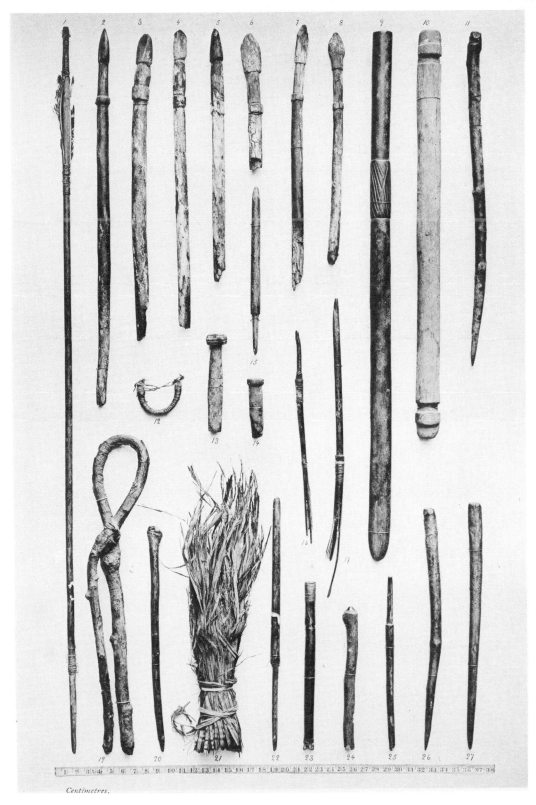

Centimetres.

Plate XLIII.

1 (626).   Awl ot hard wood.
> Found in Step House beside the bag of salt (Pl. XLIX: 3).

2 (52).   Wooden implement of dark brown colour, much worn at the narrower end. Employed probably in crushing or pounding some substance, possibly in beating out the yucca fibre.
> Found in Ruin 9.

3 (585) and **4** (584).   Concave pieces of soft wood about 2 cm. in thickness; 4 much worn at the ends and edges.
> Found in Step House.

5 (7).   Forked implement of wood.   At the lower end and at the tips of the prongs somewhat scratched.
> Found in Ruin 9.

6 (669).   Bundle of 19 sticks of hard wood, probably employed in some kind of knitting or crochet work.   The pins are pointed at one end, blunt at the other, and black with wear.   They are held together by a narrow band of yucca.
> Found in Sprucetree House.

7 (120).   Bent disk of soft wood.   Employed as a scoop or spaddle.
> Found in Ruin 9.

8 (32 and 67).   Ends of a bow.   The entire length of the bows belonging to the cliff-dwellers was 1.3—1.5 metres.   These fragments are respectively 31 and 45 $^{1}_{2}$ cm. long, of strong and fairly hard wood.
> Found in Ruin 9.

9 (29) and **17** (84).   Long, flat disks of wood, with traces at one end of wear due to their having been held in the hand.   At the same end in 17 a yucca band, at the other end a groove to receive a similar band.   The other end also worn, but dull.   Employed probably in weaving, possibly to press together the threads of the woof when inserted between those of the warp.
> Found in Ruin 9.

10 (37), **11** (40), **12** (551 *b*), **13** (603), **14** (122).   Long wands (13 is 137.5 cm. long) flattened at one end.   Longitudinal scratches, especially distinct on 13, suggest that these wands have been employed in digging in the ground, probably in planting maize (see p. 100). 10 and 12 are furnished with knobs at one end.   The material is oak, certainly in 13, and probably in the others.   12 is coloured carmine-red, especially towards the pointed end.   14 is black and sooty, different in form from the others, and pointed at both ends.   This is the most common wooden implement of the cliff-dwellers.
> 10, 11, and 14 found in Ruin 9; 12 in grave *d* and 13 in grave *g* at Step House.

15 (85).   Three-pronged (originally four-pronged) wooden fork. Surface scratched. Presumably employed as a spit or toasting-fork in broiling flesh.
> Found in Ruin 9.

16 (628).   Long, round skewer of hard wood.   At one end a knob furnished with grooved rings.   On the top of the knob a cross.   Near the middle 5 more cuts, not very deep. Burnt at the tip.
> Found in Step House.

17.   See 9.

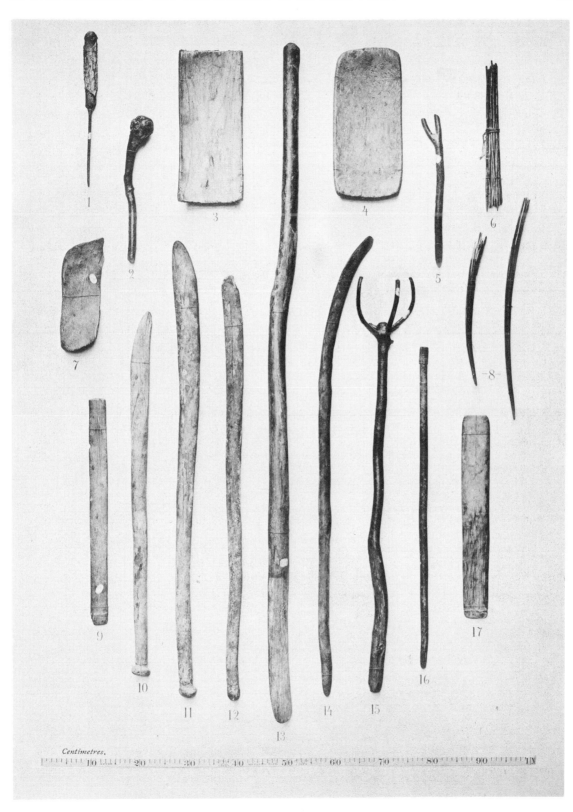

Plate XLIV.

Scale: $^1/_3$.

1 (664).   Basket of woven yucca in two different colours, a neat pattern being thus attained. The strips of yucca running in a vertical direction are of the natural yellowish brown, the others (in horizontal direction) darker.

   Found in Sprucetree House.

2 (662).   Similar to the preceding basket, but smaller.

   Found in Sprucetree House.

3 (573).   Willow basket, tightly plaited of osiers round a withe spirally coiled.

   Found in a grave (*c*) in Step House.

4 (616).   Basket lid, plaited in the same manner as the preceding object.

   Found hidden in the refuse heap at Step House.

5 (615).   Basket plaited in the same manner. It seems as though the basket had been coated on the outside with some substance stopping all the interstices and rendering it watertight. This method of manufacturing watertight vessels is still employed by several Indian tribes.

   Found at the same spot as the preceding object.

1   2

3   4

5

Plate XLV.

Scale (for 1—5): $\frac{1}{3}$.

1 (95) and **2** (663). Small baskets of yucca, of plain colour and of handsomely plaited pattern.
>Found: 1 in Ruin 9, 2 in Sprucetree House.

3 (526). Gourd, spherical. Furnished with two small round holes near each other, one on each side of the mark left by the stalk (rattle?).
>Found in Ruin 16.

4 (617). Large squash furnished with round opening and over this with a lid fastened by a cord of yucca. The crevices between the lid and the opening as well as the other cracks were originally stopped with mortar. Contents a quantity of feathers from which insects have gnawed the plumes, a complete material for the manufacture of feather cloth, consisting of loose cord, loose, long feathers, the ends of feathers, some 5 centimetres long, cut off and tied up with a cord, and lastly about two metres of two-stranded cotton twine knotted into a ring. Half of this twine is wrapped with the feather ends and ready for use in the preparation of the cloth. Through a hole in the stalk, which is still attached, a yucca cord is passed, presumably to hang up the pumpkin. (Se also p. 103).
>Found hidden in the refuse heap at Step House.

5 (19). Cup made of the end of a pumpkin. The tip of the pumpkin, forming the bottom of the cup, has been sewn together with a cord and stopped with a lump of pitch.
>Found in Ruin 9.

6, 7, 8, and **9** (587). Maize cobs of different varieties. 6 dark brown, the others yellow or yellowish gray.
>Found in Step House.

10 (419). Yucca fruit. Has been threaded and hung on a stalk, probably to dry.
>Ruin 13.

11 (72). Half of a nut (*Carya*). Pierced at the end with two holes, and probably used as an ornament or amulet.
>Ruin 9.

12 (178). Bean, dark brown.
>Long House.

13 (66). Pumpkin seed.
>Ruin 9.

1   2

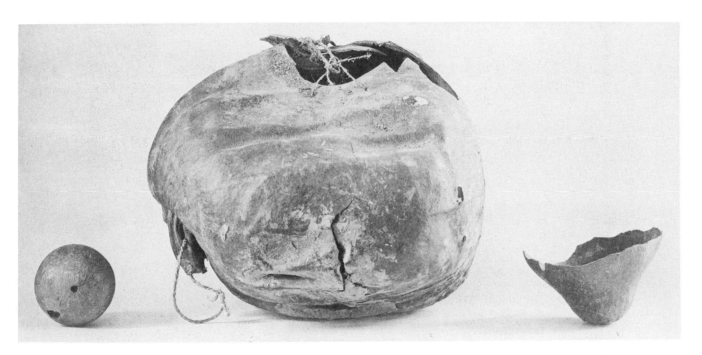

3   4   5

6   7   12   13   8   9

10

11

Centimetres.

Plate XLVI.

1 (635). Sandal plaited of entire yucca leaves; covered on the upper side, to protect the foot, with maize leaves. Attached by means of strips of yucca leaves passed over the foot. Length 30 cm.

      Found in Step House.

2 and **3** (80). Pair of sandals knotted of twined yucca cords. Kept on the foot by means of two thongs of buckskin into which the toes were passed. The holes patched with interlaced cords.

      Found in Ruin 9.

4 (216). Moccasin of raw hide.

      Found in Long House.

5 (116). Sandal of the commonest variety, plaited of fine strips of yucca leaves. Along both sides loops of two-stranded cords of yucca to fasten the sandal to the foot.

      Found in Ruin 9.

6 (553). Sandal plaited of yucca cords, but in a singular manner. The plaiting is done round 25 three-stranded cords of yucca running in the longitudinal direction of the sandal; these cords project at the toes and at the heel, and were used to bind the sandal to the foot. The plaiting is tight and firm, and a kind of pattern may be traced in it.

      Found in Step House.

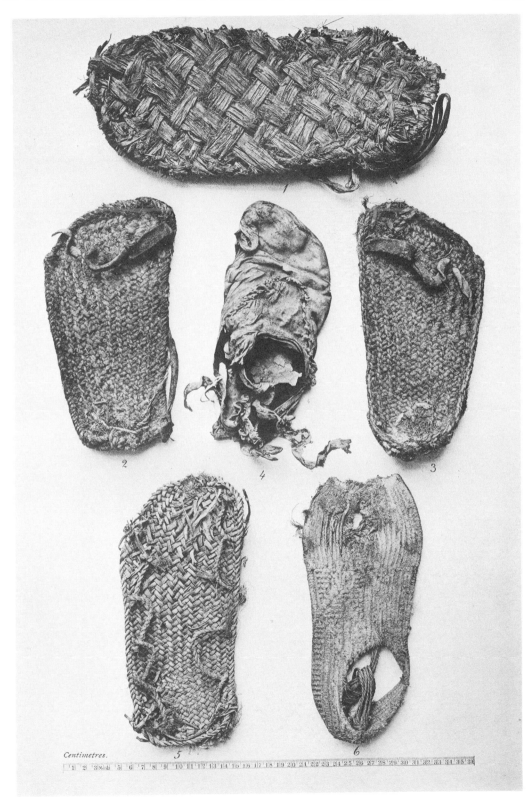

Plate XLVII.

1 (634) and **2** (294). Strips of yucca leaves wound into a double T-shaped bundle, possibly to wind cord or yarn upon.

Found: 1 in Step House, 2 in Ruin 11.

3 (265) and **10** (97). Rings of yucca fibre probably used in carrying vessels on the head or as support under the round bottomed jars. Fine strips of leaf are laid in a ring and wrapped in coarser strips.

Found: 3 in Ruin 11, 10 in Ruin 9.

4 (555). Fine yucca fibre wound round the dried leaves of some plant. In different localities I have found several of these balls. Perhaps they served as amulets, the inner leaves being considered to possess some mystical properties.

Found in Step House.

5 (631) and **9** (703). Fine leaves of some yucca species, tied up with a cord and employed in kindling a fire. At the ends, which are somewhat burnt, the fibres are separated from each other in order to render them more easily inflammable.

Found in Step House.

6 (44). Pouch of maize leaves kept together by a net of fine strips of yucca leaf.

Found in Ruin 9.

7 (263). Ring similar to 3 and 10, but of cedar bast wrapped in the soft blades of some grass. Burnt at one side.

Found in Ruin 11.

8 (58). Hairbrush of the fine, sharp leaves of some species of yucca. The points all turned in the same direction.

Found in Ruin 9.

9. See 5. **10**. See 3.

11 (152). Ball (toy?) of fine yucca fibre wrapped in yucca leaves.

Found in Long House.

12 (262). Brush similar to 8, but of fine blades of dried grass, tied together with a cord.

Found in Ruin 11.

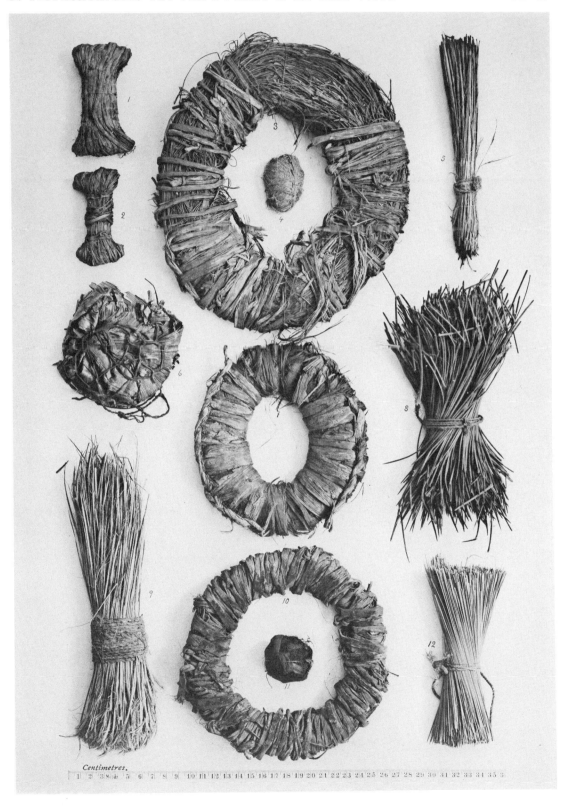

Plate XLVIII.

1 (602). Mat ($1._{78} \times 1._{08}$ m.) composed of withes split in two and held together by stiff cords of
yucca passed through holes at regular intervals in the withes. The narrow ends of the
withes turned alternately to the right and left. A mat of this description was wrapped
round a corpse when it was deposited in the grave. (See p. 39).
(See p. 39).
Found in a grave (*g*) at Step House.

2 (82). Snowshoe (?). Two frames of soft twigs, which are joined together and fastened
at two points with yucca leaves. Between them lies a loose layer of cedar bast.
Found in Ruin 9.

3 (209). A bundle of yucca leaves. Raw material for the textile industry.
Found in Long House.

4 (674). Mat of plaited reeds. Originally $1._2 \times 1._2$ m., but damaged in transportation.
Found in Sprucetree House.

Plate XLIX.

1 (261). Woven band with two round bars at the ends. Used in carrying burdens. Warp of yucca, woof of cotton.
    Found in Ruin 11.

2 (461). Double woven band used for the same purpose, material also the same as that of 1.
    Found in an estufa in Ruin 12.

3 (552). Handsome and well-preserved pouch of hide, filled with common salt (about 700 grammes) almost pure according to analysis. The pouch consists of the skin of a prairie-dog, sewn together in such a manner as to leave only the hole corresponding to the mouth of the animal open, some holes have been patched with bits of skin sewn fast with yucca fibre.
    Found in the refuse heap at Step House (at *m*).

4 (566). Large hank of yucca cord, rather finely twined of two strands. Length more than 400 m., weight 277 grammes. The cord is admirably well-preserved. looking almost new, and is extremely strong and well and evenly twined.
    Found in the refuse heap at Step House.

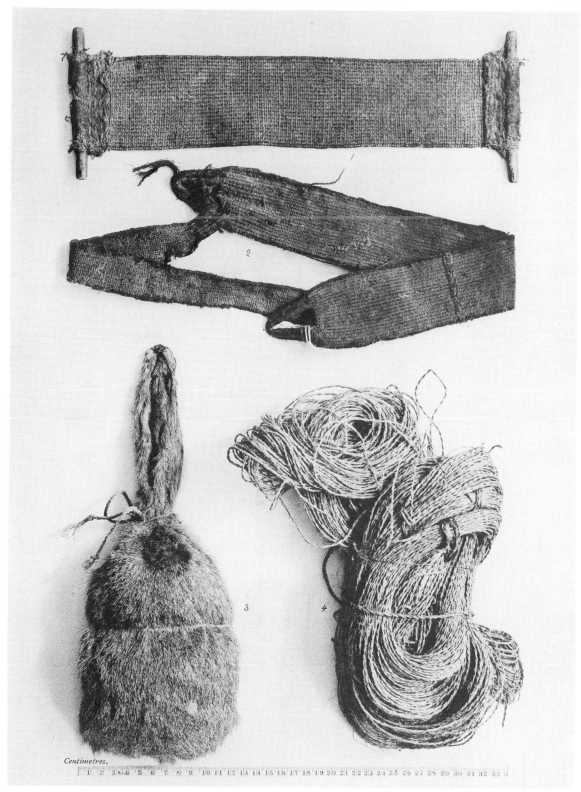

Centimetres.

Plate L.

1 (134).   Piece of cotton cloth with woven pattern.   Ends originally fastened together, so that the cloth formed a ring.   Pattern woven in threads of a dark brown colour.
Found in Mug House.

Centimetres.

Plate LI.

1 (105).   Stick with a lump of resin mixed with ferric oxide.
> Found in Ruin 9.

2 (137).   A number of perforated shells of a species still found in a fossilized condition amongst the sand on the mesa. Probably the remains of a necklace, though loose when found.
> Found in Mug House.

3 (683).   Bead, consisting of a perforated disk of horn.
> Found in Spring House.

4 (176).   Small bead of limestone (mother-of-pearl?).
> Found in Long House.

5 (639).   A pair of rats' claws, bound with yucca fibres to a stick.   A toy?
> Found in the refuse heap at Step House.

6 (92).   Head-dress of feathers tightly bound together in two rows, 5 in each row, with double strands of yucca, attached at two points and with their ends tied in a large knot.   The man figured on the potsherd p. 108 is represented with a similar head dress.
> Found in Ruin 9.

7 (381).   Black bead of jet.
> Found in Spring House.

8 (522).   Cylinder of polished hematite.   Perhaps a fetish.
> Found in Ruin 16.

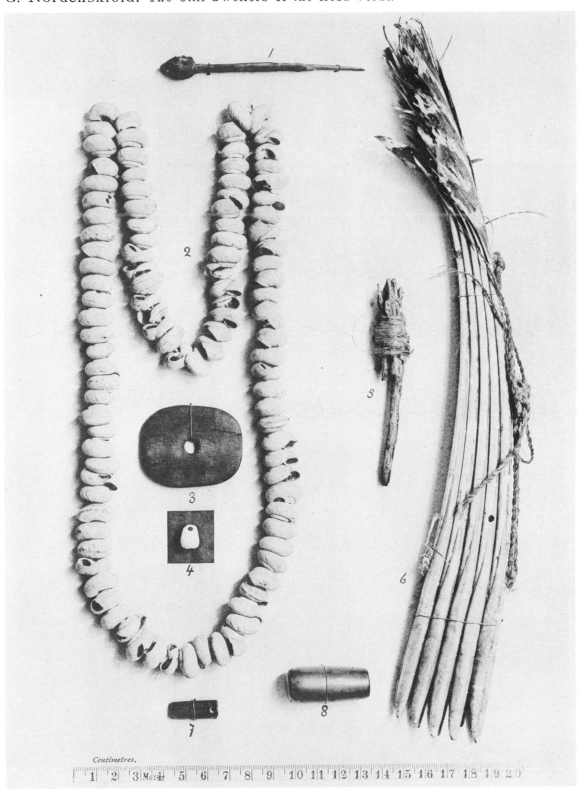

INDEX.

APPENDIX

HUMAN REMAINS

FROM

THE CLIFF DWELLINGS

OF

THE MESA VERDE

BY

G. RETZIUS

Human Remains

Collected by M. GUSTAF NORDENSKIÖLD in the Cliff Dwellings of the Mesa Verde
Described by Prof. G. RETZIUS.

With Ten Plates (Pl. I—X).

At the request of M. GUSTAF NORDENSKIÖLD I am here about to give a short description of the human skulls and other skeletal remains found and collected by him among the cliff-dwellings of the Mesa Verde.

As may be gathered from M. NORDENSKIÖLD's account, these remains consist of: —

1. *Two mummies* of adult individuals, one so densely enveloped in shrouds, bandages, and hide, as to preclude all possibility of examining the skull without the removal of the wrappings — a course which has been considered unadvisable, the other with the skull sufficiently exposed for examination and the taking of most of the measurements (No. 5 in the appended description).

2. *Seven perfect* (or almost perfect) *skulls* with the skeletons belonging to them more or less complete. From cliff-dwellings.

3. *Two defective skulls* from cliff-dwellings.

4. *Two child mummies* and *three child skulls* (the skeletons wanting).

5. *One complete skull* of an adult together with a defective skeleton, and *a defective skull*. From graves on the mesa in the neighbourhood of the ruins.

Of the above skulls I have selected for purposes of description ten which are in such a state of preservation that it is possible to measure them exactly and to give complete figures of them: 1) eight skulls of adults and one child skull from cliff-dwellings, 2) one skull of an adult from a grave on the mesa.

As it is of the utmost importance in the study of these cliff-dwellings — the origin and history of which are veiled in such obscurity — to know what race and people built and inhabited them, an examination of the mummies found there, and above all, of the skulls, possesses great interest.

All who have been engaged for any length of time in such researches, and who have followed the development of craniology with attention and discrimination, well know with how great caution we must beware of drawing too positive conclusions. But in spite of this, especially in a case so interesting as the present one, it is our duty to attempt an objective investigation. It may be thought that this duty should have been performed in a conscientious manner in the country to which the cliff-dwellings actually belong. With the assistance of M. G. NORDENSKIÖLD I have therefore searched the anthropological literature of America for works on the human remains discovered in similar ruins, but we have not succeeded in finding more than a few papers on the subject.

*　　*　　*

When SAMUEL MORTON published his great work on *Crania Americana* (1839), the ruins now in point were as yet unknown, or at least undescribed, and his book does not supply us with any information of skulls found in the cliff-dwellings. Not until much later (1870—80) were the cliff-dwellings subjected to any special investigation; and in spite of the exceeding singularity of these remains scientific literature contains only very few, meagre and cursory descriptions of the explorations in their neighbourhood. This explains the comparative failure of our efforts to collect information as to the skulls found in the cliff-dwellings. We are inclined to believe either that the number of crania collected has been very small, or that only an insignificant proportion thereof has been described.

The first authenticated discoveries of the kind seem to have been those made by the staff of the United States Geological and Geographical Survey, among the ruins described by W. H. HOLMES and W. H. JACKSON. These skulls were published in 1876 by EMIL BESSELS,[1] and are only three in number. One of them (No. 3 in BESSELS' paper) was found by Mr. CHITTENDEN in the Hovenweep, about 17 kilom. above its junction with McElmo Cañon, about 50 kilom. north of the New Mexican frontier and 10 kilom. east of the Utah line. The other two skulls were exhumed in an ancient ruin near Abiquiu, New Mexico, quite close to the place where Dr. YARROW made his discoveries.

From the measurements of these three skulls as given by BESSELS we make the following extracts:

	Length.	Breadth.	Height.	Circumference.	Capacity.	Zygom. diam.
Skull No. 1	168	144	135	508	1325	144
Skull No. 2	150	131	130	450	1020	116
Skull No. 3	—	136	—	—	—	144

No. 3, as may be gathered from these measurements, was rather defective.

From the descriptions and measurements, as well as from the woodcuts, it appears that these skulls were exceedingly brachycephalic; the anteroposterior index

---

[1] BESSELS, EMIL. The Human Remains found near the Ancient Ruins of Southwestern Colorado and New Mexico. Bull. U. S. Geol. and Geogr. Surv. of the Terr., Vol. II: No. 1, Wash. 1876.

of No. 1 being 85, 7, of No. 2 87, 3. But they showed marked artificial depression of the occipital region and of the posterior part of the parietal region, and in connexion therewith an asymmetrical form.

No. 1 was a strongly developed skull, probably male. No. 2 seemed to have belonged to a woman of about 17. Both were rather high, especially No. 1. In No. 2 the jaw was much projected, in No. 3 less so. No. 3, which consisted of several fragments (occipital bone wanting), showed a similar deformation to Nos. 1 och 2, though less marked; the frontal bone sharply receding; superciliary ridges very prominent.

For the sake of comparison with these three crania, BESSELS described in the same paper the two skulls previously collected by Dr. YARROW in the vicinity of the ruins near Abiquiu, and belonging to the United States Army Medical Museum (Nos. 1178 and 1179 in the catalogue). One of them is the skull of a child about 10 years old, the other that of an adult and exhibiting the general characteristics of a female cranium. The child skull measured 151 mm. in length and 138 mm. in breadth; it is deformed to about the same extent as No. 2, but while in the latter the deformation affects the right side, the former is compressed on the left. The skull No. 1179 is deformed so as to resemble that of an ancient Peruvian.

BESSELS finally added to his paper two crania exhumed in "mounds in Tennessee," and "showing exactly the same mode of deformation as the skulls obtained in the vicinity of the ruins." The resemblance between the crania from these two different localities is indeed so great that they might easily be confounded. The last-mentioned skulls were respectively 156 and 153 mm. long and 141 and 140 mm. broad.

"How far," says BESSELS, "the brachycephalic character is due to deformation, cannot be decided by means of the limited number of specimens on hand, but according to the general features of the skulls, we consider ourselves justified in saying that originally they were brachycephalic, and that in consequence of the deformation of the occiput the brachycephalic character is brought to view more strikingly than it would be if the skulls had not been compressed." They are also all more or less prognathous. "Now the question arises," he proceeds, "was the deformation to be found among the ancient inhabitants of the ruins generally or only in some instances? . . . . As the five skulls before us show the most unmistakeable signs of deformation, it is more than probable that the compression of the skull cannot have been a rare occurrence."

As to the tribe to which the cliff-dwellers belonged, BESSELS remarks, "Unfortunately, there are no skulls of Indian tribes that now inhabit the vicinity of the region in question within our reach, and therefore we are unable to draw any comparisons or to point out cranial affinities that might exist between the ancient inhabitants of the ruins and the people that now live near those deserted dwellings.

"According to other evidence, however, there is not much room left to doubt that the present Pueblo Indians are the direct descendants of the ancient inhabitants of Southern Colorado and New Mexico, although there are either no traditions preserved pointing toward this direction, or the few that do exist are of too vague a nature to be relied upon. As one of the arguments in favour of this view, we may take the mode of constructing the houses."

Two years later W. J. HOFFMAN [1] described a skull found in Chaco Cañon (northwestern New Mexico) in an old pueblo, at a depth of 14 ft. below the surface of the ground. The pueblos and the cliff-dwellings are supposed to have been constructed and inhabited by the same people. The skull, which is slightly damaged, and the lower jaw of which is wanting, was probably that of a young woman and is very brachycephalic. The most striking peculiarity, according to HOFFMAN, is the great flattening of the posterior portion of the skull, including the anterior portion of the occipital and the posterior superior portions of the parietal bone, especially on the left side, as may be seen from the figures.

In the *Report of the U. S. Geographical Surveys West of 100th Mer.* [2] published in 1879, MARK SIBLEY SEVERANCE and H. C. YARROW have given a description of the skulls and skeletons collected during the expeditions of 1872—74. Among these mention is made, and the measurements are given, of the two skulls from Abiquiu (New Mexico) noticed by BESSELS as belonging to the United States, Army Medical Museum (Nos. 1178 and 1179 in the catalogue). The first (1178) is here termed "Cranium of supposed ancient Pueblo Indian — from a burial-place without the walls of a fortified town," the other (1179) "Skeleton, almost complete, from same locality as last."

Lastly, in a paper on the Antiquities af New Mexico and Arizona, W. J. HOFFMAN has noticed and given several measurements of a number of skulls from Pueblo mounds in Utah, New Mexican pueblos, Chaco Cañon, Arizona, etc. Of these skulls only two, both from Arizona, were found in cliff-dwellings, some miles north-west of Camp Verde.

These are the only results of our literary researches, so that up to the present but very few skulls have been collected in the ancient cliff-dwellings and their burial-grounds. Thus the series of crania, with the skeletons appertaining to them, brought home by M. GUSTAF NORDENSKIÖLD and collected by him personally in their original localities, all the circumstances accompanying their discovery being well known, is apparently the largest and best collection of the kind at present in existence. It is now my purpose to describe these skulls. The craniological experience of years has, however, taught me that too minute descriptions, either of skulls or skeletons, are of little value; and the space allotted to this subject in the present work is very limited. I shall therefore give only the most important measurements in a tabular form, adding special remarks on the features of the skulls, and, in particular, accurate orthoscopical drawings of the most important crania, each in four normæ. In making

---

[1] HOFFMAN, W. J. Report on the Chaco Cranium. Rep. U. S. Geol. and Geogr. Surv. of the Terr. 1876. Wash. 1878, p. 453.
[2] Vol. VII, p. 391.

the drawings I have employed the regulator now in general use among cranio-logists, the German horizontal line (through the *meatus auditorii externi* and the inferior margin of the orbits). In the case of the child skull, in order to secure a natural position, I was obliged to abandon this rule. In some of the other skulls here figured, this line seems to me slightly to exaggerate the forward inclination, a fault which I have before observed.

The measurements employed are principally those of the Frankfort Agreement; but I have not throughout adhered to this method, especially as the artificial deforma-tion more or less apparent in these skulls has altered their natural form, and in some cases caused too great an abnormity to admit of the deduction of any positive conclusions as to the original habitus of the crania. In some of the skulls, however, the deformation being less pronounced, the natural form is discernible.

From M. G. NORDENSKIÖLD's collection I have selected for purposes of exa-mination and description the following skulls, numbered as below:

No. 1, Pl. I (catalogue number, 229). Skull from a room in Long House (see p. 29). No other objects found there.

No. 2, Pl. II (cat. n., 558). Skull found at Step House in the refuse heap beside the ruin (grave *h* in the plan Pl. VII). Four specimens of pottery were also exhumed there.

No. 3, Pl. III (cat. n., 608). Skull found in the same place as No. 2, toge-ther with four specimens of pottery (grave *b*).

No. 4, Pl. VI (cat. n., 598). Skull found in the same place as Nos. 2 and 3, together with three vessels of earthenware and a long wooden implement (grave *g*).

No. 5, Pl. V (cat. n., 568). Skull found in the same place as Nos. 2—4, together with a ladle of earthenware (grave *e*).

No. 6, Pl. VI (cat. n., 648). Skull from a cave in the sandstone cliff below a small ruin in Pool Cañon (see p. 48). Three earthen vessels also found there.

No. 7, Pl. VII (cat. n., 300). Skull found under a jutting rock below Kodak House (see p. 30). The grave contained two specimens of pottery.

No. 8, Pl. VIII (cat. n., 643). Skull exhumed in a small, isolated ruin (see p. 45). No other objects found in the grave.

No. 9, Pl. IX (cat. n., 646). Child skull belonging to one of the three ske-letons of children found in a room at the very back of Sprucetree House (see p. 55).

No. 10, Pl. X (cat. n., 368). Skull from a grave on the mesa in the neigh-bourhood of the ruins (see p. 75). No entire pottery was found here, but numbers of fragments were strewn about.

All these crania are in a fair state of preservation, with the lower jaws remaining, though some of the teeth are lost. The collection also contains, as I have mentioned above, the head of a mummy enveloped in a complete shroud, and some calvaria, which I have thought it unnecessary to describe. Of the child skulls I have con-sidered a description of one example to be sufficient.

To the eight skulls from cliff-dwellings, seven those of adults and one that of a child, I have added in the above series one of the two crania exhumed by M. NORDENSKIÖLD on the mesa, as it may be of interest to compare this specimen with the others.

Before proceeding to general conclusions, I will now give the measurements etc. of all these ten skulls, which are arranged in the following table:

No.	No. in G. Nordenskiölds catalogue.		Capacity.	Greatest length.	Greatest breadth.	Smallest frontal breadth.	Height (vert. to the horiz. line).	Auricular height.	Craniobasal length.	Intermastoidal diameter.	Circumference.	Longitudinal arch.	Interauricular arch.	Facial breadth (Virchow).	Zygomatic diameter.	Facial height.	Nasal height.	Orbital height.	Orbital breadth.	Sup. palatine length.	Sup. alveolar breadth.	Interangular mandibular breadth.	Breadth-index.	Height-index.
1	229	From a cliff-dwelling	1280	171	142	96	144	124	105	134	510	355	335	97	141	122	48	32	42	60	70	97	83.0	84.2
2	558	,, ,, ,,	1460	167	150	97	147	133	99	133	512	365	352	99	137	115	53	36	40	51	63	105	89.8	88.0
3	608	,, ,, ,,	1440	170	144	92	146	132	102	129	505	365	350	93	135	122	53	38	38	55	63	101	84.7	85.9
4	598	,, ,, ,,	1320	165	149	97	145	125	106	130	505	351	343	100	133	118	49	35	42	60	61	97	90.3	87.9
5	568	,, ,, ,,	1075	166	147	91	0	121	0	127	503	360	342	91	128	118	48	36	40	0	0	89	88.6	0
6	648	,, ,, ,,	0	164	137	91	134	121	100	125	485	345	325	97	128	118	49	34	40	55	65	97	83.5	81.7
7	300	,, ,, ,,	1305	161	150	94	134	118	101	140	502	350	342	100	139	0	49	32	37	0	0	100	93.2	83.2
8	643	,, ,, ,,	1275	143	145	79	141	119	84	129	455	335	330	104	125	115	50	34	38	53	67	88	10.1	98.6
9	646	,, ,, ,,	0	119	135	79	129	124	74	82	410	230	360	69	86	77	32	30	32	33	49	65	11.3	10.8
10	368	From a mesa grave	1480	169	154	91	138	123	97	135	518	350	350	103	139	123	52	35	37	54	66	95	91.1	81.7

No. 1 (229). Well-preserved, strongly developed skull, apparently that of a middle-aged *man*; it is stoutly built, heavy and has well-developed muscular processes (tuber occipitale, proc. mastoidei, etc.), arcus superciliares, and facial bones; the remaining teeth seem to be in excellent condition and uniformly worn, but in the upper jaw 8 are wanting, in the lower 3, all lost apparently after death.

The skull shows traces of some artificial depression at the occiput, the lambda region (i. e. the upper portion of the squama occipitalis and the posterior parts of the parietal bones) being slightly depressed on the right side and behind. This deformation, however, has not altered to any considerable extent the general form of the skull, nor has it affected the condition of the sutures, the latter being nowhere obliterated. The lineæ semicirculares ascend high on the vertex and are well marked. The orbits are comparatively low. The upper jaw is projected, the lower rather strongly developed.

This skull represents the most powerful type of all, with very prominent arcus superciliares and sagittal elevation of the vertical region.

No. 2 (558). Fairly well preserved and stoutly built skull of an elderly individual, probably a *man*. In the upper jaw only one tooth, in the lower the remains of 6, much worn and defective; from the condition of the jaws it may be inferred that most of the teeth were lost during life, the alveoli being contracted.

This cranium is very brachycephalic and hypsicephalic. A pronounced depression of the lambda region indicates artificial deformation, though here, as in No. 1, the flattening has not exercised any important influence on the general conformation of the skull, or caused any marked obliquity. The height is considerable, especially in the anterior vertical region, at and behind the confluence of the sut. sagittalis and the sut. coronalis, where there is a ridge. The forehead is high and broad. Arcus superciliares little developed, but the muscular processes prominent, as well as the arcus jugulares and the lower jaw. Orbits high and large. So many teeth being lost, it is impossible to determine the prognathism.

The sutures are partly open, partly obliterated, which is the case with the lateral parts of the sut. coronalis, the posterior part of the sut. sagittalis, and part of the upper posterior portion of the sut. lambdoidea. The sut. nasalis is also obliterated.

No. 3 (608). Well-preserved skull of less development than Nos. 1 and 2, with pronounced artificial depression behind and on the right side, some obliquity being thus caused in the general conformation of the cranium. An intercalated bone of some size is situated at and to the left of the point of the lambda suture, but the upper suture of this bone is for the most part obliterated. The remaining sutures are open, only the lateral portions of the coronal suture being partly obliterated. The cranium as a whole is rather heavy, indicating a robust structure. In the vertical region, along the anterior portion of the sagittal suture, lies a ridge. The skull is on the whole fairly high; the forehead high, but not very broad; the arcus superciliares but slightly developed. Face high, but rather narrow. Orbits high; nasal bones prominent; alveolar processes very prognathous with receding chin. Teeth in an excellent state of preservation, evenly worn, but not to any great extent; a canine wanting, lost evidently after death. Probably the skull of a young *man* of weak development.

No. 4 (598). Well-preserved skull, distinctly brachycephalic, with rather strong posterior flattening (of the lambda region and the parts above this region), causing an obliquity in the form of the cranium; a few intercalated bones at the point of the lambda suture, to the right.

Sutures in general open. Forehead broad and high. Arcus superciliares not much developed. Face rather broad, but not very high. Orbits large and high. Alveoli prognathous, but less so than in No. 3. Teeth much worn and partially damaged by caries; several missing, some of them lost during life, others after death.

No. 5 (568). Head of an entire mummy. Cervical vertebræ with their dried muscles and connective tissue still adhering to the skull. Hence neither the height nor the cranial base could be measured. Apparently the skull of an elderly individual, probably a *woman* (the sex could not be ascertained by examination of the mummy). Pronounced brachycephalism. Skull high and round. Regular, but not very strong flattening behind. Sutures for the most part obliterated, this applying to the whole upper part of the lambda suture, the greater part of the sagittal and coronal sutures. Arcus superciliares but slightly developed. Orbits high. Facial bones little developed, jugular breadth not great. Marked alveolar prognathism. Lower jaw weakly developed, with very long, pendent chin. Teeth only partly preserved, partly worn and damaged by caries; most of them lost during life.

No. 6 (648). Skull of a full-grown but young individual, with the sutures open, the teeth for the most part preserved and comparatively little worn. Probably *female*, the cranium showing some resemblance to No. 5. Parieto-occipital (lambda) region flattened, most distinctly on the right side. Forehead rather narrow; hardly any arcus superciliares. Facial parts little developed. Jugular breadth not great. Strong alveolar prognathism. Lower jaw of weak development, with long, pendent chin.

No. 7 (300). Skull of toothless, aged individual with effaced alveoli. Cranium strongly brachycephalic and rounded, with marked depression of the parieto-occipital region, especially on the right. Most of the sutures still open; hind part of the sagittal suture obliterated. Face broad (jugular breadth considerable). Atlas coalescent with the occipital bone, the confluence extending to its anterior arch, its condyloid processes, and the left half of its posterior arch.

No. 8 (643). Greatly deformed skull, the deformation seeming to affect not only the occipital region (especially on the left side), but also the frontal; forehead and face flattened. Orbits not deep. A small defect in the occipital bone to the left of the foramen magnum. Lambda suture open. Squamosal sutures of the sagittal, coronal, and temporal bones entirely obliterated. The possessor of the skull was apparently young, for the remaining teeth are little worn, and the wisdom teeth in the upper and lower jaws not yet developed. Many teeth lost after death. Marked alveolar prognathism. Facial bones rather feebly developed; but the jugular breadth rather great, and the alveolar breadth considerable. Nose broad. Lower jaw rather weakly developed.

No. 9 (646). Skull of a child (3—4 years old). Very brachycephalic. Great flattening of the parieto-occipital (lambda) region. Several small Wormian bones at the point of the lambda suture. Teeth partly lost.

No. 10 (368). Skull from a mound on the mesa, probably *male*. Very brachycephalic, rather heavy and massive. Marked depression of the lambda and posterior occipital regions. Most of the sutures open, only the posterior part of the sagittal suture and the lateral parts of the coronal suture being slightly obliterated. Wormian bones in the lambda suture. Arcus superciliares rather large. Frontal, jugular, and alveolar breadths great. Teeth partly lost, some during life, others after death; the remaining ones strong, but rather worn. Slight alveolar prognathism.

*   *   *

On a general review of the skulls described above, we find that men as well as women, adults and young individuals, middle-aged and old persons, are represented in the series. We observe that in nearly all these crania an *artificial deformation* has been caused in early infancy by the application of pressure to the *superior parieto-occipital region*, this part (the superior occipital and posterior parietal regions) having been depressed with some flat object. But this depression *varies greatly in degree*, its influence on the cranial conformation being in some instances very slight, in others, as for example No. 8, considerable, causing great deformation, increased probably by the coalescence of the sutures, a process which may with reason be assumed to have been promoted by the artificial flattening.

No conclusions as to the original normal type can be drawn from the shape of the most deformed skulls, especially as in these instances a compensatory development, more or less advanced, seems to have affected other parts of the cranium. In the least deformed skulls, on the other hand, we may be able, even if the natural type be in some respects distorted, to discern the essential characters. To me it seems evident, as M. BESSELS was inclined to conclude from the few skulls which he was enabled to examine, that, though the brachycephalism may have been more or less augmented by the artificial treatment, we have here to deal with a *distinctly brachycephalic race*. It should be kept in mind, however, that the inferior occipital region, the occiput proper, has not been directly influenced by the deformative pressure; it rather seems in several instances that, owing to the retarded development of the superior region, the inferior occipital region has bulged out in compensation.

From the male skulls we may conclude that this race was fairly robust, with heavy skeleton and strong muscular processes. The facial bones are rather well developed, showing considerable breadth, with heavy lower jaw. All the crania are more or less prognathous.

The skulls in general are of considerable height. The capacity of the crania found in cliff-dwellings, in the cases where it is possible to measure them, varies between 1,075 (i. e. nannocephalism, R. VIRCHOW) and 1,460 cub. centim. (thus affording no instances of kephalonia), the intermediate grades being 1,275, 1,280, 1,305, 1,320, and 1,440 cub. centim. Considering that not only well developed men, but also delicate, less developed women and aged persons, seem to be represented among these individuals nothing unusual strikes us in the capacity of the crania.

In order to learn the ethnological relations of the extinct cliff-dwellers to other peoples, it would be of great importance, for the sake of comparison, to possess a series of skulls belonging to Indian tribes who inhabit or have inhabited the adjacent tracts. Such a collection is not at our disposal; only a few crania of North American Indians are within my reach. But among the skulls in MORTON's *Crania Americana* there are several similar in character to those described above. No doubt, the builders and inhabitants of the cliff-dwellings were *Indians of the same ethnological type* as those who lived in the surrounding regions. The ancient Mexican skulls which I have been enabled to examine possessed closely analogous characters.

Whether the few surviving Indians who now inhabit the neighbouring country are the descendants of the cliff-dwellers or otherwise related to them, is a point which craniology cannot at present decide, for of these remnants of Indian tribes, so far as I am informed, we as yet know next to nothing.

A scientific anthropological examination of the interesting Moki tribe, whose dwellings M. NORDENSKIÖLD visited, would no doubt be of great service in the unravelling of problems affecting the obscure history of the cliff-dwellers and their relations to the other aborigines of North America.

Until this has been accomplished, it is too early to draw general conclusions. Nevertheless, the skulls carefully collected by M. NORDENSKIÖLD and briefly described above, are valuable as material and of great importance with a view to the final solution of the question.

*   *   *

In *Crania Ethnica Americana*, the great work recently published by RUDOLF VIRCHOW, the author has discussed with profound thoroughness the question of the deformation of the skull among American tribes. He points out that this deformation may originally have been caused not with a design to produce distortion, but from a wish to protect the new-born child from violent concussion with the board to which it was tied, and where it thus suffered pressure of protracted duration on a part of the occipital region, the bandages and the pillow which was probably placed under the occiput having complicated the deformation. Gradually this practice became a custom, the process being regarded as conducive to beauty and as beneficial both to the individual and the family.

The occipital deformation thus claims precedence and is the original form, the next stage being the occipito-frontal flattening. The occipital depression is the more widely spread in America; it chiefly affects the superior portion of the occipital bone (squama occipitis), and is often accompanied with plagiocephalism, one side of the upper part of the occiput, together with the posterior angle of the parietal bone, beeing laterally compressed. A further step is thus taken towards deformation of a pronounced type, the occipital pressure being applied not to the real convexity of the squama occipitis, but rather to its upper angle and the adjacent parts of the parietal bones. In the same instances, adds VIRCHOW, signs of frontal depression are to be found.

On examination of the skulls from the cliff-dwellings, we observe in most of them a greater or less degree of this occipito-parietal flattening; in two cases (the child, Pl. IX and the full-grown man, Pl. I) the depression has extended somewhat further down the occipital bone, and the cranium is rather more like the specimen figured by VIRCHOW (l. c., p. 11, Fig. IV, aus einem Hügelgrabe von Vicksburg). But the other skulls from the cliff-dwellings as well as the cranium from the mesa (Pl. X) show the superior occipital (occipito-parietal) flattening, combined with a greater or less degree of plagiocephalism. No instance of frontal depression, however, was observed in any of these skulls.

*   *   *

In the above I have confined my remarks to the crania. I have still to give a brief description of the other *skeletal remains*.

Besides the mummies still enveloped in their wrappings, and therefore impossible to examine without damaging the shrouds, the collection contains more or less complete skeletons appertaining to 6 of the crania described above, namely those numbered 1, 2, 3, 4, 7, and 10.

The bones belonging to skull No. 1 (229 in G. Nordenskiöld's catalogue) are almost complete in number and well-preserved; all the long bones and the pelvic bones in an excellent state of preservation. Length of the humeri 27.3 cm., of the femora 38.7 cm. Pelvis of a male type.

No. 2 (catalogue number, 558). Skeleton almost complete, and the bones generally in a good state of preservation. Apparently the remains of an old man. Length of the humeri 28.2 cm., of the femora 39.8 (39.7) cm.

No. 3 (cat. n., 608). Ossified parts of the skeleton still held together by ligaments and bits of skin, this being particularly noticeable in the vertebral column, the pelvis, and one femur. Length of humerus 25.3 cm., of femur 38.9 cm. The skeleton seems to be fairly well preserved and almost complete. Sex not easy to determine.

No. 4 (cat. n., 598). Skeleton fairly complete; all the long bones, the pelvis, etc. still preserved. Length of the humeri resp. 27.7 and 28.7 cm. (the right), of the femora resp. 40.8 and 39.9 cm. (the right). Pelvic bones of female character.

No. 7 (cat. n., 300). Long bones in a rather good condition; length of the humeri resp. 25.8 and 25.9 cm., of the femora 38.5 cm. Pelvic bones wanting; of the rest of the skeleton there remain the scapulæ, the clavicles, a great number of vertebræ, ribs, etc. Sex not easy to determine.

No. 10 (from the mesa). Bones in a pretty good state of preservation and fairly complete; pelvis and scapulæ present. Length of the humeri resp. 28.6 and 28.9 cm., of the femora resp. 40.1 and 40.6 cm. Apparently male.

*   *   *

The following plates (Nos. I—X) give *orthoscopical* figures in the natural size of the crania described above as Nos. 1—10, preserving the same order of arrangement.

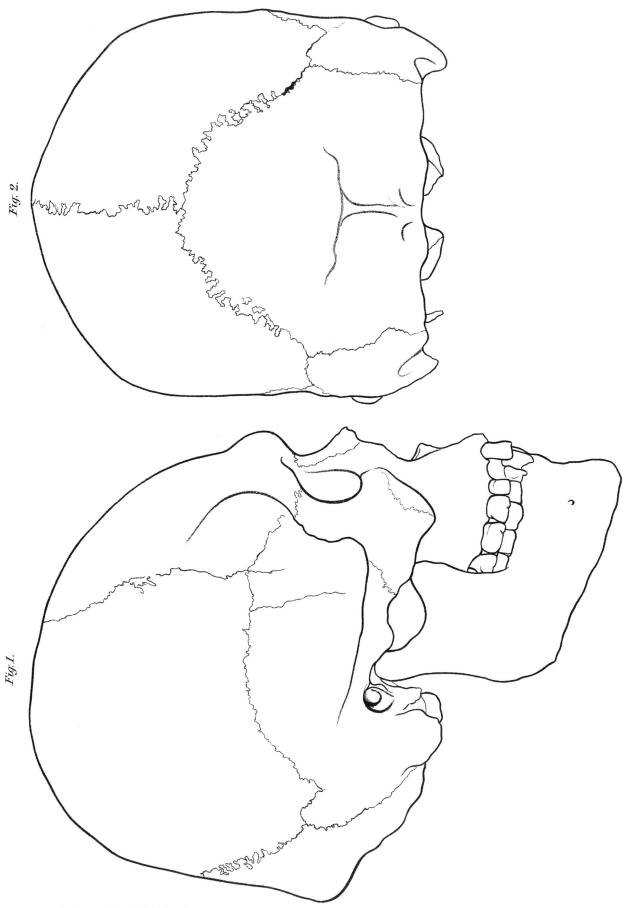

Fig. 2.

Fig. 1.

Sigrid Andersson del.   G. Tholander lith.

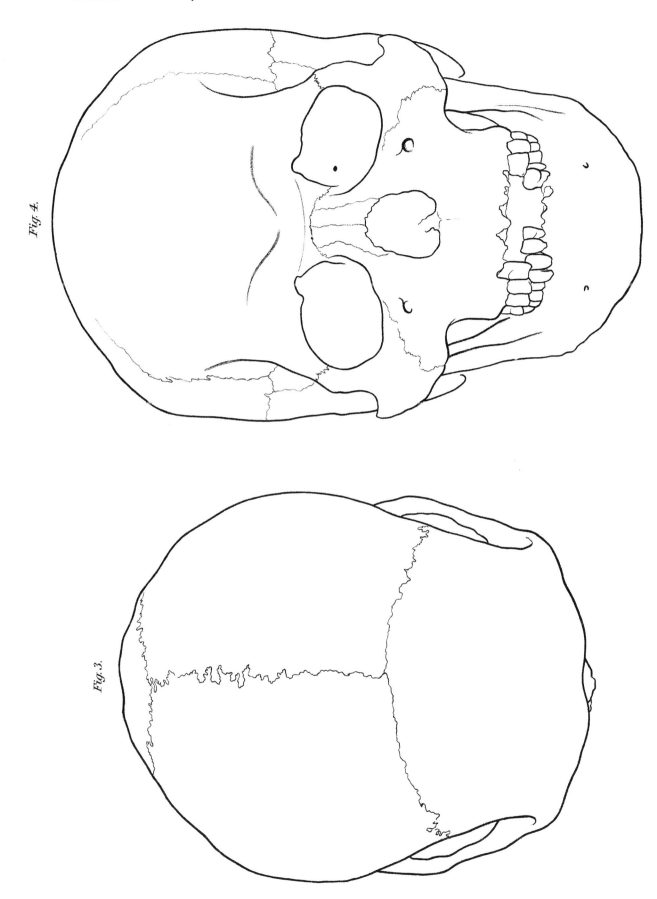

W. Schlachter, Stockholm.

Fig. 2.

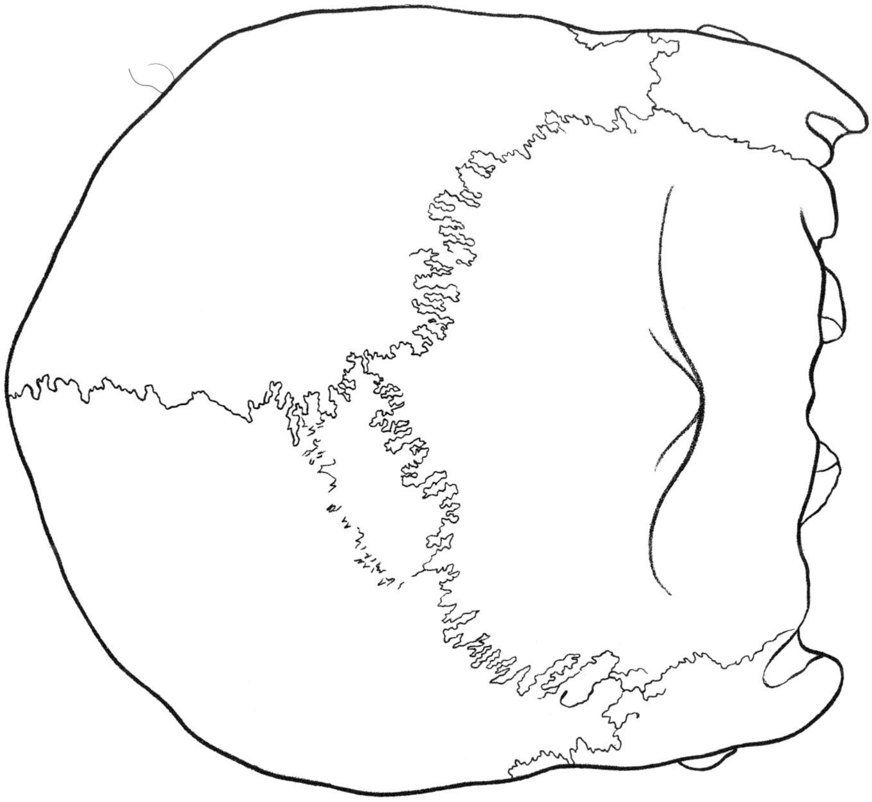

Fig. 1.

Sigrid Andersson del.   G. Tholander lith.

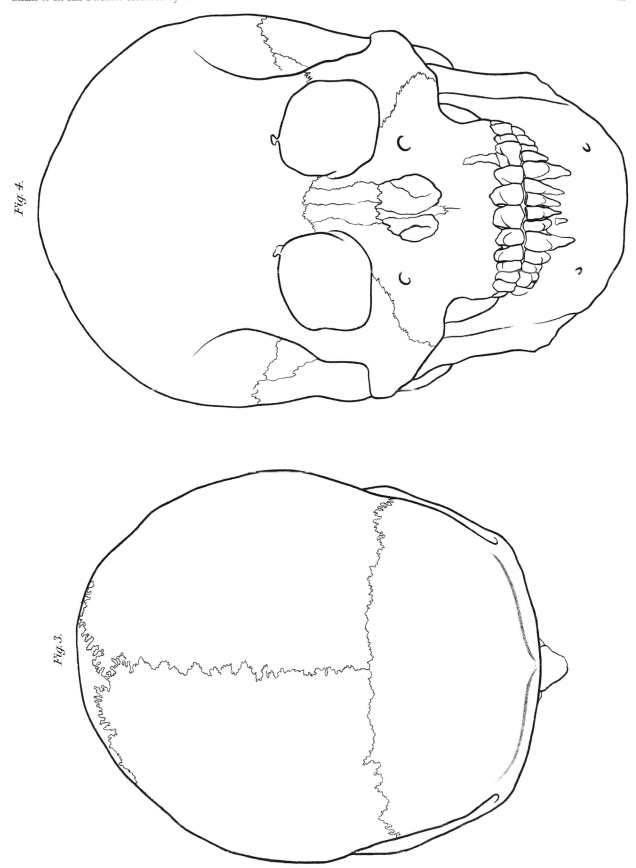

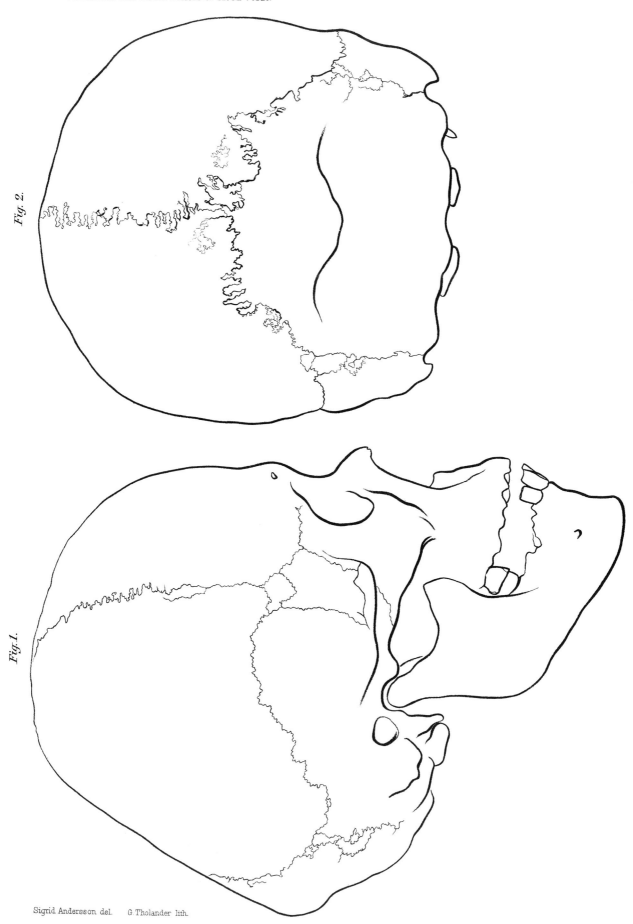

Fig. 2.

Fig. 1.

Sigrid Andersson del.   G. Tholander lith.

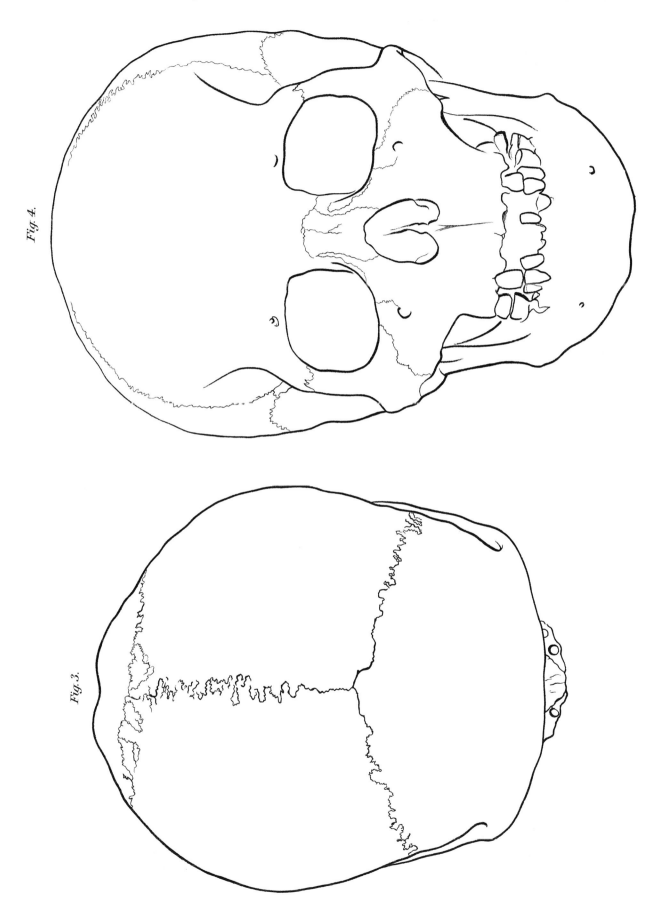

Fig. 4.

Fig. 3.

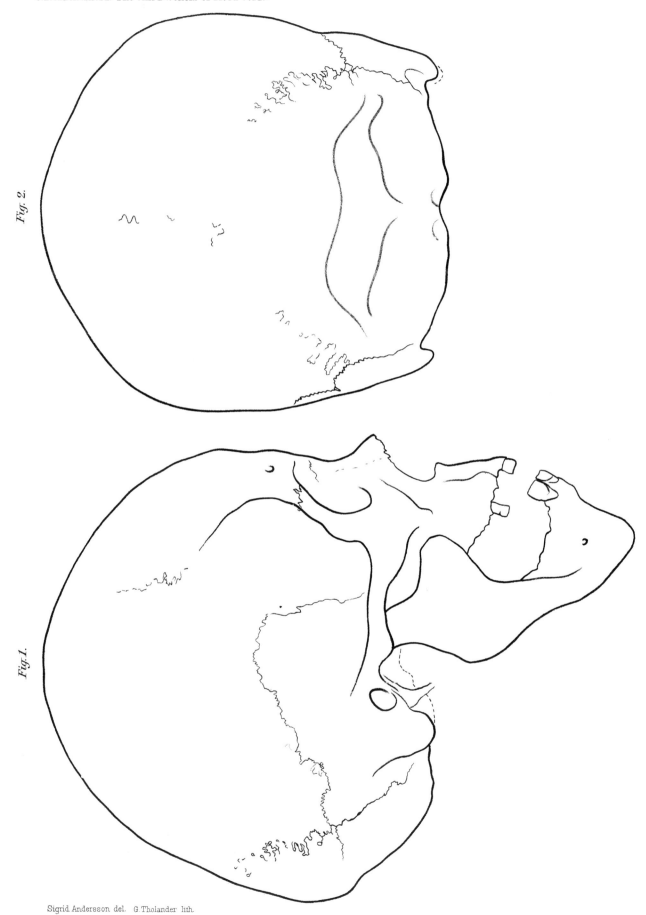

Fig. 2.

Fig. 1.

Sigrid Andersson del.   G.Tholander lith.

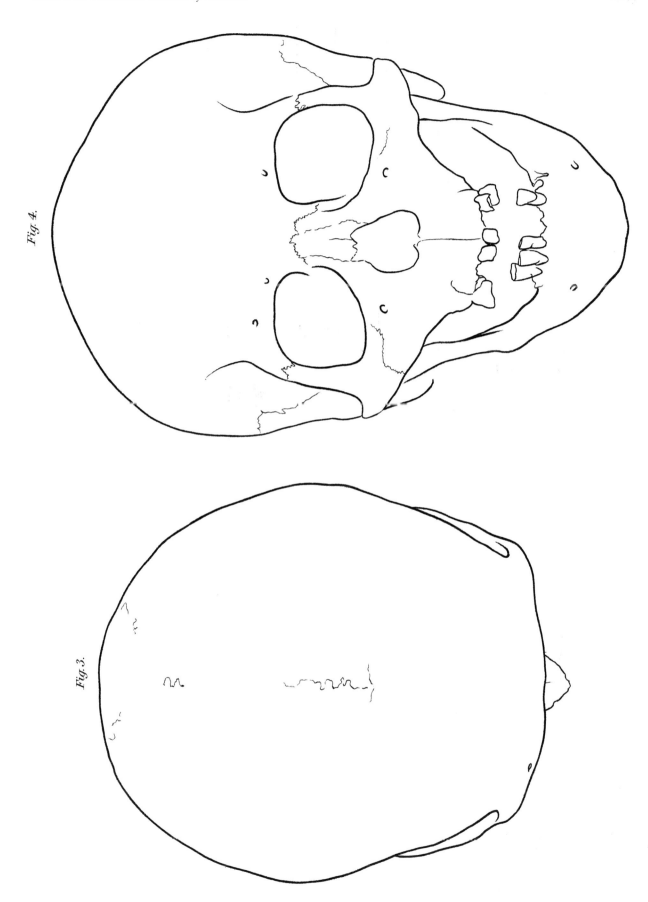

Fig. 4.

Fig. 3.

W. Schlachter, Stockholm.

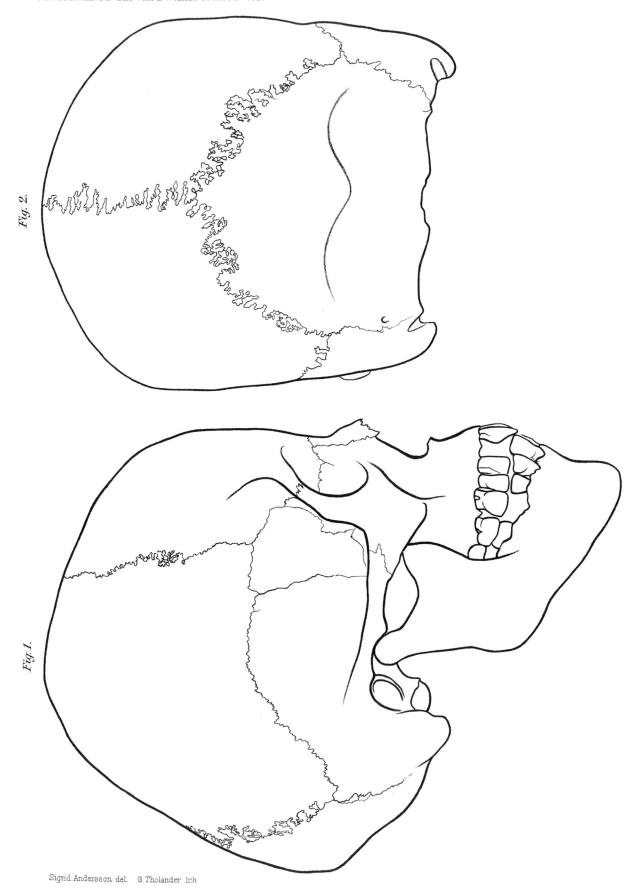

Fig. 2.

Fig. 1.

Sigrid Andersson del.   G. Tholander lith

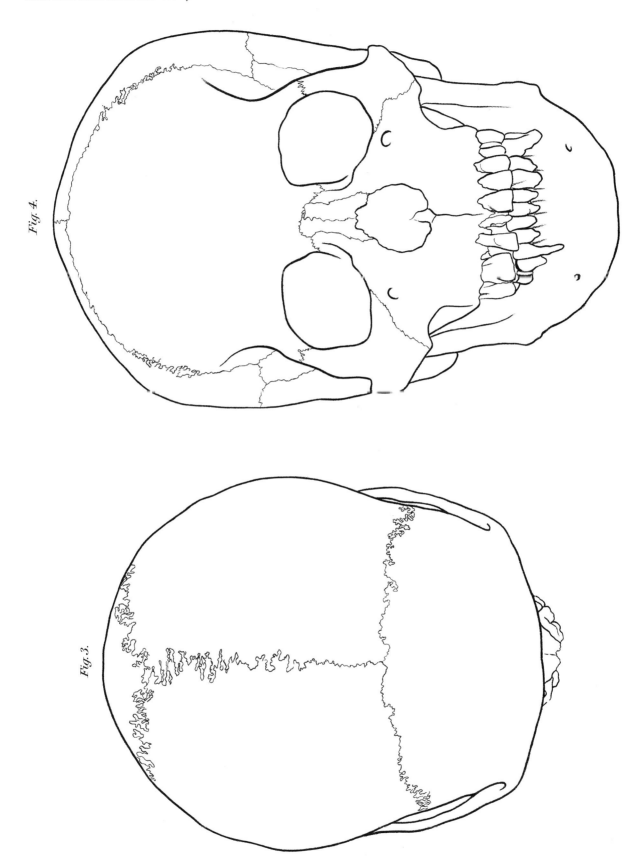

Fig. 4.

Fig. 3.

W. Schlachter, Stockholm.

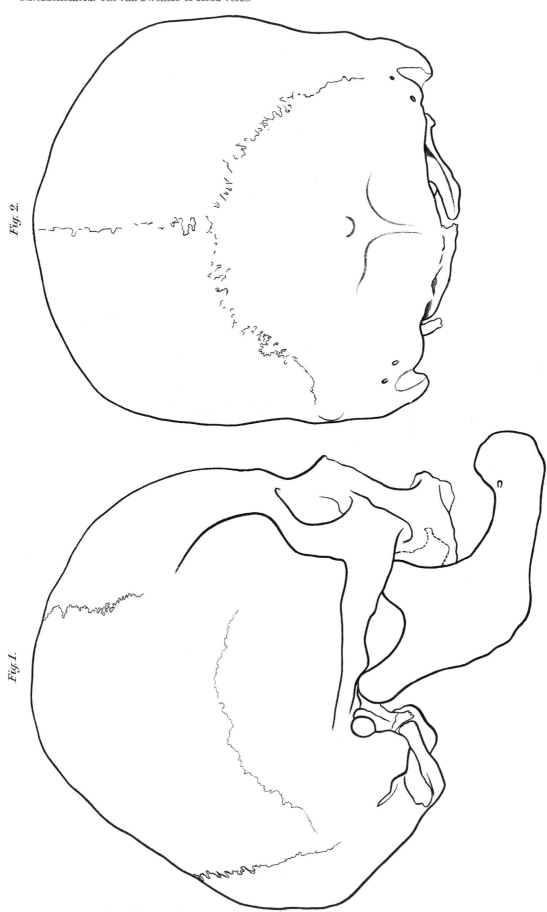

Fig. 2.

Fig. 1.

Sigrid Andersson del.   G. Tholander lith.

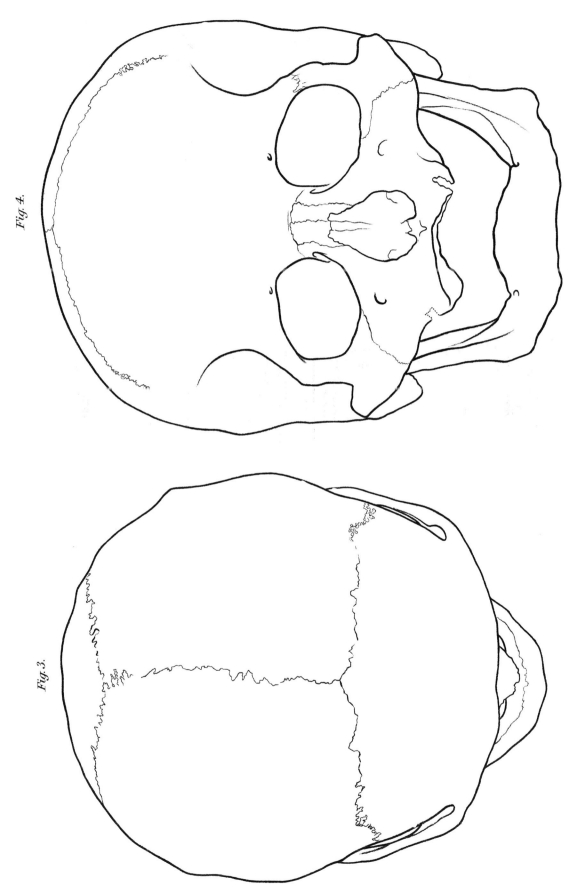

W. Schlachter, Stockholm.

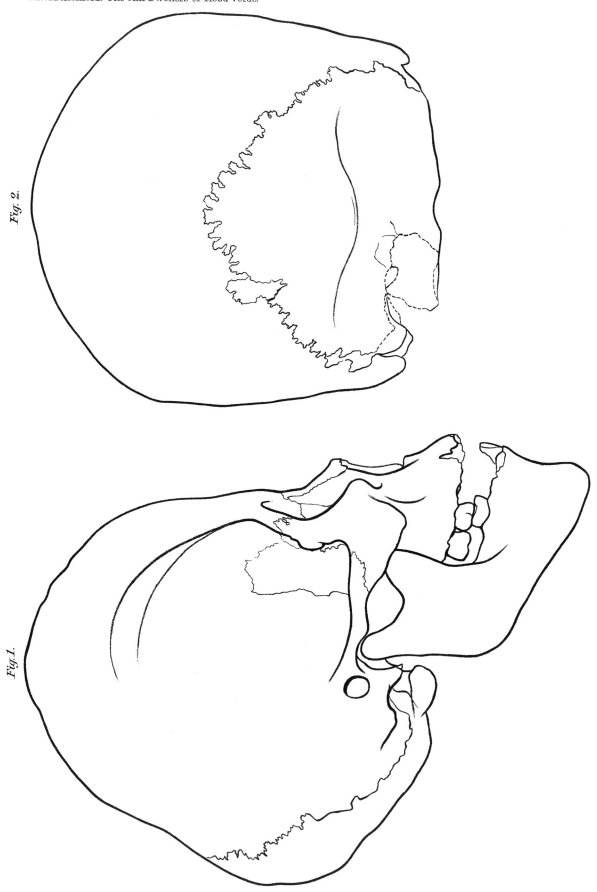

Sigrid Andersson del.   G. Tholander lith.

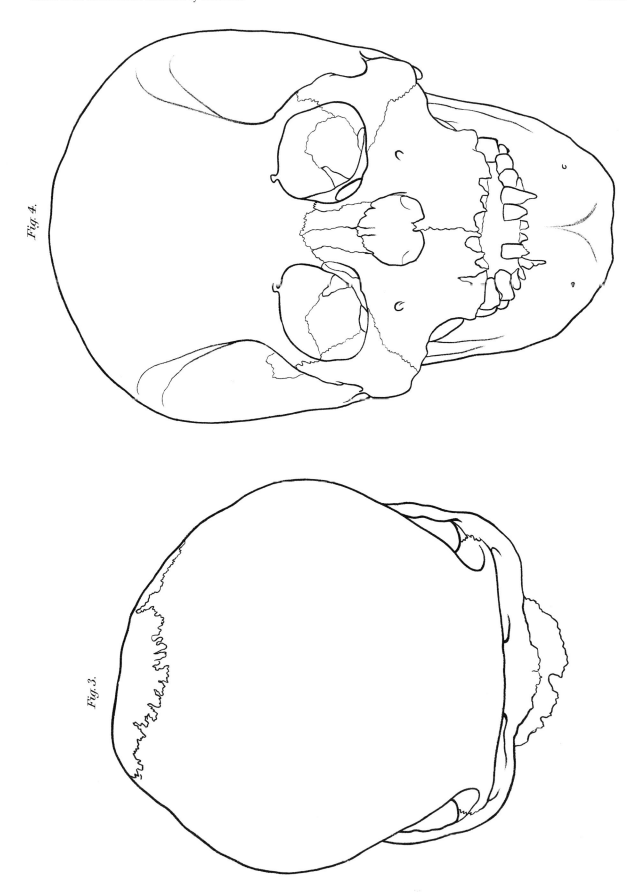

Fig. 4.

Fig. 3.

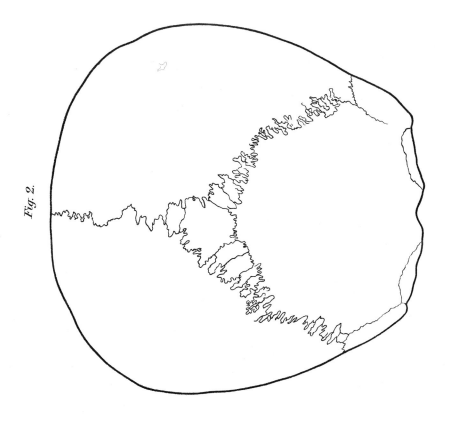

Fig. 2.

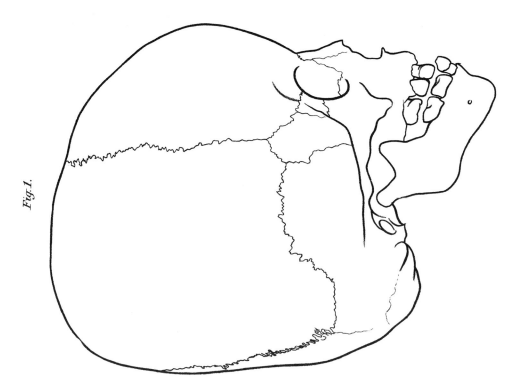

Fig. 1.

Sigrid Andersson del.   G. Tholander lith.

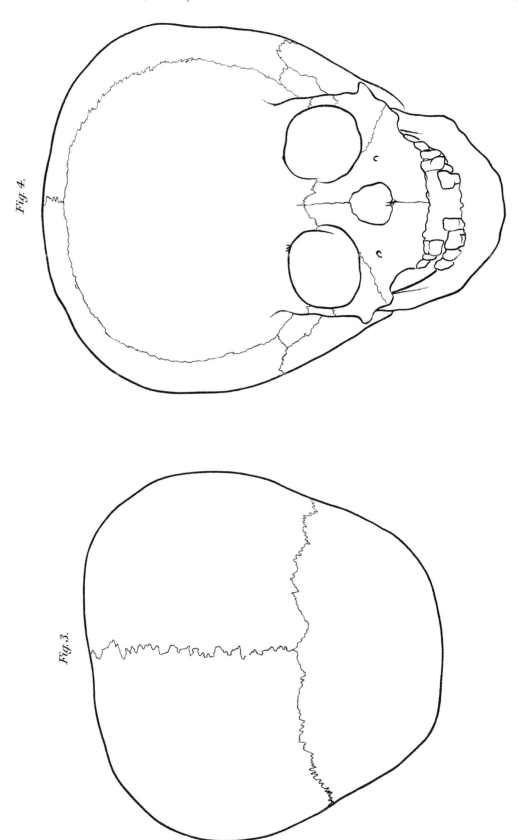

W. Schlachter, Stockholm.

38

37

36

35

34

33

32

31

30

29

Gen. S.